Acclaim for Eyetracking Web Usability

"Always ahead of the curve, always provocative, always insightful... if Jakob Nielsen and Kara Pernice have something to say about the way the Web works, you should listen."

—Seth Godin, Author, *Linchpin*

"Designing great interfaces requires more than creativity and mere consistency. The information and tools on the Web are made for people. The more a designer knows about how people perceive, read, think, scan, prioritize, skip, and absorb, the more effective their designs will ultimately be. This eyetracking usability study, the largest ever held, provides powerful and very practical new insights on how real people, trying to get real things done, see those interfaces. The results are, well... eye opening. This is a great example of meticulous research and crisp data analysis, leading to deeper understanding with a set of practical, clear-cut rules and recommendations that will make your designs better."

—Tjeerd Hoek, Executive Creative Director, frog design

"Jakob and Kara demystify eyetracking Web usability by delivering common sense and practical advice. This book is a critical tool for anyone that wants to improve how to organize and treat Web content for maximum usability and efficiency."

—Armando González, UI Design Director, eBay

"This book has something for everyone: important Web design principles, eyetracking research methods, and relevant business issues and examples. Whether you are a Web designer, user researcher, or business owner, you will benefit from *Eyetracking Web Usability*."

—Christian Rohrer, Ph.D., Senior Director of User Experience Design, Move, Inc.

"Expert usability practitioners Nielsen and Pernice offer Web page design guidelines from a unique perspective of users' recorded eye movements. Compelling gaze visualizations over actual, active Web pages are included and amassed from an impressive number of studies and participants. The authors provide interesting insights into user behavior, Web page content and layout, as well as giving guidance for future eye tracking research. The book will be an indispensable addition to eyetracking and Web usability bookshelves."

—Professor Andrew Duchowski, School of Computing, Clemson University;
Author, *Eye Tracking Methodology: Theory and Practice*

"Finally a book about Web design where the guidance given is derived less from the authors' opinions and more on real research data using the Eyetracker! As an executive responsible for implementing global learning technologies, Kara and Jakob provide simple and insightful ways to ensure that we take smart approaches to every screen and task we want people to perform on a Web page. It's a great tool for anyone trying to drive performance out of their Web site."

—Rob Lauber, Vice President, Yum! University, Yum! Brands, Inc.

Jakob Nielsen
Kara Pernice

Eyetracking
Web Usability

New
Riders

New Riders, An Imprint of Peachpit, Berkeley, California USA

Eyetracking Web Usability

Jakob Nielsen and Kara Pernice

New Riders
1249 Eighth Street
Berkeley, CA 94710
510/524-2178
510/524-2221 (fax)

Find us on the Web at: www.newriders.com
To report errors, please send a note to errata@peachpit.com

New Riders is an imprint of Peachpit, a division of Pearson Education

Project Editor: Susan Rimerman
Development Editor: Camille Peri
Copy Editor: Kim Wimpsett
Production Editor: Hilal Sala
Compositor: WolfsonDesign
Indexer: James Minkin
Cover design: Peachpit
Interior design: Peachpit

ISBN-13: 978-0321-49836-6
ISBN-10: 0-321-49836-4

9 8 7 6 5 4 3 2 1

Printed and bound in the United States of America

For the next generation, Oskar and William.

—Jakob Nielsen

For the members of the Lotus Graphics Products Group circa 1991, especially MaryKate Foley and Betsy Fortin. I am grateful for the introduction to usability and the encouragement to experiment, fail, and succeed in the name of making simple designs to be proud of.

—Kara Pernice

Acknowledgments

Many people generously shared their experience, time, and knowledge to help us bring this book to fruition. We feel such gratitude to them all.

None of this would have been possible without our gifted, talented, and ridiculously hardworking research assistants: Sukeshini "Suki" Grandhi, David Shulman, and Tatyana Nikolayeva. They wholeheartedly labored on this project—running studies, writing code, and quantifying and analyzing data—even longer than they had initially promised and ever pleasantly. If they ever apply for a job with you, hire them immediately at top salary.

Along those lines, Nielsen Norman Group's Susan Pernice did anything and everything, from recruiting testers to drawing about a million "areas of interest" boxes to filling in spreadsheets with success scores and questionnaires. For this and more, we thank her.

Thanks to our colleagues at NN/g: Jen Cardello provided unselfish feedback in IA and layout-related chapters. Luice Hwang magically juggled our non-ET schedules so we could do this work. Amy Schade consulted with us on e-commerce-related ET research. And the rest of Nielsen Norman Group showed support throughout this project: Raluca Budiu, Janelle Estes, Susan Farrell, Garrett Goldfield, Hoa Loranger, Dr. Julie Moran, Chris Nodder, Don Norman, Sherrill Saxer, and Bruce "Tog" Tognazzini.

We are also thankful to Hannah Kain and her team at ALOM in California.

Thank you to Andrew T. Duchowski, PhD, of Clemson University, for his comprehensive book *Eye Tracking Methodology*, an easy-to-understand primer for anyone delving into eyetracking research. His work and answers to our questions were much help when we were forming many of our initial research ideas.

We thank Peter Brawn, PhD, from eyetracker in Australia for rounding out our ET library of ideas with information about eyetracking in a real-world, non-Web environment.

Thank you to Rob Stevens at Bunnyfoot for being an obliging sounding board and for sharing his own ET research initiatives.

Thanks to Michael E. Goldberg, MD, at Columbia University College of Physicians and Surgeons, for answering questions about how the human eye works in very specific situations.

Thank you to everyone at Regus at One Penn Plaza in Manhattan, where the studies were conducted.

To the good people at Tobii Technologies in Sweden, thank you for your support with the equipment so we could conduct these studies and analyze the information. We appreciate your patience with the challenges that come with dealing with a vast amount of data.

Kara thanks her family and especially her wonderful parents, Mary and Robert Pernice, for their unwavering encouragement and love. She thanks sweet Jeff Nichols for his ever offbeat and surprising humor. (And Columbo thanks him for making sure he was fed, was watered, and got to chase squirrels while Kara was working long hours.) She also thanks her dear friends for their encouragement, especially Danny Petrocchi, Sharon "ShaRON" LeBlanc, and Cecilia Ott for convincingly acting interested in her ramblings about the eye and the Web for years. Your stamina is incredible.

Finally, big thanks to our editors, Susan Rimerman, Kim Wimpsett, and Camille Peri. Camille should probably be bronzed and raised for the hours she put in on this work. We hope the blue dots you are seeing go away soon.

—Jakob Nielsen and Kara Pernice

About the Authors

Jakob Nielsen

Jakob Nielsen, PhD, is a principal of Nielsen Norman Group (NN/g). He is the founder of the "discount usability engineering" movement, which emphasizes fast and efficient methods for improving the quality of user interfaces. Nielsen, noted as "the world's leading expert on Web usability" by *U.S. News and World Report* and "the next best thing to a true time machine" by *USA Today*, is the author of the best-selling book *Designing Web Usability: The Practice of Simplicity* (New Riders Publishing, 2000), which has sold more than a quarter of a million copies in 22 languages.

Nielsen's other books include *Usability Engineering* (Morgan Kaufmann, 1993); with Robert L. Mack, *Usability Inspection Methods* (Wiley, 1994); *Multimedia and Hypertext: The Internet and Beyond* (Morgan Kaufmann, 1995); *International User Interfaces* (Wiley, 1996); with Marie Tahir, *Homepage Usability: 50 Websites Deconstructed* (New Riders Publishing, 2001); and with Hoa Loranger, *Prioritizing Web Usability* (New Riders Publishing, 2006). Nielsen's Alertbox column on Web usability has been published on the Internet since 1995 and has about 200,000 readers at *www.useit.com*.

From 1994 to 1998, Nielsen was a Sun Microsystems Distinguished Engineer. His previous affiliations include Bell Communications Research, the Technical University of Denmark, and the IBM User Interface Institute. He has been awarded 79 U.S. patents, mainly on ways of making the Internet easier to use. Nielsen holds a PhD in human-computer interaction from the Technical University of Denmark.

Kara Pernice

Kara Pernice is the managing director at Nielsen Norman Group and heads the Company's East Coast operations. *The Wall Street Journal* has called her "an intranet guru."

Pernice has more than 18 years of experience evaluating usability and is well versed in the usability areas of collaboration, document management, multimedia, database design, print materials, and consumer-oriented products. She has done numerous studies on the effects of aging, accessibility, and low literacy. She has also designed products ranging from Web calendar applications to dictation devices for radiologists to server monitoring programs.

Before joining Nielsen Norman Group, Pernice established successful usability programs at Lotus Development, Iris Associates (an IBM subsidiary), and Interleaf. She managed the first user experience program for Lotus Notes, and after the first usability release, *PC Magazine* wrote, "If this were summer camp, Lotus Notes would walk away with the Most Improved Camper award."

Since joining NN/g, Pernice has worked with clients in a variety of industries and has led many intercontinental research studies, generated design guidelines, and coauthored study reports. She has presented countless seminars and conference keynotes on Web and intranet design, usability research techniques, usability management, and the politics of usability.

With one usability method or another, Pernice has watched thousands of people using software and the Web over the years. She may be best known for practicing and championing usability videos as a tool for analyzing, presenting, and teaching about usability and design.

Pernice chaired the Usability Professionals' Association 2000 and 2001 conferences and served as 2002 conference advisor.

Pernice holds an MBA from Northeastern University and a BA from Simmons College.

She lives in New York and Cape Cod with her zealous terrier, Columbo.

Contents

Preface

How do your customers see your Web site? This is one of the most fundamental questions in doing business on the Internet, and it's one that most companies can't answer. You know how *you* see the site and how other people on the design team see it, but what about people outside your company? You may even know how people use your site or what they say about it, but you have no clue about how they actually *look* at it. This book aims to answer that question.

Of course, no book can answer questions specifically about *your* Web site. For that, you need to conduct your own usability studies. But there is a lot of commonality in the way customers look at Web sites and how that impacts what they do on sites. That's something we *can* write a book about.

This book has a very clear focus: what we can learn about Web usability from eyetracking research. In other words, we recorded exactly where users look on the screen as they use the Web, and we used these very specific (and yes, sometimes tedious and granular) findings to deduce guidelines for making Web sites better for users and more profitable for companies.

Although this is our first book that includes eyetracking technology, eyetracking is certainly not a new method of research. Scientists in the field of perceptual psychology have conducted eyetracking research to find out how the eye works since the 19th century. In the 21st century, eyetracking has finally become a practical technology that can be used for commercial studies, not just for academic research. Now we can watch people as they use the Web and exhibit naturalistic behavior, such as going shopping.

We conducted what we believe is the world's largest eyetracking study, in terms of the breadth and number of Web sites examined and the types of tasks observed with hundreds of users. There have been other good studies, but they have focused on narrow categories of Web sites, such as newspaper sites, or even on a single site, such as Google.

The findings from these studies are usually very specific to the topic at hand and are difficult to generalize to other types of sites.

Our goal was to study people's common viewing patterns and behaviors as they use purposeful Web sites. We mainly focused our testing on company Web sites, though we also covered government and nonprofit sites. All these sites have a common business goal: to get users to do something on the site.

Because most of our consulting experience is commercial, we tend to use commercially biased terminology such as *company*, *customers*, *business goals*, and *profit*, even when we talk about concepts that apply equally to government agencies and nonprofit organizations. For example, a government tax site may not necessarily think in terms of "business goals." But if you want taxpayers to be able to download tax forms from your Web site, we would say that is your business goal, even if your agency doesn't make a penny from the downloads. And these taxpayers are your customers, even if your organization uses a term like *citizens* instead. Similarly, if your site aims to educate patients about a health condition and ways of coping with it, these are your business goals, even if you're giving away your medical expertise. And the patients are your customers, even if the health-care sector rarely uses customer-centric terminology.

Eyetracking, Not All Usability

In this book, we stayed focused on the goal at hand: to study look patterns and how they relate to Web usage. This is not a general book about Web usability. We have studied many topics with other research methods, and through 16 years of testing sites and conducting field studies, we have discovered 2,503 usability guidelines for Web sites, intranets, social network postings, and e-mail newsletters that are not eyetracking related and that we don't have room for here. If you are familiar with these guidelines, you will discover as you read this book that our eyetracking research supports and enhances many of them. For an overview of the most important findings about general

Web usability, we refer you to *Prioritizing Web Usability* by Jakob Nielsen and Hoa Loranger (published by New Riders). Or visit our Web site for a list of comprehensive reports about Web usability, intranet usability, and usability research methodology: *www.nngroup.com/reports*.

Supplementary Reports

Despite our tight focus, the manuscript for this book got bigger and bigger as we were writing. We have many findings from our research, and the nature of eyetracking demands scores of screenshots to visualize these findings. In numerous cases, we needed two screenshots just to make one point: a plain screenshot and one that shows the look pattern.

To keep this book at a manageable size, we cover two topics in separate reports instead of discussing them here. They are available online:

- "Eyetracking Methodology: How to Conduct and Evaluate Usability Studies Using Eyetracking" is available at *www.useit.com/eyetracking/methodology*.

- "How People Read on the Web: The Eyetracking Evidence" is available at *www.nngroup.com/reports/reading*.

The first report covers methodological aspects of running proper eyetracking studies that will result in valid usability findings. Sadly, many eyetracking studies don't ask users to use Web sites in free navigation to perform real-world tasks. The results of studies like these can often be deceptive and should not be used as the basis for designing business sites that aspire to make money from real-world customers.

Because it's so important to promote correct research methodology and because our methodology report provides much more detail about our approach than we can include in the short chapter about our research in this book, we are giving away the report as a free download.

The second report covers how people read on many kinds of pages, including search engine results pages. There is a modest charge for this report to help us defray the high cost of doing the detailed eyetracking research needed to understand users' reading behaviors.

What This Book Doesn't Cover

Beyond the topics of eyetracking methodology and reading and searching, there are other areas we do not cover here.

We usually tested Web sites that have a business goal and that aim to support users in getting something done. If you have a personal weblog that covers your latest dating exploits and is targeted at your five closest friends, many of our findings won't apply. That's not the type of site we studied or the type of user we included in our testing. (Some of our findings do apply to personal sites, but there's no business model for us to find out which ones; after all, one of the major purposes of usability is profit, so site creators who don't have a business goal for their site won't pay to fund usability research.)

Our findings also don't apply to purely artistic sites that people may visit to admire the design or content, not to use.

We did test entertainment-oriented sites, such as the Warner Bros. site for a Harry Potter movie. And in our consulting business, we have worked with many clients in the entertainment sector to improve the usability of sites that sell or promote movie tickets, concert tickets, theater tickets, music downloads, theme park vacations, television characters, and several other entertainment products. Our usability guidelines apply very well to these types of businesses, even if people usually say they like entertainment sites to look more glamorous than we recommend for more staid types of sites. A Harry Potter site should be more "magical" than the investor relations site for a Fortune 500 corporation, but on either of them, it should be easy to play the video—whether it's a movie trailer or a CEO talking about a company's latest quarterly results.

So, our findings apply to the business side of entertainment but not necessarily to sites that are purely entertainment for its own sake. We have tested game sites for our research report on how children use the Internet, but those findings are quite different from our findings for business sites and are not covered here. And we did not conduct those tests using eyetracking. We know that the way children use Web sites differs strikingly from the way adults do, leading to highly different usability guidelines, but we don't discuss that in this book.

Just as we don't cover young users, we don't cover older users in this book. It can be difficult to track the eyes of senior citizens because regression lenses, bifocals, or various eye diseases that often come with age can trip up current eyetracking technology. Additionally, usability studies with seniors tend to take a little longer to run, and our sessions were already very jam-packed with the logistics of facilitating an eyetracking study. From our other research studies with seniors, we know that they require special considerations in Web design, so we caution you against applying the findings in this book to people who are older than 65.

This book also does not cover users with disabilities. In the past, we have studied people who are deaf, are blind, have low vision or low literacy, or have cognitive or motor-skill challenges. But the scale and complexity of eyetracking research prevented us from being able to include users such as these at this time. It may also be impossible to track the eyes of people with low-vision.

Finally, because of our focus on Web sites, we did not cover two important areas of design: e-mail newsletters and intranets. Our colleague Amy Schade has conducted intensive eyetracking studies of email newsletters. (Go to *www.nngroup.com/reports* for the results of our research with children and teens, seniors, and people who use assistive technology, as well as our research with e-mail newsletters.)

Intranets are often similar to Web sites in form and navigation behavior, though different in information architecture, and the two types of design share many usability guidelines. But intranet user groups and tasks differ from those of Web sites. We have conducted many elaborate studies of intranets and discovered 614 independent usability guidelines for them. Unfortunately, however, these were not eyetracking studies because we did not drag the eyetracker around to dozens of companies around the world.

Many of the Web-centric findings in this book do apply to intranets, but if you're designing an intranet, you should take them with a grain of salt and reinterpret our guidelines according to the needs of your internal design project.

In summary, this book presents information about how people aged 18 to 65 look at and use Web sites that have a business goal. This focus leaves us with many interesting eyetracking usability findings and advice for improving the design of mainstream Web sites. Some of our findings are quite broad and easily interpreted. Others are specific and somewhat intricate, but stick with them because they all have good stories to tell about people's look patterns on the Web. Users do look at your site differently than *you* do—that's for sure. We hope that you will apply our findings about what attracts, repels, assists, and confuses the typical Web user to enhance your own site.

—Jakob Nielsen and Kara Pernice, November 2009
Silicon Valley and New York City

1 Eyetracking and the Eye

Eyetracking is simply following the trail of where a person is looking. With current technology, it is fairly easy to observe the path where users look on a computer screen. Eyetracking equipment can be built into the computer monitor, and eyetracking software can keep track of what's displayed on the screen while the user is looking at it.

We shouldn't take eyetracking advancements for granted. In the old days, eyetracking was done by truly tortuous means, such as physically gluing something to a test subject's eyeballs. Newer eyetracking technology all works on the same basic principle: focusing a light and a video camera on a person's eye. The light, along with some back-end analysis, helps deduce in which direction the person is looking. The video camera records the interaction.

In addition to knowing how the eye is turning within the socket, you need one more piece of information to calculate where the person is looking: where the head is. The first eyetrackers we used in the 1980s solved this problem by strapping the user's head into a fixed position. In doing this, they eliminated the need to calculate where the head was because it always was in the same spot. This was not a very pleasant experience for test participants, however.

In the 1990s, eyetracking equipment was miniaturized enough to be placed in a cap or a headband that was strapped onto the user's head. It was still easy to calculate the position of the eyetracker relative to the user's head because the eyetracker and the head moved in parallel. Thus, users were allowed some amount of free movement. But this was at the cost of making them look like dorks and making them strain their necks and backs because of the heavy stuff on their heads. And there was still the problem of having to match up the recorded screen session with the separately recorded eye movement session. This was time-consuming and error-prone.

How Modern Eyetracking Works

Finally, in the 2000s, computer power improved to the extent that it is now possible to assign a separate video camera to look at the user's head and calculate the head's position in real time. Other cameras are zoomed in to gather close-up views of the two eyes. Since almost everybody looks in the same direction with both eyes, the eyetracker draws its conclusion about where the user is looking by averaging the calculations for the two eyes.

One more ingenious trick most modern eyetrackers use is to bounce a beam of invisible infrared light off the user's face. This wavelength is reflected much better by the retina than by the rest of the eye, since the retina absorbs visible light but reflects infrared. This helps the eyetracker identify the position of the pupils without having to do intense image recognition.

When you put all this information together, it's a fairly simple geometry problem to calculate the direction of a user's gaze. Hindsight is 20/20, though, eh? It's even simpler to calculate what the user is looking at by finding the intersection between the gaze direction (a straight line) and the plane of the computer monitor. (Since eyetracking cameras are built into the monitor, the system certainly knows where the screen is relative to the cameras.)

Using more advanced technology, it's also possible to track where people look in paper documents, such as newspapers, and where they look in physical environments, such as while shopping in a supermarket. But the problem with eyetracking in a noncomputer environment is that there's no automated way to know what the user is looking at, except by utilizing artificial intelligence to perform image recognition. So, most analyses of these eyetracking studies are done by tedious manual reviews of video recordings. These projects are fascinating, but we confine our discussion here to eyetracking computer use.

Other Books on Eyetracking

We present only a very brief introduction to the theory of eyetracking in this book in order to dedicate most of these pages to our findings and what they mean for your Web site. To learn more about the physiology of the eye, perceptual psychology, and the mechanics of eyetracking equipment and its storied history, we recommend *Eye Tracking Methodology: Theory and Practice*, second edition, by Andrew T. Duchowski (Springer, 2009).

For more about eyetracking of the printed page, we recommend a book that documents a large research project about how people read newspapers: *Eyetracking the News* by Sara Quinn, Pegie Stark, Rick Edmonds, and Julie Moos (Poynter Institute, 2007).

Foveal Vision vs. Peripheral Vision

The human eye may seem to be a lot like a camera: It has a lens that can focus on items at a range of distances, an iris diaphragm in the form of the pupil to adjust for various levels of lighting, and a "film" or sensor in the form of the retina to record the image. But the eye sensor doesn't provide the same resolution across an entire image as film does. Photos look about equally sharp at the center and the edges, but human vision is only good in the center; it's inaccurate at the edges. For example, in peripheral vision, the eye sometimes interprets movement when there is none. And it is not very good at deciphering colors or details.

The wonder of the human visual system is that you *think* you have a clear image of your entire environment even when you can hardly see most of it. This works because the instant you want to pay attention to a particular part of your surroundings, you point your gaze straight at it, and it comes into sharp focus. Your brain stitches together these bits and pieces of small, sharp images to form a mental picture of your surroundings that's much better than anything you actually see at any one moment in time.

Roughly speaking, human vision has two parts: a small central area with very high resolution, called **foveal vision**, and the vast majority of the visual field with crummy resolution, called **peripheral vision**.

The really high-resolution area covers only about 2 *degrees* of the visual field—about the size of a thumbnail at arm's length or one to two words on a computer screen under most viewing conditions. This is as much as you can see clearly. Anything else is blurred because it falls within the peripheral rather than foveal vision.

Fixations and Saccades

To stitch together small areas of good visibility into a larger, sharp mental image, a person's eye moves across the items of interest. There's one more important thing to know about this process: The eye's multiple observations don't happen as one smooth, panning movement—the way they would if we were filming a scene with a video camera on a

When the eye is resting on something, it's called a fixation.

Eyetracking Web Usability

tripod with great shock absorbers. Instead, the eye moves in spurts and rests between each movement. Of course, this happens so fast that you're not aware of it (well, now you may be painfully aware of it), but psychologists have run countless experiments for more than 100 years to nail down the details of this movement.

When the eye is resting on something, it's called a **fixation**. The eye's rapid movements from one fixation to the next are called **saccades**. Because the eye moves so fast, each saccade lasts only between one-hundredth and one-tenth of a second. The optical image on the retina blurs so much during this fast movement that we're effectively *blind* during a saccade: We don't actually see what the eye is moving across. We see only during fixations, while the eye is holding still.

Fixations typically last between one-tenth and one-half second, so they're also pretty fast. In fact, the first thing people notice when watching a video recording of an eyetracking session is how fast the eye moves. To analyze what happens during this time, we typically need to watch replays in slow motion—slowed down to at least one-third (and often one-tenth) of their real-time speed. And even then, we need to rewind them several times to follow and understand just small segments of the user's viewing paths. Because people are virtually blind during saccades, we do not analyze them. Instead, we consider only fixations when we discuss the results of eyetracking studies.

In the figures in this book, users' fixations are blue spots (big for long fixations and small for short fixations) in the gaze plot of their viewing behavior on a given Web page. The thin blue lines connecting these dots represent a user's saccades between fixations.

Why Do Users *Not* See Something?

Throughout this book, we point out when users did not look at a certain design element. But how can there be a usability explanation for why something wasn't seen? And if users *didn't see* a design element, how could it possibly have impacted their behavior?

> *The eye's rapid movements from one fixation to the next are called saccades. The optical image on the retina blurs so much during these movements that people are effectively blind during a saccade.*

This paradox is explained by considering the difference between foveal and peripheral vision. Our eyetracking equipment records what parts of the screen the user's foveal vision fixates on. It does not record peripheral (or the in-between parafoveal) vision. Because foveal vision is the only high-resolution part of the human visual system, only the screen elements that receive fixations are seen by users in sufficient enough detail to read text or notice fine components of visual design. This is why we say that users only *saw* the screen elements they fixated on. Since they did not fixate at all on some items, they didn't perceive enough information from other parts of the screen to really understand their content.

However, through peripheral vision, users sometimes still perceive—in a rough, low-resolution manner—design elements they did not fixate on. Even though peripheral vision isn't good enough for reading or interpreting details, it's sufficient for perceiving the general shape and color of screen elements. For example, users can tell that there's a big photo on the screen even if they don't fixate on it. They won't be able to tell who is in it, but they can tell whether it is a photo of a human face. (Of course, in some cases, a sea otter's face may also peripherally look like a human face.) That's the difference between high-resolution viewing (foveal vision) and low-resolution viewing (peripheral vision).

You can demonstrate this phenomenon yourself by letting your gaze rest on the last words at the bottom of this page. When you do this, you will be able to read the words you're staring at. While keeping your eyes locked at this position, mentally consider what's within your visual field. If you have reasonably good vision, you should be able to perceive that there's text at the top of the page within your peripheral vision. But because your foveal vision is fixed on the last world on the page, you won't be able to read any of the words up there.

As we discuss in the next section, it's unnatural to retain your gaze on one element while you are trying to perceive another one. Normally, you simply switch your gaze to the other thing if you want to look at it. However, for the sake of the experiment, you can force your eyes to practice this weird behavior for a short time.

Peripheral vision allows users to be aware of the general layout of a Web page even though they are not looking at all the elements. The elements they don't fixate on are those they don't care about for various reasons—correct or erroneous—that we discuss in future chapters. And only those design elements that they do fixate on are perceived in sufficient detail for users to see their content.

The Mind–Eye Hypothesis

Knowing where people look would be worthless if it didn't tell us something about their behavior. Fortunately, it does, thanks to the **mind–eye hypothesis**, which holds that what people are looking at and what they are thinking about tends to be the same.

If taken to the extreme, the mind–eye hypothesis may seem ludicrous. *Looking at* and *thinking about* are certainly not always intertwined. You can think about pink elephants without looking at one. And your thoughts may be on freshly deep-fried donuts while you're sitting in your car when the stoplight changes. You may not be paying attention to whatever happens to be within your foveal vision, such as the light turning green, until a honk from the car behind you wakes you from your donut dream.

According to the mind–eye hypothesis, people are usually thinking about what they are looking at. They do not always totally understand or engage with it, but if they are looking, they are usually paying attention, especially when concentrating on a particular task.

In general, though, the mind–eye hypothesis holds true often enough for eyetracking to tell us what users pay attention to on Web pages. People generally do tend to look at the same thing they're thinking about. That's the way the human visual system works, and that's why it fools us into believing that we have a high-resolution image of the world. We can therefore conclude that fixations equal attention: People look at the design elements they are concerned about, and the more they look at something, the more they think about it.

We are not claiming that looking always indicates understanding or actually processing on the user's part. Many times users briefly (or not so briefly) fixate on the very item they need but do not select it. In these cases, they aren't registering what the designers intended the words, image, or link to mean, even as they looked at it.

Are Looks Good or Bad?

By itself, eyetracking can do one thing and one thing only: discover what users look at. But a pure count of fixations can't tell us whether users are productive, happy, or confused when they look at certain things and not at others.

For example, users may look a great deal at a certain paragraph of text because the content is relevant and interesting. Good! Or maybe it's because the writing is convoluted and hard to understand. Bad!

Conversely, if users don't look at certain parts of the navigation, it could be because these design elements don't seem like navigation, and users erroneously assume they are useless. Bad! Alternatively, users don't waste time looking at navigation elements that are consistently repeated from page to page because they know where to find them when they need them again. Good!

So, it is not inherently good or bad for a certain design element to attract fixations or be ignored. Any judgment of the design implications of eyetracking data must include knowledge of users' intents and the usability impact of their behaviors. Overlooking something you need is bad, but saving time by bypassing stuff you don't need is the hallmark of good page layout. The Web is too big for users to attend to everything, and those sites that allow them to focus on what they want are the ones people return to again and again.

Visualizing Eyetracking Results

There are three main ways of visualizing eyetracking results. The very best approach is to watch slow-motion gaze replay videos, but that's very time-consuming and not suited for print. We do have a few video clips on our Web site (*www.useit.com/eyetracking*), and we show many gaze replays in our seminars, but in this book, we focus on two static representations of users' viewing behavior: heat maps and gaze plots.

As you look at them, it's important to remember that they represent movements in time as users' eyes move very rapidly across a Web page and as they navigate through the site. Real behavior is time-sensitive, and usability analyses require us to consider the time dimension as one of the most important components in a study. We have sat through hundreds of eyetracking sessions, observing users as they navigated the Web sites we discuss in this book. And we've watched countless slow-mo replays of these sessions as we worked on translating raw user behaviors into usability insights. We can show you only static depictions of these behaviors, so you have to trust that our analyses accurately reflect what actually happened in the sessions.

Viewing the Heat Maps and Gaze Plots in This Book

Heat maps are the best-known visualization technique for eyetracking studies (**Figure 1.1**). In a heat map, a screenshot is color-coded according to the amount of looks each part attracts: The red areas are where users looked the most, the yellow areas indicate fewer fixations, and the blue areas indicate the least-viewed areas. If an area is gray, it didn't attract any fixations. Heat maps got their name because the choice of colors metaphorically indicates hot zones and cold zones on a page.

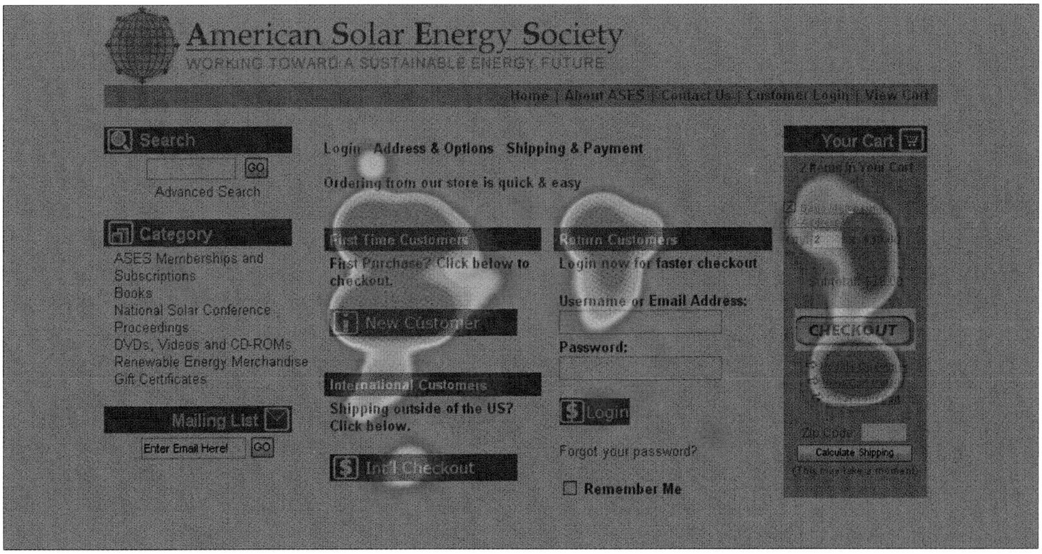

Figure 1.1 A heat map showing a standard step in the checkout process: separating new customers from returning customers. Since first-time shoppers tested this site, people appropriately allocated most of their attention to the *First Time Customers* area of the page.

Heat maps can represent either the *number* of fixations or the *duration* of fixations. In practice, there's typically not much difference between these two approaches, especially when averaged across many users. We have chosen to base the heat maps in this book on fixation duration because we are interested in the amount of attention allocated to each part of a Web page. Thus, the heat maps show how many seconds users look at different screen elements, not how many times they look at them.

Heat maps are typically aggregated across multiple users. This visualization lends itself to huge studies because it doesn't depict individual users' viewing behaviors. The color-coding represents the average behavior for all users.

However, although it's useful to get an overview of many people's behaviors in a single image, heat maps also smooth over differences in individual behaviors. People approach the same Web page in different ways. Ultimately, a design needs to cater to one user at a time, and usability is determined by the success or failure of each single user. So, there is also much be gained from visualizing individual users' viewing patterns. This is done in gaze plots.

In a **gaze plot**, a single user's visit to a page is depicted as a series of blue dots, each indicating one fixation (**Figure 1.2**). The size of each dot represents the duration of that fixation, with bigger dots indicating longer looks. The dots are numbered, showing the sequence of the fixations, and thin lines connect the fixations, indicating the saccades as the eye moved from one location to the next. Remember that humans are blind during saccades, so the user didn't see the elements under the thin lines, only those under the dots.

It's possible to draw gaze plots to visualize a user's entire visit to a page, but they can be difficult to follow if the user pays close attention to a particular part of the page. It's also possible to draw different gaze plots for different parts of a user's visit—for example, to see what the person did during the first few seconds on a page. We use gaze plots like these most often in this book.

Figure 1.2 A gaze plot of one user's fixations on the Web site of *GQ* and *Details*. It shows intense reading of the text and less attention to the photo, including a single look at the dog's face.

Note that a few screenshots in this book show just a moment of a gaze replay, displaying only one blue dot and no number on it. This is the only way to capture the eye gaze of dynamic elements such as animations.

Tasks Determine Looks

The mind–eye hypothesis implies that the way people look at any given artifact—such as a Web page—is determined by what they're trying to do with it. In other words, the task the user has chosen or been asked to do determines their looks.

Obviously, it's important to test the right tasks: to conduct eyetracking studies while users are trying to do the same things on a Web site in a lab as they would at home or work. If you ask users to do an unrealistic task, you'll get unrealistic eyetracking data, and your study will be worthless. It is also important to give people some open-ended tasks, such as reading the news, and to let them create their own tasks. Doing this helps us learn where people choose to look when we did not impose even the slightest influence on them.

Let's look at an example from an eyetracking study we conducted of our own Web site (*www.nngroup.com*). This study is not included in this book and involved a different group of 30 participants recruited from our customer base. (In other words, we are hopeful they were similar to you, dear reader.) These users visited our site to research our annual Usability Week conference and also browsed sites for several competing events.

We gave them two main tasks:

- To decide which conference they would rather attend
- To decide which seminars they would choose at that conference

As the two heat maps of one of our seminar descriptions show, people looked very differently at the same information, depending on what they were trying to accomplish (**Figure 1.3** and **Figure 1.4**).

Usability is always relative to two questions: Who are the users, and what are they trying to do? The same design may be great for one type of user and horrible for another. For example, we often find user interfaces that assume a level of technical expertise that's far beyond regular folks. Such a user interface (UI) might work well for the engineers who designed it, but it'd be a disaster for a broad consumer audience.

Similarly, a design might support some tasks very well but be terrible for others: A drop-down list is OK for selecting between a dozen options or so, but it's awkward for selecting between scores of options—and completely impossible with hundreds of options.

It's not a weakness of eyetracking that people look at the same page differently. It's a fact of usability and something you would find no matter what research method you employed. User interface designs only make sense in the context of actual use, and that's how they should be tested.

> The tasks a user is trying to do and his experience on other pages of the site greatly impact how he looks at a page.

Figure 1.3 A heat map showing how potential conference attendees looked at a seminar description page for our Usability Week conference when trying to decide whether to attend this conference or another. People allocated most of their attention to the summary of the seminar and didn't read much of anything else.

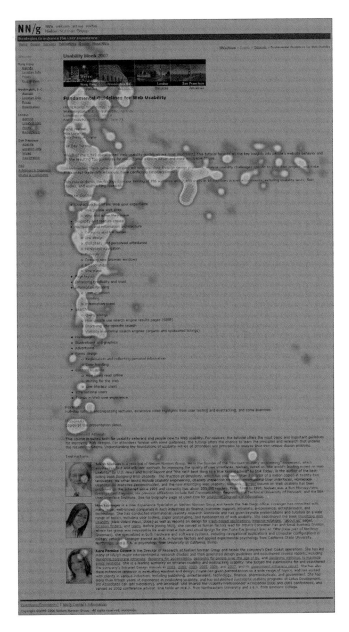

Figure 1.4 A heat map showing how potential conference attendees looked at the same seminar description page when trying to decide which seminars to attend at the Usability Week conference. In this case, they read the detailed course outline carefully and spent substantial time on the *Who Should Attend* section. They also scanned the speaker photos, perhaps trying to determine how competent they were or how fun their class might be.

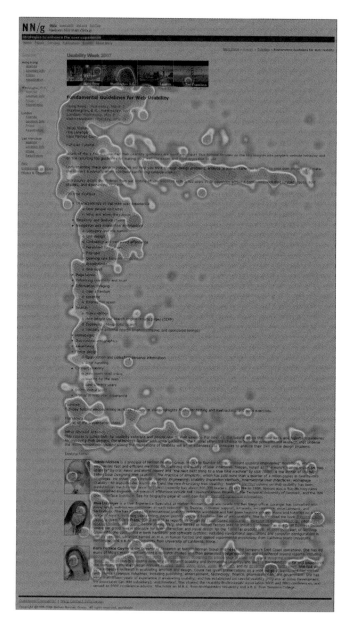

Other Uses of Eyetracking

This book is about the use of eyetracking to study Web usability, but there are many other interesting applications of this technology. Two obvious ones are to study the usability of application software and to study the effectiveness of advertising on the Web.

There's not much difference between eyetracking for Web usability and eyetracking for application software usability. In fact, sometimes applications are implemented as Web pages, and then the difference is even smaller. In both cases, we run software on the computer and track users' eye movements as they look at the information displayed on the monitor. If we're testing Web sites, the software is a Web browser, but it could as easily be anything else, such as a spreadsheet or photo-editing program.

The main difference between Web usability and application usability is that application designers are often interested in optimizing minute aspects of an interaction in order to create a highly optimized, flowing user experience. So, in application design, it might be a goal to shave a few tenths of a second off the time it takes users to activate a frequently used command. For Web sites, we rarely strive for such extreme optimization because we'd rather get people to the right link first and worry later about getting them to click that link 0.1 seconds faster. If you can get users to click a link 0.1 seconds faster, you have done them a disservice if it turns out to be a link that leads to a page the user doesn't actually want.

The main difference between studying Web usability and Web advertising usability is that although interactive ads exist, display ads (such as the ones printed in magazines) are more common, and people don't *use* them as they do the UI components of a Web site. They may watch them, but they don't have to interact with most of them. Therefore, eyetracking studies of advertisements rarely ask users to perform tasks. Instead, the ads are simply displayed on the monitor, and the eyetracker measures what elements attract the users' eyes first and how much time they spend looking at different areas of the ad.

Online advertisements that include interactive elements, such as drop-down menus or small games, should be tested like any other user interface: by giving users a task, even a very open-ended one, to see how they interact with the UI. These advertisements, which are embedded within a larger interactive environment such as a Web site or a video game, should be tested within the context of the pages that users will be seeing them in. (And see the Chapter 7, "Advertisements," for what we learned about Web advertising during our studies of Web sites.)

Even though it's much easier to use an eyetracker that's embedded within a computer screen, that's not the only way to track people's eye movements and gaze direction. It is also possible to ask users to wear a head-mounted eyetracker that tracks their gaze while they are moving around the world and looking at three-dimensional objects. Such equipment is useful for studying real-world shopping behaviors and for usability studies of physical devices. For example, manufacturers of anything from PCs to mobile phones to plasma televisions should run out-of-the-box studies to observe users unpacking their product and trying to plug it in.

Eyetrackers as Input Devices

Finally, eyetrackers can go beyond testing to become part of the user interface itself. If the computer knows where the user is looking, the software can adjust the display to present more information about the things the user cares about most. As a simple example, if a user was staring intently at a thumbnail photo on an e-commerce site, the site could automatically display a bigger version of the photo instead of waiting for the user to click a zoom button.

Using eyetracking as an input technique is a long-standing research topic in human–computer interaction, but it has not made it into practical products yet. The first time we encountered eyetracking as an input technique was at the Naval Research Laboratory (NRL) in the late 1980s when Dr. Robert J. K. Jacob showed us his experimental system for allowing Navy officers fast access to information about ships in the vicinity. While an officer worked with the radar screen, the eyetracker would determine what ship he was looking at, and intelligence information about that ship would immediately come up on a display, saving the officer the time of manually calling up the information from the database.

This early use of eyetracking as an input device was not only a compelling demonstration; it was also a good example of the types of applications it is most appropriate for. As we have discussed, it is not always the case that people look at an object because they have a particular intent regarding that object. Sometimes their gaze just happens to point in that direction while they are pondering something else. In the NRL system, the officer might be looking at the radar image of a ship because he is worried that it's an enemy ship about to come within attack range. Or his gaze might be resting on that part of the radar screen while he's pondering next week's mission.

As long as the system doesn't do anything except display information about the ship on the secondary monitor, it doesn't matter why the officer is looking at the ship. If he is interested in the ship, the information will be available faster than would otherwise be possible—perhaps crucially so. On the other hand, if he is not really interested in the ship, the computer made an extra database query that wasn't needed. No big deal. But what if the eyetracker was tied into the weapons targeting system instead? Then the user's intent would be critical.

The fact that we can't know precisely why users are looking at objects on the screen is a limiting factor in using eyetracking as an input device for practical computer applications. Some applications will probably hold great promise for improving usability once eyetracking technology gets inexpensive enough to embed in all computer monitors, not just the expensive ones we buy for computer-related usability studies. For now, though, these ideas remain in the research labs, with one important exception: use of eyetracking as an assistive technology.

This is a powerful, though expensive, advancement in using the Web for people who have use of their eyes but not their arms or hands. Rather than using a mouth stick—a device resembling a long pencil, which people hold in their teeth to type and click—or a head wand or other home-fashioned substitutes, they just have to look. Eyetracking can be of great help to these users because it allows them to point to objects on the screen and activate them with just the blink of an eye.

2 Our Eyetracking Research

We have conducted usability studies using eyetracking for clients and for our own research reports. But this book is based on a series of large-scale studies that had four goals:

- To use eyetracking to test our theories about usable and unusable Web design

- To investigate eyetracking data for new usability findings

- To determine which, if any, findings can be collected with eyetracking only

- To collect information about good eyetracking usability practices and methodology

We believe this to be the largest eyetracking usability study ever done.

To study vastly different Web sites and many of the kinds of tasks possible on the Web today, we needed to do this study with a lot of people. Several hundred may not seem like many if you are thinking in market research terms, but in behavioral research terms this is a huge sample. (A basic qualitative usability study requires only five people to find many of the usability issues with a system.) We watched every one of them use Web sites and learned all about where they did and did not look, what was helpful in the designs, and why.

Also, we wanted to determine how many users' visits are needed on a page to make a valid heat map of that page. We could do this only by having many different people use the same sites and do various tasks on them.

Data Collected

The findings in this book are based on 1.5 million fixations.

More than 300 people participated in this study. We assigned 85 tasks—some very specific and some very open-ended. This resulted in 1.5 million fixations, or **looks**. The recordings we reviewed and retain comprise more than 300GB of data.

Since we planned to measure some behaviors quantitatively, it is important that these sessions were conducted in exactly the same way. For consistency's sake, only two Nielsen Norman Group facilitators conducted all the tests for this study using the same methodology: observing people in a lab and following a predefined, specific protocol. The lab was set up in an office in midtown Manhattan in New York.

Study Participants

We recruited primarily working people with these demographics:

Age	18–29: 20%
	30–49: 64%
	50–64: 16%
Web experience	Low: 39%
	Medium: 29%
	High: 32%
Gender	Female: 58%
	Male: 42%
Employment	Full-time: 81%
	Part-time: 15%
	Unemployed: 1%
	Homemaker: 3%
	Retired: 0%
Household income	Less than $20,000: 3%
	$20,000 to 50,000: 32%
	More than $50,000: 65%
Education	Some high school: 2%
	High school graduate: 4%
	Some college: 25%
	College graduate or more: 69%
Ethnicity	White: 58%
	Black: 21%
	Hispanic: 11%
	Other: 10%
Residence	City: 83%
	Suburb/rural: 17%

We chose these demographics because they represent those of users who comprise most of the business among our clients. The number of usability problems uncovered could have been greater had we included more people with less

Web experience. This could include people with few years of formal education, the unemployed, retirees who did not use the Internet much during their professional careers, and possibly low-salary workers who do not use a computer at work.

To make the study feasible, we conducted all the sessions in one location. Fortunately, because it was New York, we had access to people with a great variety of backgrounds. However, had this study been conducted in other countries (particularly where people read from right to left or respond differently to color and animations), some results would likely differ.

Qualitative and Quantitative Sessions

Traditionally, usability methods can be divided into quantitative (sometimes abbreviated as "quant") and qualitative approaches. Quantitative studies measure usability data numerically, whereas qualitative studies aim to collect richer insights and observations. We employed both kinds of studies in our eyetracking research.

For example, a quantitative study might show that it takes users an average of 5.2 minutes to buy 12 yellow roses on a flower site, whereas a qualitative study might show that users can't figure out how to specify the delivery date for the flowers because of a certain design weakness. Both are interesting insights, but if you want to sell more flowers, a qualitative study is the way to go. Of course, a quant study may yield some rich insights, but they are secondary to the numbers and, because of the way quant studies are run, are less commonly uncovered.

Eyetracking adds another twist, because there are two main ways of analyzing the data: by aggregating viewing behavior across a large number of users to form a heat map or by analyzing individual users' viewing behaviors through gaze plots and gaze replays.

Eyetracking Web Usability

To create an effective heat map for a given Web page, we made sure to include eyetracking recordings from 30 users on that page.

Our free report gives more information and tips about eyetracking usability methodology: www.useit.com/eyetracking/methodology.

For a heat map to be robust, it needs to be averaged across many users because of the large variability in individual users' eye movements. Our studies indicate that it's best to have eyetracking recordings from 30 users to plot a heat map for a given Web page. This means that about 39 participants need to test the sites because you won't get good recordings from all users.

We present more detail on how many users to include in an eyetracking study in our separate report on eyetracking methodology, which is available for download at *www.useit.com/eyetracking/methodology*.

When collecting numeric data and in sessions aimed at generating heat maps, we did not ask participants to think aloud because that could impact how long they looked at something. We used consistent task-timing methods and predetermined success scores.

When collecting richer qualitative feedback, we sometimes did ask participants to think aloud to further illuminate their behavior. But extra fixations while talking spoils eyetracking data, so we discounted these instances when doing fixation counts or using heat maps.

Test Sessions

Each test session lasted between one-and-a-half and two hours. Users were asked to indicate when they were finished with a task or if they wanted to stop. Users gave answers for all tasks in various ways (depending on the task): verbally, via a questionnaire, or by writing an essay. For open-ended exploring, they just said when they were finished.

All tasks were captured by the eyetracker and timed and scored by the facilitators. The user's face was sometimes also videotaped. But this crashed the system on occasion, so we did not always do this. We did tape people via a video camera on a tripod as a backup, however.

Session Logistics

Each user session consisted of the following activities, which were always done in the same order:

- Welcome/setup
- Consent form
- Interest questionnaire
- Calibration of eyetracker
- Tasks
- Web experience observed score
- Post-task questionnaires (users rated their satisfaction, frustration, and confidence after each task)
- Retrospective (seldom), in which we asked people to watch parts of their test session and comment

Web Sites and Test Tasks

The assigned tasks were a combination of open-ended tasks, in which users could choose any sites they wanted (in some cases doing something specific and in others doing something very open-ended), and closed tasks, in which users were asked to use a particular site and do something specific.

The eyetracking system opened the Web site to be tested or another site or blank page for users. When users were told to go wherever they wanted on the Web, we sometimes opened a blank document as the homepage, a news Web site, or another site that was unrelated to the task in order to not bias where they went first.

Quantitative Tasks

This is a sampling of the tasks that we tested with large numbers of users, using quantitative test methodology.

Web search/research

- Google: Which professional sport and position did George Brett play?
- Google: What was the date of Groundhog Day 2006?
- Yahoo: What is the top speed at which a mako shark swims?

- Yahoo: Find out which, if any, identification a U.S. citizen should have to drive across the Canadian border.

- About.com: Your friend gets heartburn a lot. Read and tell me the advice you would give your friend.

Reading

- *New York Magazine:* Find the restaurant you would most like to go to.

- *New York Times*: Two Australians recently won a Nobel Prize. Read "Australians Win Nobel Prize in Medicine" to learn the details and any interesting points about their research.

- *New York Magazine:* Read "Will Wait for Food." Tell me which food establishments the reviewer feels merit the wait time.

- Danceworksonline.co.uk: Your friend is a big fan of Mikhail Baryshnikov. Learn enough so you can talk with your friend about him.

Corporate

- Agere: Find the company's headquarters.

- Adelphia: Learn about digital video recording (DVR).

- BNSF: Read the latest news about BNSF Railway.

- BNSF: What are some of its corporate values?

- JetBlue: Which stock exchange is it listed on?

Shopping

- JCPenney: Buy a present for a fictitious friend's new baby girl.

- Kiehl's: Buy yourself something.

- Headset Zone: Buy a headset that will work well for your needs.

- Sears: Buy an air humidifier for a room that is 2,000 square feet. Spend less than $125.

- Rapid-fire for specific sites: Click the specific item as soon as you find it.

Qualitative Tasks

This is a sampling of the qualitative tasks we tested with a smaller number of users who were asked to think aloud as they used the Internet:

- Who was Fiorello LaGuardia?

- You and a friend want to go skiing in Colorado this winter. Plan the trip.

- What major event happened in Galveston, Texas, in 1900? And what were the effects?

- Tie a bowline knot. (We gave people a piece of rope to tie the knot.)

- You are considering investing $10,000 in a retirement plan. Find the best way to invest your money.

- Which of these two dog breeds would be better for you: Cairn Terrier or Pharaoh Hound?

- Your friend is worried about contracting the bird flu. Find some information to calm his nerves.

- You are buying a new home and need to finance it. Find the mortgage company that will provide the best service and rates for you.

- Use the Sony Web site to buy yourself a small digital camera for less than $450.

- You are thinking about buying a digital music player. Use the Sony site to choose the one that would be best for you.

- Find the Sony store nearest you.

- Buy yourself (or a friend) something good at *mrchocolate.com*.

- Buy a few T-shirts for yourself or for someone else at *panic.com/goods*.

- Buy yourself a shirt at *neimanmarcus.com*.

- Is there a Neiman Marcus store close to you?

- You are thinking of buying a phone with T-Mobile. Choose the options that would work best for you.

- Check to ensure that T-Mobile will work in all the places you go.
- Assume that you filed your tax return five weeks ago. You expect a refund, but have not yet received it. What should you do? Use *irs.gov*.
- You gave $100 to the Good Dog Foundation. Is it deductible?
- Buy yourself something you (or a friend) would like at *mrcoffee.com*.
- Your friend broke the coffee pot for his model: ECDT84. See whether it is possible to get a new one. Use *mrcoffee.com*.
- See whether there is anything you are interested in (on *usatoday.com*).
- See whether there is anything you are interested in (on *youtube.com*).
- See whether there is anything you are interested in (on *vogue.com*).
- What is the *Vogue* Fashion Fund?
- See whether there is anything you are interested in buying at Victoria's Secret.
- Do your grocery shopping (on *freshdirect.com*).
- What is Skype? Is it something you might want to use? Why or why not?
- Does a mallard duck dive for food? If so, does it usually stay underwater long?
- Look for a flat-screen TV that you might want. Use the Panasonic Web site.
- Get a flight on United Airlines for you and a friend to San Francisco for a week in June or July.
- Which teams are currently leading in college basketball? Look on the *Sports Illustrated* site (*si.com*).
- How does a windmill generate power?
- Which systems does *GQ* magazine recommend for playing video games?

Measures

As with several of our studies, we measured many of the results from this one in a qualitative way: We watched users' behavior as we considered what they were trying to do. In this study, we also focused on what people looked at, how much they looked at elements, and what they did not look at. Finally, we worked to determine why they did or did not look at things. To a lesser degree, we listened to the comments users made either as they worked or between tasks.

In addition to qualitative measures, we used four basic quantitative measures that we often employ in our usability work: task time, success score, errors, and users' subjective satisfaction. We also considered the number of fixations people spent at different stages of tasks and whether they were desired or wasted.

Subjective Satisfaction

While collecting objective measures, it's also important to get users' perspectives on the task they have just worked on. This can help us see where users were most happy and least happy. Sometimes a user may complete a task quickly but is unhappy with it, or they might spend a long time on a task but not be bothered by that.

So, we asked people to answer three questions just after they finished a task and before we asked them for comments or asked specific questions (at least in our quantitative studies with a larger user sample). The questions usually were as follows:

■ How easy or difficult was it to complete the task?

	Very Easy						*Very Difficult*
	1	2	3	4	5	6	7

This question (easy or difficult) allows people to say how much trouble they had, if any.

■ How satisfying or unsatisfying was it to work on this task?

	Very Satisfying						*Very Unsatisfying*
	1	2	3	4	5	6	7

At first glance, this question (satisfaction) seems to ask the same thing as the first question. But we often get very different answers to it because it actually relates more to content and feature set than to usability. For example, a user may have found some very interesting information about how to apply for a passport while learning what identification is needed to drive across the Canada/U.S. border. Maybe the task was difficult to do, so the person circled "6" in answering the first question. But since the user got some interesting tidbits, she was kind of happy with her work. So, for the second question, she circled a satisfied "3."

- How confident or not confident are you that you completed the task (or gave the right answer)?

Very Confident   *Not Confident*

1   2   3   4   5   6   7

This question (confidence) captures those situations in which users did a task but weren't really certain that they gave the correct answer. Or they brought a task to fruition, but they did not realize or trust that they did everything they needed to complete it.

For example, maybe a Web site offered conflicting information or different sites offered different information, and the user was not sure which source to trust. If a user rates low confidence in the lab, we anticipate that out of the lab, if the information was really important to him, he would probably look further or call someone. Conversely, a Web site may give misleading or incorrect information packaged in a very credible way, so the user believes it. She may be very confident in her answer although she did not really complete the task successfully. This information is then balanced with the actual success score, so we can make statements such as, "The site gave users a good impression, though they were only 50 percent successful." Or, we might say, "Customers will be surprised and probably upset when their order never arrives because they were unable to submit it correctly, but the interface led them to believe that they had."

We write these questionnaires so the users can see the rating scale and physically circle a number. Saying a rating scale aloud is often hard for users to keep straight. We like to use a seven-point Likert scale simply because people have more difficulty choosing a number on a five-point scale. It's easy to see why. With only five choices, there is not much room for nuance. So, respondents often create their own numbers, like this:

Very Easy   *Very Difficult*

    1 *2* *3* *4* *5*

        ↑

       3.5

On the other hand, an 11-point scale offers too many choices, and it takes people a long time to choose or they circle more than one:

Very Easy   *Very Difficult*

   1 *2* *3* *4* *5* (*6* *7*) *8* *9* *10* *11*

Seven is the least number of choices that make users feel they have enough of a selection.

Notice that we also use signpost words to anchor the two ends of the scale. The words match the language used in the actual question because consistency helps users move ahead quickly and confidently. The text signposts appear only above the numbers at either end of the scale, not over each number in the scale. This enables users to choose their own definitions and not get hung up on the words we use. For example, all the text signposts on this scale make it limiting and potentially confusing:

Very Easy	*Easy*	*Pretty Easy*	*Neither*	*Pretty Difficult*	*Difficult*	*Very Difficult*
1	*2*	*3*	*4*	*5*	*6*	*7*

Rather than having people tell us their choices, we give them a pen to circle their answers. This allows us to check the answers for anything that seems interesting (or wrong—sometimes people forget which end of the scale is positive and which is negative). Having the information on paper also allows us to easily enter the data into a spreadsheet later, freeing us during testing to advance faster and fit in more tasks.

A seven-point rating scale makes it easier for users to choose a number than a five-point or eleven-point scale.

We averaged each user's three answers to get the user's overall subjective satisfaction for the task. We administered this questionnaire after every quantitative task.

Time

To measure how long it took a user to complete a specific task, we started the clock after the person had read (or was told) the task, understood his marching orders, and "addressed" the system. In Web studies, this is when he has his hand on the mouse and is looking at the screen. (Note that the screen we started the timer on varied, depending on the exact task we were measuring.) We paused the timer if there was an interruption such as a system crash. We also stopped it when the user stated that he had finished. We didn't stop it when the user had actually finished unless he said he had, because sometimes the user wasn't sure he was done and wanted to keep working.

Considering the importance of the task's end point, it is imperative to explain to testers before the session begins that they must announce when they are finished, or we would continue writing and observing. After the first task, some users needed to be reminded of this. For this reason, we found it a good idea to give users a throwaway, or practice, task in this and other quant studies. We didn't tell users it was practice; we just counted it as such.

We typically used a standard athletic stopwatch to time our sessions. Technologists will undoubtedly think we are nuts and there must be a better way. But while managing a session, especially an eyetracking session, facilitators must keep so many things going smoothly that having a simple stopwatch at their side makes it easier for some. The only problem is that most modern stopwatches beep when you stop and start them. That's good for checking your splits but not great for making users relax and forget they're in a lab. Fortunately, our colleague Amy Schade and her husband took the stopwatch apart and removed the little piece of aluminum foil in the back that causes the beep.

Success

Success was measured by how much of a task the user completed in the end. When the user said she was finished, had she completed the task? And if so, what percent did she complete? We did not score tasks as pass/fail because this yields a slanted picture that designs are worse than they actually are.

Errors

We kept track of how many times users selected the wrong feature in the interface. For example, a user might select the *view shopping cart* button thinking it was really the *add to shopping cart* button. Or he might click the *Investor Relations* link to find a press release when press information is really located under the *Media* link on a site. Or an intranet user might type a colleague's name in the intranet site search to find his phone number when he really needed to type in the employee directory search to find this information.

To capture errors accurately, test facilitators must be very fast and have thorough knowledge of the Web site they are dealing with or watch the test recording after the fact. Cataloguing errors is time-consuming and, ironically, error-prone. This is mainly because cross-linking and convoluted information architecture result in so many avenues for getting to pages and information on Web sites. For example, though a press release may be located in the *Media* section of the site, there is also a link to *Media* in the *Investor Relations* section. So, was it actually an error when the user selected *Investor Relations*? This is very difficult to determine. And we come across the same issues when trying to determine miscues.

Miscues

The notion of **miscues**, elements that attract the user's eye and attention at the wrong time, is important. But counting every miscue is extremely difficult, if not impossible. You simply cannot always tell whether someone is looking at something because they are just interested or because they are erroneously drawn to it. It took many viewings of user sessions to determine when miscues truly occurred in our studies.

Recognizing miscues is even more difficult than recognizing errors. Because it is so time-consuming and error-prone, we recommend that only very advanced usability teams bother with this. It would probably be difficult for many design teams today to deeply study and use feedback regarding miscues. Most teams are not quite primed for this, because they are still learning and trying to respond to basic usability findings without eyetracking. Miscues should probably only be pursued by advanced design teams that have already found and fixed problems pertaining to more serious usability issues—such as misclicks (clicking the wrong links or buttons) and unsuccessful tasks.

Why Many Eyetracking Studies Are Bogus

Our studies are not the first to use eyetracking to research Web site usability. But this is the first large-scale eyetracking study to use valid usability methodology to record the gaze of representative users as they performed realistic tasks on a wide variety of Web sites. Note the three important criteria:

- Representative users
- Realistic task performance
- A wide variety of Web sites

We believe all three are necessary to form conclusions that can be generalized and serve as useful design guidelines for other Web sites.

Representative Users

Academic studies that use students as subjects are irrelevant for the design of corporate Web sites, e-commerce sites, government sites, and any other type of sites that primarily target adult users and business professionals. And even if your site targets teenagers or other young users, you can't rely on the findings from academic studies that use undergraduate psychology students from elite universities as test participants—unless that narrow audience happens to be your only target.

Realistic Task Performance

Academic papers are also irrelevant for commercial design projects because they are not about realistic, business-oriented task performance. Usability is always highly context-dependent, and Web usability is even more dependent on the richness of the informational environment than other areas of usability, such as the design of airplane cockpits. When people use a Web site, they typically need to navigate a hyperspace with tens of thousands of pages, and they are aware that there are probably hundreds of competing sites they could visit as well. In contrast, academic studies usually test a very narrowly construed information environment in order to control the variables of that environment sufficiently stringently to get the theoretical findings needed for a publishable research paper. If you're interested in fundamental advances in perceptual psychology, that's indeed the way to run an experiment. If you're interested in generating more leads from a business-to-business site, a tightly controlled experiment won't give you findings that relate to real-world sales, even in the unlikely case that you tested corporate purchasing managers instead of students.

Even commercial eyetracking studies are usually conducted with weak methodology that makes their findings suspect. The most common mistake is to conduct studies without giving users realistic tasks to perform. People look at a Web page very differently depending on whether they're just passing through on the way to meeting a goal elsewhere or checking out the page for its own sake. Many studies collect useless data by asking users to "review this Web page, and let us know what you think about it." This is not a realistic task because users normally don't go to a Web site in order to analyze its design. Only Web designers do this. But when people are looking at a page to review it, they're going to pay attention to design elements much more carefully and systematically than they would if they were on the move.

When researchers assign the unrealistic task of commenting on a page, they end up recording many more fixations on elements such as advertisements than are likely in realistic user behavior. They also find that users read the text much more carefully than they would do during real use.

Even assigning realistic tasks can yield invalid findings if the test environment is too narrow. Say that you are interested in finding out how shoppers enter information in the address fields on shipping information pages during checkout. To get a nice heat map of this page, you might be tempted to take 30 users straight to the point where they would enter their shipping information and then ask them to start typing their address. You could then record how people look around the Web form as part of the real-enough task of getting something shipped to their house.

However, this would actually generate a bogus heat map, and its conclusions would not help us design an e-commerce site that helps users complete the purchasing process. The problem is taking users to a specific page and out of the real-world context within which they normally progress through the flow. People's behavior with an individual page is very different from their behavior within a flow.

OK, you might think, then instead let's have users complete the full checkout process and record their eye movements on all of those pages, even though we're interested only in how they deal with the address form. This would be better but still not truly valid. The best study is one in which users are asked to shop on the site, starting with finding a product and adding it to the shopping cart. Only then can you ask them to check out and observe how they look at the address fields, because their behavior on this page will be primed by their experience on the previous pages they've encountered during the entire shopping process.

There's a tension between eyetracking studies and real user behavior. Eyetracking records behavior within a single page, but Web usability is dominated by movement between pages. The way to resolve this tension is to conduct eyetracking studies with users who are navigating normally because they are using the Web to perform a realistic task. Only then can you get realistic data about how people look at each of the pages they encounter.

Unfortunately, many eyetracking studies are conducted by showing one or two pages to users and then recording how they look at them. But the very act of showing users a specific page biases the way they will look at it. When users are aware that the facilitators are interested in a particular page, they consider it much more carefully than they would if that page were just one out of many they happened on while navigating.

On the Web, there are no silver bells that ring when users arrive at the page they are looking for. In countless sessions, we have observed users getting to the correct page only to abandon it within a few seconds because it didn't look right to them. In normal Web use, people have to judge pages quickly and cut their losses if they are on the wrong (or at least what they believe is the wrong) page or site. Only after people have determined that a page is of high interest will they start studying it in detail. If people studied all pages on the Web in great detail, they would never get anything done, and they know this. So, researchers alter people's behavior (and invalidate their study results) if they put them on a particular page instead of allowing them to navigate freely.

Wide Variety of the Web Sites and Tasks

The third criterion for judging the validity of an eyetracking study is the breadth and variety of the Web sites that are tested. There's nothing wrong with testing a single site—in fact, that's what we do in most of our consulting projects. But you can't generalize findings from one site to many others.

If you identify a usability finding on a single Web site that was tested with its target audience, you have no way of knowing whether that finding is a peculiarity of that site or its audience. Perhaps it *is* a generally applicable usability insight, but with only one data point, you can't know for sure.

This is why it's important to test a wide variety of sites and audiences. Only after you see the same pattern of behaviors repeated on multiple sites can you start feeling confident that you have discovered a usability guideline that is likely to apply to a site that you have not tested.

Weigh the Evidence

In Nielsen Norman Group, we have tested more than 1,250 Web sites with more than 3,600 users in 16 nations on 4 continents. Certainly, our eyetracking study was smaller than our generalized user testing—for example, we collected eyetracking data in only a single nation. But in interpreting our eyetracking findings, we could draw on experience from thousands of other user sessions we have observed and compare them with documented behaviors for an enormously diverse range of other designs.

The need to generalize across a broad variety of Web sites and users presents another problem for the practical applicability of most academic studies and even presentations at trade shows and industry conferences. Academic studies almost always target an incredibly narrow range of designs —often just one or two Web sites or two variations of a single site. And industry presentations are even narrower because they usually involve a speaker talking about his own project. When a speaker at an industry event says, "We did an eyetracking study of this page, and here's what we found and how we improved our site," you're usually going to get a positive spin on what actually happened. Companies often claim great success for their own designs without much evidence that their sites actually make money.

Most of the eyetracking reports we have read have not been very convincing because they violated one—or usually all three—of the requirements for producing valid insights. Still, across a large number of studies, one can derive some insights. As long as each study includes representative users performing realistic tasks, its findings are likely to be true, even if they apply only to the Web site tested. And if you combine the findings of many limited-scope studies, you are in effect conducting a broader-scope study by generalizing across each of the reports.

In essence, you have to weigh the evidence. If you read 20 reports from 20 studies of 20 sites and 19 of these reports have more or less the same finding, then you've probably hit on a true usability guideline. Remember that usability guidelines are just that: guidelines, or rules of thumb. They do not always apply to every design. Because interaction design is so context-based, special circumstances may dictate that a certain design project deviate from an otherwise valid usability guideline.

In this hypothetical example, if 19 studies had a common finding and one study found the opposite, it is almost always safe to go with the majority. The deviant study was probably conducted with poor research methodology, which is all too common. But even if the methodology was sound, the results could have been a statistical fluke caused by randomness. This is particularly common for quantitative studies that base their conclusions on statistical analyses. Usually, the criterion for "statistical significance" is $p<.05$, which means that there is less than 5 percent probability of being wrong because of random factors. But if you have 20 studies, then a 5 percent probability of being wrong translates into one erroneous study. (And you don't know which one, so you have to distrust all of them.)

Ultimately, even if the methodology was sound and the results were not skewed by random error, you might still be able to discard the one deviant finding in our example. Most likely, that particular report studied one of the exceptional designs that are indeed different from the majority because of some contextual peculiarity.

There are so many reasons eyetracking studies can go wrong. It's even more difficult to get an eyetracking study right and analyze the findings correctly than it is to work with traditional usability methods. Considering how many studies have been done, it's no wonder that there are a lot of questionable results around.

When deciding which eyetracking results to trust, remember to consider these three criteria: users, tasks, and breadth of sites.

When deciding what eyetracking results to trust, remember the three criteria: users, tasks, and breadth of sites. And weigh the evidence: When many different studies say the same thing, they're probably right. If one sensational study claims to invalidate all existing findings, it's probably wrong.

Cost of Eyetracking Research

Currently, the overall cost of doing eyetracking research is still relatively high. There are the costs of renting or buying the eyetracker and of setting up and running a good study. Before embarking on any study, run some pilot tests to check your protocol as it works with the system so there are no surprises when you start the actual study or try to analyze the results.

The costs of our study are summarized here. Please keep in mind that we conducted a very large and expensive study. Since many of the costs in eyetracking studies are variable —affected by the number of sessions and users and the amounts of data and storage management—a smaller study would cost less. The large fixed costs, which are consistent no matter how large the study is, are those associated with eyetracking equipment purchase or rental and space rental. For organizations that have space in their buildings or that have already purchased an eyetracker that is amortizing as we speak, these particular costs may be unimportant.

Overall Study Costs

The following table shows the overall study costs (not including usability specialists' time/salary or analysts' time).

Item	Cost
Lab space in Manhattan (five months)	$11,000
Eyetracking equipment rental (five months)	$10,440
Recruiting costs (including $2,000 advertising)	$18,000
Honoraria for participants	$17,900
E-commerce task allowance	$ 1,750
Hard drives to store data	$ 2,000
Total	**$61,090**

Recruiting Costs

The tangible recruiting costs are summarized in the above table. In addition to these, we turned away five percent of the people we called for the study because of eye issues we learned of during recruiting. So, there is an unmeasured cost, namely, that of the screening calls, associated with this.

We were able to keep recruiting costs down to about $50 per user because people employed by our organization conducted the recruiting. Hiring external recruiting firms can be helpful and save time but usually costs more like $100 to $200 per user.

Because the studies were so large, the system sometimes crashed and would not work properly in time for the next scheduled session. In those cases, we had to turn away the test participants. In addition to the recruiting costs already mentioned, we spent thousands of dollars more on recruiting due to eyetracking technology issues.

Why Scheduled Sessions Did Not Occur	Cost of Recruiting
No Shows	49 people: $2,450
Sent home related to eyetracking issues	18 people: $900 + $1,800 = $2,700
Total	$5,150

In addition to extra eyetracking-related recruiting costs, we paid participants whose eye couldn't be calibrated by (work with) the eyetracking system. For example, most eyeglasses that do not have regression lenses will work with the eyetracker. But glasses that have very thick rims sometimes impair calibration. Or if users' irises are almost the same color as their pupils, sometimes the eyetracker cannot find the pupil to track. Those people who made it past the screening process were paid the $100 honorarium for arriving at their scheduled time in the lab, even if they could not do the eyetracking study because of eye calibration issues.

The usual rate for people not showing up for their scheduled sessions is about 20 percent when the lab study has components that may scare people off at the last minute, such as finding out they have to use their own credit card during the study. This was about the rate for our studies, plus we needed to cancel or postpone 7 percent of the sessions because of eyetracker technology issues.

Lost Eyetracking and Recorded Data Costs

Because the system sometimes crashed, all the data for some tasks was lost. We had still observed and taken notes on the sessions where this occurred, and we had backup videotapes, but we were unable to refer to the eyetracking data after the sessions. So, we had to recruit more users to ensure we had enough.

Also, we discarded or didn't collect eyetracking data when the user's eye would not calibrate well.

Breakdown of Task Data Lost by Reason	Percentage of Task Data Lost
Poor calibration	15.83%
Eyetracking technology crash	7.19%
Total	23.02%

Eyetracking-Related Costs

There are costs associated with any usability study, especially those that involve more than 50 users. This study included those and eyetracking-specific costs. The following table summarizes only the costs associated with the eyetracking part of this study. Most of these costs are mentioned in previous tables. (Not included are the usability specialists' time/salary).

Eyetracking-Related Item	Cost
Users sent home, related to eyetracking issues	$ 2,700
Extra users to make up lost data (recruitment, honorariums)	$ 9,450
Eyetracking equipment rental for five months	$10,440
Hard drives to store data	$ 2,000
Total	$24,590 (43% of total study costs)

Equipment

We used the Tobii 1750 Eyetracker and a high-powered PC connected to the Internet. The screen resolution was set to 1024x768 with 16-bit color depth. (Tobii recommended this, and we found that using any higher resolution and large color depth was too resource intensive.)

On a separate monitor, we could see (and record for review) the point on the screen that falls in the center of the fovea of users' eyes. The system did not track peripheral vision.

Tobii ran at a constant frame-rate of 50Hz. It employs the Pupil Center Corneal Reflection (PCCR) eyetracking technique in which, basically, a barely perceptible light makes a glint on the user's eye. A camera picks it up and records it.

Two major eyetracking issues that the system accommodates are drift and head-motion compensation error. Either can result in poor eye gaze capture.

Drift is a weakening of a participant's eye calibration. It can happen because of environmental changes in the test lab, such as light conditions or humidity. We watched for this and recalibrated users as needed.

Head-motion compensation error can occur if the user moves or turns the head. The field of view of the camera is about 20 x 15 x 20 cm (width x height x depth) at 60 cm from the screen. This is enough to compensate for head positions that are comfortable when sitting in a normal posture in front of a computer screen. If the user moved drastically, began to slouch, or leaned very far forward or back, we corrected the situation and recalibrated as necessary. For more information about Tobii Technology, go to *www.tobii.com*.

3 Page Layout

Web pages are not bank accounts: Full is not better. Cluttered or difficult designs make people less likely to find what they want. Only a person who really needs something on a particular site will grin and bear it through an unpleasant user experience.

In this chapter, we consider how people look at Web pages and which elements tend to draw their eyes. We also discuss where and how to place the most important content and how to keep the items on a page from competing for users' attention.

Politics and lack of priorities are responsible for much of the cluttered Web design today. The problem is often that too many people in an organization want too many things to appear in the premier location. This is usually on the homepage, in the main page of a section, "above the fold," or in the topmost menu.

If there is only one important piece of content and one priority piece of real estate on a page, there's no problem. Even if a couple of important items are called out in an area, no problem. But when campaigns require that five of them be called out, the designer must cram in all five elements and hope that they will somehow be seen. Most likely, they won't be.

Organizations need to find a balance between what they want people to do at their sites and what people actually want to do.

Organizations can combat these issues by systematically planning the pages and menus of their Web sites, allowing for changing content. They should determine the following:

- What people want when they come to their site

- What they want people to see and do when they come to their site

- What the priority real estate sections (areas users are most drawn to) are in their design

This would be easy if user goals and business goals always matched, but they don't. A classic example is that users don't scream for ads on newspaper Web sites. They go to newspaper Web sites to get the news. But to stay in business, newspapers accept ad revenue. People, in turn, tolerate the ads because they get to read newspapers every morning for little or no money. It's not complete harmony, but it's a tune you can tap your foot to just the same.

Other times site goals can truly fit in with users' interests. In an example from our testing, the content one person was looking for was in a lower-priority area of the page, while the business priority content took center stage. But in the end, this turned out to be positive for everyone.

Using the Circuit City Web site, Dori had put an iPod nano and a dock for it in her shopping cart (**Figure 3.1**). She indicated that these two items cost more than she initially wanted to spend, but she started the checkout process. Her items appeared in an *Order Summary* area on the far right of the page. But the main content area showed additional recommended products and a protection plan. In the first moments on the page, she seemed confused, but then she looked at the nano accessory items such as a starter kit and armband. After a few more looks, she was won over and added the armband to her cart.

What originally seemed like a borderline dodgy move on the part of the vendor, trying to sell more, enabled Dori to find a useful item that she hadn't even known existed. Whether or not the designers actually had the user's best interests in mind in this case, the result married the seller's and the buyer's needs.

Figure 3.1 The test user Dori had wanted to purchase only an iPod nano and dock at this site. But at checkout, she was presented with several up-sell items in the main content area. After a few moments, she discovered a new item there and decided to buy it too.

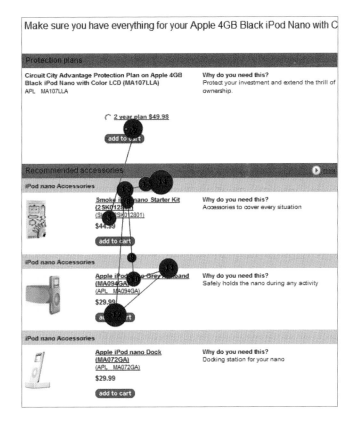

Beyond this balancing act, we have a simple piece of advice for good page layout design: Use discipline. Remember discipline? That thing we learned in second grade when we wanted to play Atari after school and our parents told us to go study our times tables? We did learn long division after all—not from playing Pong but from discipline.

Designers today need to make choices about which content and how much belongs on each page and then have the guts to drop what's less important. Give that Wii a rest, and go prioritize your Web page layout design. You can do it!

How Do People Look at a Page?

There is no universal way that people look at Web pages. We cannot say, for example, that they look first in the upper-left corner or finish in the middle of the page. People sometimes look first at the middle of the page because an application or image draws their eye. Sometimes they specifically look for the logo to understand or confirm what site they are on. Other times people look to the upper right for the search function or to the top or left for global navigation. Or they may decide to read some content and scan headings first.

People are more likely to have similar look patterns if they are attempting to do the same task on the same Web site, hitting the site from the same search engine results page (SERP), and have had the same or very similar past experience with the site. But even in these similar situations, the way people look at the features such as global navigation still varies.

Users Looking for News

Even on a news page, where most visitors have a similar goal—to learn what's new—some people look at the menus to choose the type of news they want while others look at the main headlines. For example, we asked people to read anything they were interested in on the CNN news site, and then we compared their initial look patterns.

Boris—a self-described "news junkie"—wanted to get right into the suggested stories and looked at the *Latest News* links in the top-center section of the homepage (**Figure 3.2**). When he didn't see anything he wanted to click immediately, he looked at the search function for just a few fixations and then at the large headline of the featured story.

Figure 3.2 Boris looked first at the list of links on this news homepage to find a story that interested him. He stayed "above the fold" for his first few moments on the site.

Another user, Gloria, also scanned the *Latest News* items in the top center of the page first (**Figure 3.3**). Then, without clicking any link, she looked to the lower right of the visible page at the area with videos.

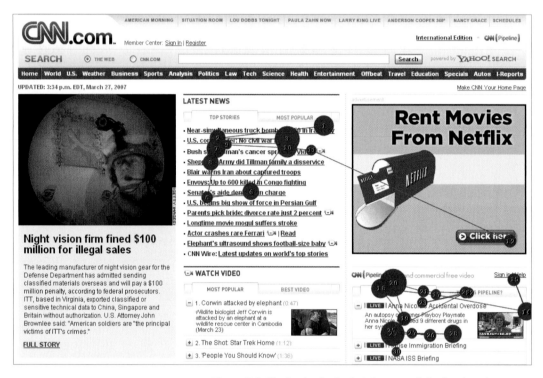

Figure 3.3 Gloria also looked at the news links first but then to the lower right.

Renee, on the other hand, checked out the featured story (**Figure 3.4**). She was first drawn to the image for just one fixation. (This fixation may have been residual, however, based on the way her eye moved from the previous page.) Then she scanned to the text below the image and was not interested. She skipped the *Latest News* items altogether and instead looked at the department headings. Then she looked up at the date and the menu.

Figure 3.4 Renee looked at the featured story and then at department headings and the menu in her first moments on the CNN site.

So, where do people look first on a news site? It depends on the layout of the site, whether they are attracted to the featured story and image, and whether they want to read suggestions or pick a topic themselves.

Users Looking to Buy

In another example with a slightly more directed task, people were asked to choose something to buy on the Mr. Coffee Web site. This task requires a person to first investigate what the site offers.

In trying to get a sense of the company and its offerings on the homepage, the user Bill first looked in the lower-middle part of the content area at the *American Favorites* promotion (**Figure 3.5**). He read the clear text in the orange badge and below it, and then he looked left at the limited-edition Jeff Gordon helmet replica mug—another promotion with clear text. After that, he looked at the image of the coffee-maker and finally at the menu.

Figure 3.5 Looking for something to buy on this site, Bill first looked at the promotions in the lower part of the screen.

Whether or not it was the designer's intent, the white in the large image of a snow scene seemed to push Bill's eye down to the first important-looking thing, in this case the clear promotions.

Toni also chose to look first in the lower section of the content area, skipping past the white in the image to the note in the blue box (**Figure 3.6**). She then looked at the *American Favorites* promotion Bill had looked at first and finally up to the company logo and the horizontal menu.

After considering the gaze patterns from these two people, we might conclude that the big white area in the large image acts as a visual conduit to usher people's eyes down past the image, making the promotions or blue text box the most eye-catching content area (at least initially). But when we examined the initial look patterns of other users doing the same task on the same site, we saw that this was not always so.

Eyetracking Web Usability

Some people started at the top, initially taking an inventory of the horizontal menu. For example, Lauren first looked at each menu option in the global navigation (**Figure 3.7**). She looked left to right and then right to left. She then looked at the corporate logo, confirming what site she was on.

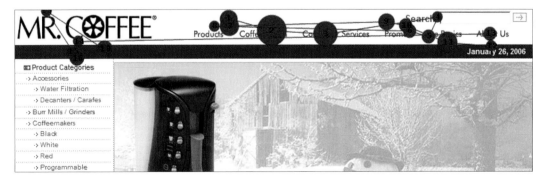

Figure 3.7 Lauren took a different route on the Mr. Coffee site, doing an inventory of the global navigation at the top of the page first.

Like Lauren, the user Nancy initially looked at the global navigation, but only at the first and second commands (**Figure 3.8**).

Figure 3.8 Nancy also looked at the top navigation briefly before going on to the search and then the left navigation.

A combination of layout and content almost always dictates what draws or repels people's eyes.

Now, the initial gaze patterns of Lauren and Nancy might suggest that the top horizontal area is most arresting to users. But then we see that other users, such as Susan, go first to the left-side menu (**Figure 3.9**). And Susan looked at several links in the menu multiple times.

The left-side menu was set up with expandable categories in gray text. The text used for the main categories was larger and darker than the subcategory and the sub-subcategory text. On the menu, *Product Categories* was expanded by default.

For the user Jim, the long list of light gray links formed a visual tunnel at first, causing his eye to look downward to the larger, bolder text links at the bottom of the menu (**Figure 3.10**). So, Jim first looked at the end of the menu, not the beginning. Then he looked at the large, clear image of the coffeemaker.

Figure 3.9 Susan looked at the left-side menu exclusively for the first few seconds of her visit to this site.

Figure 3.10 Jim's eyes were coaxed first to the bottom of the menu by larger, bolder text.

In this sample, the initial gaze patterns of six users were not alike even though they attempted the same task on the same site. What factors determined where they looked?

- The clear, high-quality image of the coffeemaker
- The lackluster, faded gray and white section of the main image
- The color, size, and boldness of the menu items
- The legible text with bright, contrasting background in the promotions

In sum, a combination of layout and content almost always dictates what draws or repels users' eyes.

Users Buying a Specific Item

On some sites, users may have similar initial look patterns as they try to complete the same task. Let's look what people did during their first few seconds on the Neiman Marcus site when we gave a more specific, though still somewhat open, task: to buy a shirt or top.

Most users looked at the global navigation menu within their first few fixations. This probably was partly because of the page layout, but more likely it was because of the task at hand. Most people got right down to business. Some people looked at the menu first to get a sense of the offerings on the site and scanned other page elements afterward.

Lisa, for example, began by looking at the first two menu links on the left and then quickly went into scan mode, skipping the third link and looking at the fourth, eighth (two times), ninth, and seventh (two times) (**Figure 3.11**).

Bill first looked at the sale promotion below the menu for just one fixation (**Figure 3.12**). Then he looked up and slightly left to the *Men's & Electronics* link for two fixations and further left to the first three links in the menu, each for one fixation. Then he looked back to *Men's & Electronics* and the link to the right of it.

Figure 3.11 The Neiman Marcus homepage offers global navigation across the top and images of products in the middle. Initially, Lisa looked at the first two menu links on the left. Then she jumped around on the rest of the menu.

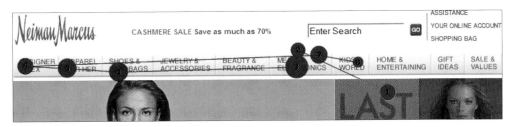

Figure 3.12 Bill looked toward the upper-right section of the content area, then to the second half of the menu, and then back to the first menu links during the first moments of his visit to this site.

A third user, Damon, looked to the search area at the top right for six fixations and then skipped over the menu altogether and looked at the text in the content area and then at the model's skirt (**Figure 3.13**).

We see from these examples that people doing the same task on the same Web site sometimes gravitate toward the same general area—in this case, the global navigation. But they still don't necessarily look in the same spots within that area.

Figure 3.13 Damon looked at the search area first for six fixations and then down to the text in the content area.

Users Doing a Very Specific Task

Now let's consider what happened when we gave people a very specific task: to learn about the board of directors at Gateway, a computer hardware company. All of them seemed to look for some kind of menu on the homepage to get this information, but the assignment was complicated by the fact that the main menu was in an unconventional place—toward the lower half of the visible page, just below the main image.

Some people found the main menu here in just a few fixations, despite the unusual location and the risk that it could be mistaken as part of the image. The drastic color change—a mocha-colored bar below a primarily green and blue image—probably helped prevent this.

The user Tamara first looked at the menu just below the main image (**Figure 3.14**). Not seeing anything that would help her learn about the management team, she directed her gaze downward, pausing on the *Home & Home Office* small text block. She skipped over the monochrome boxes

Figure 3.14 Tamara first looked at the menu below the main image and then scanned further down the page.

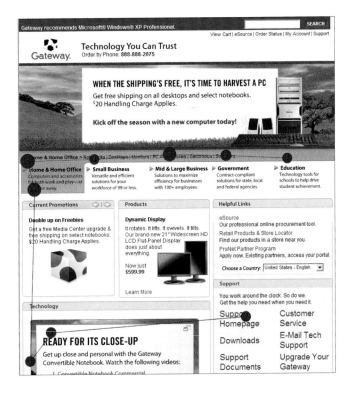

below that and gave two fixations to the white *Technology* box with the big, bold, capitalized heading. She then looked right, possibly thinking the links there might be menu.

Valerie also looked below the center image but first at three of the four small text blocks there (**Figure 3.15**). She then looked up at the mocha menu bar and to the monochrome section boxes below.

Figure 3.15 Valerie also looked below the center image but at three small text blocks, not at the menu.

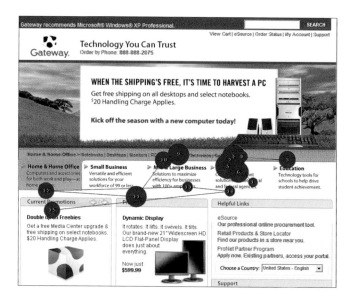

Susan looked at the small green border at the top of the page, likely thinking this was the menu (**Figure 3.16**). Instantly realizing it was not, she skipped past most of the page to the bottom, where she looked at the menus and links. She assumed the menu would be either on the top or on the bottom of the page.

Figure 3.16 Susan looked at the top green bar. Realizing it wasn't a menu, she quickly scrolled to the menus and links at the bottom of the page.

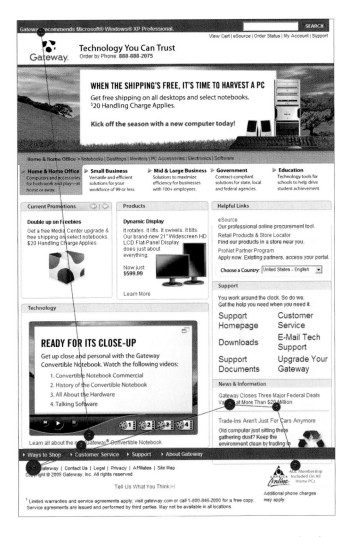

Susan was not the only person who seemed to mistake the green bar at the top of the page for a menu. Mikki first looked below the center image (as it loaded) at the mono-chrome *Current Promotions* and *Products* boxes and then up at the text in the green border at the top of the page (**Figure 3.17**). After just one fixation, she dropped that like a hot potato and looked to the right at *Search*, perhaps thinking there was no navigation to be found.

Figure 3.17 Mikki looked at the boxes toward the bottom part of the visible page and then at the green border over the main image, possibly wishing this was the menu. She then looked right at the search function.

We have hundreds of examples like these. They reveal that gaze patterns on the same page may be alike or entirely different, depending on the design, the users' tasks, and their expectations from previous experience. This may sound complicated, but from a design standpoint, it really all comes down to making sure that people see and register what they need on a site—whether it's a menu, some text, or an image. Guiding people's eyes to that "right" place means employing Web design standards and designing each element on a page with that in mind.

Web Design Standards That Users Look For

Designers have almost no control over some factors that determine how users look at a page. But using consistent Web conventions that match users' experience and expectations makes features more visible and attractive to them. Designers have known this for many years—and now eyetracking research confirms it.

Page elements that designers should consider using include the following:

- Perceptible menus, with some graphic or color delineation, across the top and usually on the left

- A *Home* button in or near the menu on the far left of all pages except the homepage
- A logo in the upper-left corner of all pages
- An open search field in the upper-right corner of all pages
- A shopping cart icon in the upper-right corner of all pages
- A login/out feature in the upper-right corner of all pages
- Utility navigation at the very top or very bottom of pages that is subtle and visually weaker than the main/global navigation

The Problem with Top-Down Design

Deciding what belongs on a homepage or any Web page can be grueling—or at least it should be. Many Web designers painstakingly consider this, but others succumb to forces that may be pulling the design in many directions—forces such as the marketing department, upper management, or simply the content that is available to them.

Many of the questions we get from Web designers at our seminars have to do with managers telling them that everything needs to be on the homepage or another particular page. Imagine the vice president of a major corporation telling an experienced designer what to put on the homepage and where! Certainly, most VPs are not Web designers, nor do they necessarily understand the notions of design balance and usability.

Even worse, sometimes an outside design firm is hired to come up with a design that supports a message that appeals to these same VPs—though not necessarily to users. Or a higher-up tells a designer, "Pretty up the page. Add some pictures." Based on our experience, we have concluded that some of the most egregious Web design—specifically, wildly cluttered homepages—are because of organizational political pressures, not unqualified designers.

To this we say: Rebel.

Don't turn a blind eye to top-down design because it's easier. You must be the one to stop it. Specifically, you must say "no" to tacking on more and more features and to features that do not match the overall design or are unusable.

In our experience, one of the best ways to do this is for designers to create guidelines for their site. So when people ask you to add something, you can answer as an agent for the guidelines.

The conversation might go like this:

Internal client: "I need you to add this big, blinking, bright pink promotion on the homepage."

Web designer: "OK, but our research and balanced design allow for just two promotions on the homepage. We found that this makes the promotions most visible without making the overall page design too cumbersome. There are two promotions on the homepage now. Which of those can we take down?"

Internal client: "Let me get back to you."

This conversation may be a bit oversimplified, but the idea can work. With research and an established plan for promotions, new features, and new links, it won't seem like just your opinion against theirs.

Snooze? We think not. If you are of the mind that your site needs to be groundbreaking and different from all other Web sites, think again. Unless it is a showpiece—not a place where people need to find information, get something done, or buy something—don't focus just on art awards. Make the site easy to use too.

In addition to being consistent with the few intersite Web conventions that exist, providing a consistent intrasite design helps users. Thorough task analysis and knowledge about your users will help you create a site with the elements people want in the places they expect to find them. And pages can be designed in such a way that features attract the user's eye at the right time. Some examples and suggestions follow.

Task analysis and knowledge about your users will help you create sites with the elements people want in the places they expect to find them.

Organization of Pages

Gluttonous Web pages are overfilled in the hope that something in the content cornucopia will speak to a user. But we cannot design good Web pages like an all-you-can-eat buffet, with everything from roast beef to cream puffs. People will look at a brimming page only if they absolutely need or truly want to be there. The experience is not enjoyable, however, and if they have a choice, they will leave. If they stay, like the buffet patron, they'll feel sick and fat and disillusioned by the end.

Light Pages Encourage Looking

In one example, we asked people to shop for dinner place settings on the Web site for Dansk, a tableware retailer (**Figure 3.18**). They found it pleasurable. Why?

- The navigation looks like navigation, is located in an expected place (at the top of the page), and is offset by a horizontal border.

- The open search field is in the upper-right corner of the page, a standard place and presentation.

- The shopping basket and a few other general commands, such as *Contact Us* and *Store Locator*, also appear in the upper right.

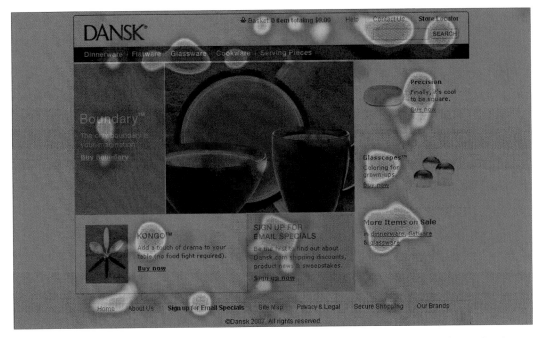

Figure 3.18 The heat on the top and bottom utility navigation shows that users wanted to scan the entire homepage of this site—even the less likely areas—because it is uncluttered and easy to use.

- There is no background behind these links in the upper right, and the text is small, but the good use of white space around them and the highly contrasted text against the background make them visible enough. They don't distract the user but are obvious and easy to ignore or find, as appropriate.

- The company logo appears, like most, in the upper-left side of the page. It acts as a reminder or signpost for where the user is on the Web and how to navigate to the homepage from anywhere on the site.

- The topmost utility navigation—*Help, Contact Us,* and *Store Locator*—appears above the logo, the search function, and the main horizontal navigation. It is in small text, with very subtle borders and no background. The utility navigation at the bottom of the page has the same look. Both are visually weaker than the main navigation, so people know these commands are secondary.

All of these simple and expected elements make the site easy on the eyes. The clean design and few choices encourage people to look at more of it. Users do not typically look at utility navigation unless they are trying to do tasks such as find a store location or read the privacy policy. But they looked here—not because they were confused or tortured—but because they knew it wouldn't take long and they might actually find something worthwhile.

The Web site of FreshDirect, an online grocery service, also presents a simple homepage (**Figure 3.19**). The menus run across the top, and types of food appear in the content area, accompanied by attractive supporting images. There are no gimmicks such as a sexy woman caressing a pork chop. Instead, the site zooms in on the actual pork chop or other grocery item.

People looked at much of this homepage and were neither frustrated nor desperate. One user, Laura, said afterward, "I like this. It's a fresh, clean kind of thing. There's so much to choose from, but I like the way it's organized."

Figure 3.19 People explored much of this homepage because it is relatively simple and sparse, despite the many grocery items it displays.

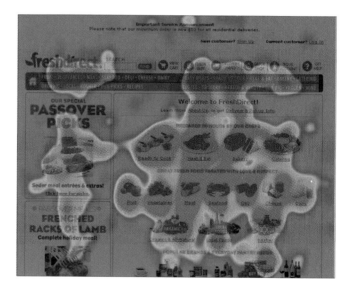

Similarly, users looked all around the page on the JetBlue Airways Web site (**Figure 3.20**). Even though they happily—and quickly—completed their tasks, they were willing to explore further because the page was so simple and they didn't fear getting bogged down in it. The simple look and wise use of white space also made it attractive and approachable.

Figure 3.20 People looked all over this site, encouraged by its light, simple design.

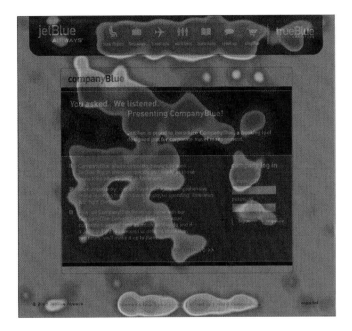

In contrast, the busy site for Headset Zone, which sells telephone headsets, was not welcoming (**Figure 3.21**). It repeated items in the top and left menus. This made for unpleasant scanning, forcing users to look twice as many times and concentrate harder when they needed to use the menus.

Figure 3.21 The same menu commands at the top and left side of this made users work twice as hard on this site.

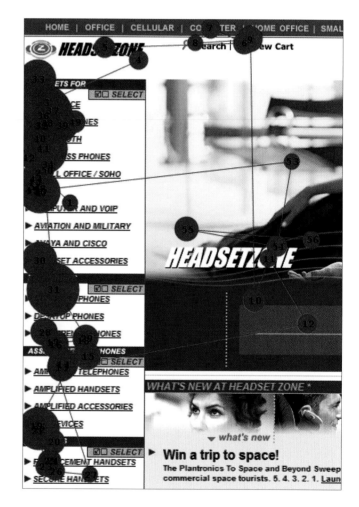

Content Placement and Visual Indicators

Eliminating or at least demoting the less important items on a page will help users see more important options more quickly. But sparseness is not the most important factor in page layout.

To test the effect of clutter alone, we judged the density of content on 35 random Web pages by counting the number of different elements they included and how often these appeared (**Figure 3.22**): rows of graphic "banner" sections or borders at the top; rows of menus at the top; visible links in top navigation (not hidden links in graphics or the logo); logos at the top (usually one, but sometimes more); right-side menus; visible links in left navigation; sectioned-off areas (excluding menus or empty margins); different colors; different color fonts (in buttons, not graphics); different typefaces/fonts (including different sizes and treatments, but not including a logo); links in the content area (excluding the top, left, and right menus); lines of text in the content area, including links (but excluding top, left, and right menus); images, graphics, or icons in top banners (not including a logo); images, graphics, or icons not in top banners; ads or promotions (not including top banners already counted); buttons; open fields; and applications or tools (such as drop-down lists).

Each visible element on a page was assigned one point; the sum of all the points was the page's density score. We then compared the density rating with the average number of user fixations on the pages. Surprisingly, page density alone had little to do with user fixations. The specifics of the design elements had more impact.

The placement of content and usable visual design are more important than page density in Web design.

Figure 3.22 A chart depicting the average number of fixations on each page in a 35-page set and the density rating for each page (each dot represents one page). It shows that density only determines 8% of the variability in how much people look at a page.

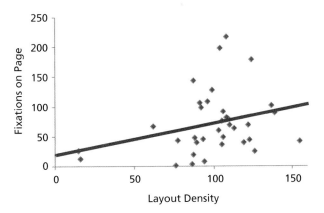

Use Priority Spots

People expect information that is most important, most basic, or most related to a page title or topic to appear in **priority spots**—areas of visual priority on the page. Areas appear to be high priority based on the following:

- **Location.** In most cases, the upper content area, below the global navigation, is a higher-priority spot than the lower content area. The highest-priority area is the uppermost section of the content area, after the menus.

- **Size and emphasis.** Bigger or bolder type, underlining, or colored type or background connote importance. But there is a fine line between drawing users' attention and losing it. Designers need to find the balance between making important information stand out and making it look like a promotion or other item that users might ignore.

- **Appearance in relation to the rest of the page.** Even an understated area can look like a high-priority spot if the rest of the page is even more understated. Purposeful visual funnels, such as elongated sections of white space with an attractive element at the bottom, can also direct people's eyes past other features to the place where you want them to look.

Each page design determines which areas are its priority spots. Let's look at how well one site succeeded in conveying priority content to users in our testing.

Rob was looking for information about scheduling a ski trip to Colorado for two. Searching Expedia.com for hotels and flights, he was presented with many elements—at least ten different text styles; loads of tiny icons; very small images of the resorts; a lengthy listing of resorts; and various links, tools, and colors (**Figure 3.23**). The page is full, for sure. But it really is not disorderly, and it doesn't look as if the elements were randomly littered all over it. They are placed consistently and thoughtfully.

Specifically, the information for each package, including the price for hotel and air, is perceptibly contained in a purple box. The boxes are clearly defined by contrasting colors, dark purple at the top and light gray at the bottom, with adequate white space between them. The name of each resort appears in bold in the upper left of each box, a priority spot in this design. Useful information, such as resort descriptions and ratings, is also encapsulated in the boxes. Because of the page's consistent arrangement, Rob looked quite far down the page.

Figure 3.23 This page on Expedia.com (shown cropped) was full but orderly.

Hotel price and proximity to the ski area were priorities for Rob. He said he just wanted to whisk away his girlfriend for an inexpensive ski getaway. Aaaaww. And he didn't want to waste a lot of time traveling to and from the slopes each day. On this page, he was able to locate the general information that he needed relatively easily (**Figure 3.24**). He could see each resort's proximity to the skiing and its price compared to that of the others.

Figure 3.24 Despite its almost cluttered appearance, the thoughtful, consistent design of this page made it easy for Rob to scan for the information he needed.

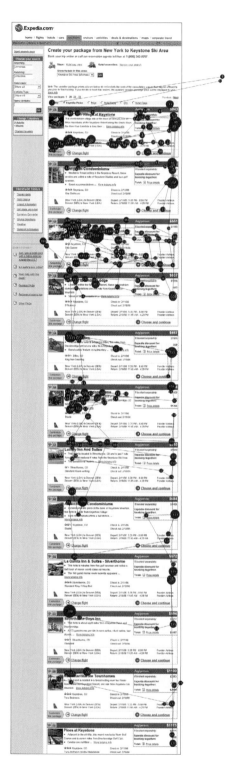

Eyetracking Web Usability

Rob looked at the airline information in only the first and third boxes. He fixated on it in the first box because it was the first time he saw the information and in the third because he was very interested in that resort and wanted to confirm that the air travel dates coincided with the hotel's availability. But he seemed to learn rather quickly that the airline information was the same in each box, so he didn't bother looking at it repeatedly.

Rob fixated much on only one package that cost more than $700—the very first one. And that occurred when he was acclimating himself to the format of the offerings on the page.

So far, so good—the site gave proper priority to the resort name, general information, and airline information in each box. It also maintained a consistent look for the 19 offerings on the page, and Rob looked at these. But now let's look closer at the price-related information in the faintly shaded yellow box in the upper right of one resort box (**Figure 3.25**). We can almost consider this little box to be its own mini-page.

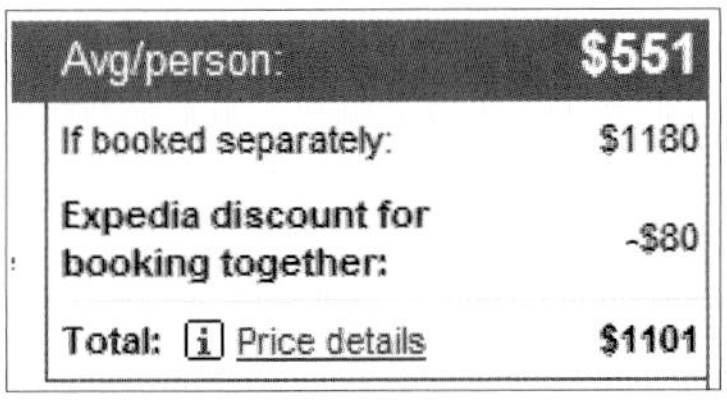

Avg/person:	**$551**
If booked separately:	$1180
Expedia discount for booking together:	-$80
Total: ⓘ Price details	$1101

Figure 3.25 The wording and design of this price box made it difficult for Rob to ascertain the price of a ski trip for two.

The price per person appears in large white text in the purple banner; additional price information is listed in smaller text below. Because of the consistent layout, the user could easily find which package is the most or least expensive, but finding the price Rob was looking for—for two people—was surprisingly difficult. The per-person price is first, in the highest-priority spot in the blue banner, and it's larger and bolder than the other prices in the box. This would suggest that this is the price for the user's personalized package.

But users could miss a price placed in this spot because of *banner blindness*—the tendency to ignore items that are bold and inside a border. That's what seemed to happen with Rob. Initially, he did not look directly at the large price but at the smaller prices below it. In the second and subsequent boxes, he did look at the large, one-person price.

The unclear wording of the price label is another potential problem. Does *Avg/person* mean that this price is an *estimate* —the average price people pay for this package—or is it the *actual* price of the package for one person? The user's several fixations in the first two boxes suggest that he was unsure.

Below the price in the banner, the labels for other prices were also perplexing. The user fixated on these labels, especially in the first few boxes, probably trying to figure out what they meant. For example, it's uncertain what *If booked separately* means—if the two people book their trips separately, or if they book their hotel separately from their air travel?

After looking at the four different prices for each entry, Rob didn't seem to know which one to believe. His eye focused on the price associated with the *Total* label more than the others, but throughout the page he looked at the different prices. In the price box, the priority spot should have been labeled better, and the price given should have been for what the user was looking for—the cost of the trip for two.

Though the price box fell a bit short, this page's excellent overall design highlights the importance of design elements in relation to page density. Overall, the user was able to move smoothly around the page, despite its density, because of its clear and consistent layout.

Unclear Priority Spots Leave Users Out in Left Field

Let's look at layout priorities in relation to page density in another sampling from our study. We examined five commonly hit pages on five baseball Web sites where users had the same task: to find out what position George Brett played. Our density scores for the pages were 106, 85, 81, 77, and 65. But the average user fixations were quite varied: 92, 250, 88, 123, and 41 (**Figure 3.26**).

Figure 3.26 The density scores for five pages on five baseball sites ranged between 65 and 106. But the average user fixations were much more varied—between 41 and 250—and did not seem to correspond to density.

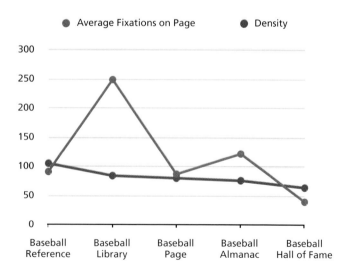

Eyetracking Web Usability

Users spent the fewest fixations on the Baseball Hall of Fame site. Why? That's where they were most successful finding the answer they were looking for in the least amount of time and fixations—41 on average. In other words, this was a highly usable page. The obvious chunking of text and bold titles helped, but the placement of vital information in visually escalated areas was probably the most important reason for their success.

In the design, there are no background colors, borders, or other elements to denote importance or demand attention. Priority content is shown simply by bold text and its position on the page. The bold text toward the top of the page, in the priority spot, naturally drew users' attention first. Alvin, for example, scanned the areas of the page but especially perused the bold words near the top (**Figure 3.27**).

Figure 3.27 Alvin looked mostly at the top and at the bold words in the priority spot on this Baseball Hall of Fame page.

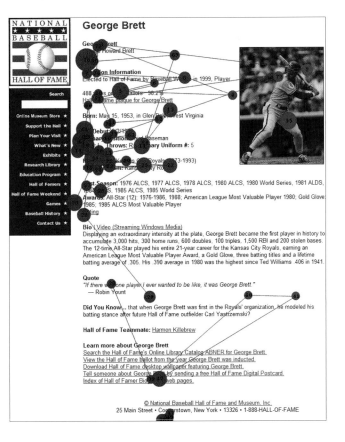

Users spent 88 fixations on average on the Baseball Page site—more than twice as many as on the Baseball Hall of Fame site. The page is very long and full of text, but it has two things going for it: The text is broken up into sections, and each section has a clear heading (**Figure 3.28**). Users could scan to the *Position* heading, where they found the answer they wanted, without reading all the text before it (**Figure 3.29**).

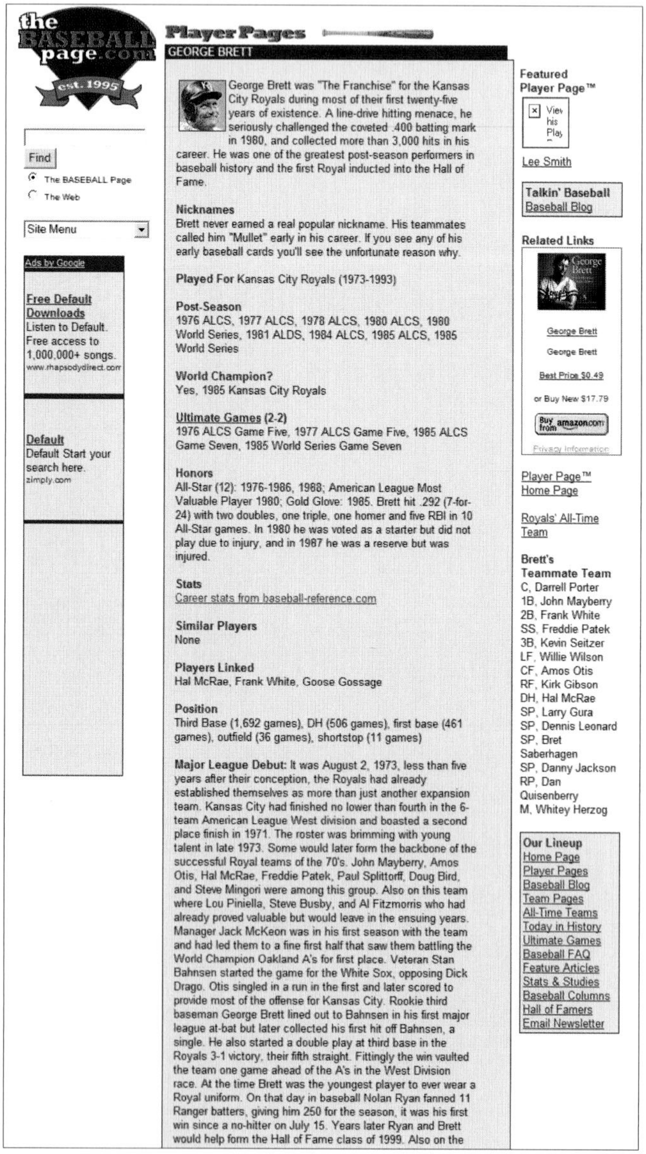

Figure 3.28 This Baseball Page page was very long and had a lot of text, but it also had headings which help people to scan with less effort.

Eyetracking Web Usability

Figure 3.29 The headings enabled users to scan the long text section for the information they wanted without having to read all of it.

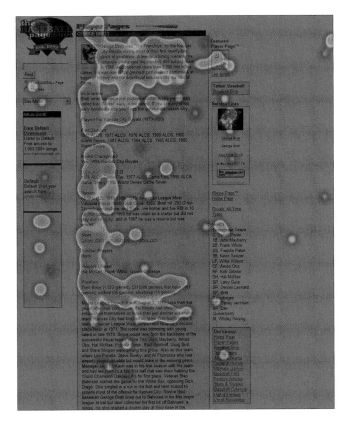

The third site, Baseball-Reference, averaged 92 user fixations—only a few more than the Baseball Page—but the layout creates user expectations that are not met. When content does not match location in terms of importance, we call it **mismatched priority**.

The first two baseball sites call out priority content with bold text and sections. This site uses colored boxes to divide areas of the page, which seems like a more advanced visual treatment. However, the color inadvertently elevates the importance of the content in the boxes. The user experience is not improved by the visual treatment because the most important content is not where users expect it to be.

People expected to see information about Brett's position in the top two or three color blocks (**Figure 3.30**). A grid of statistics filled the rest of the page. Whether or not they found the answer (it was in Brett's quote in the top yellow box, but not displayed separately), they left the page after an average of 92 fixations.

Figure 3.30 Betsy looked at the colored blocks at the top of the Baseball-Reference page, expecting George Brett's playing position to be there. She found the grid below off-putting.

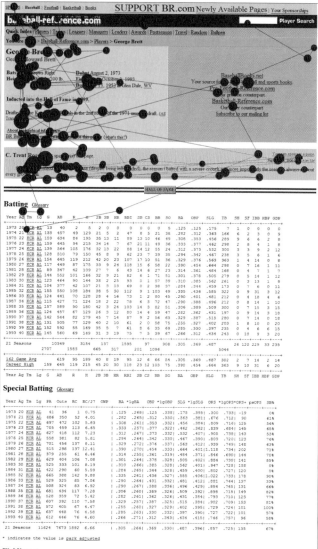

Although the color blocks may have been misleading, at least the grid of statistics below them wasn't. People knew immediately that the answer they were seeking was not there.

One user, Betsy, gave about 130 fixations to the page, mostly in the top gray, blue, and yellow priority spots. After exhausting them, she gave just three fixations to the beginning of the statistics grid and quickly abandoned it.

Mark also spent time looking at the top three sections but gave just two fixations to the grid and then left the page (**Figure 3.31**). When he returned, he continued to inspect the priority spots only, completely ignoring the grid (**Figure 3.32**).

Figure 3.31 During his first visit to the page, Mark looked at the top three sections extensively but gave just two fixations to the table.

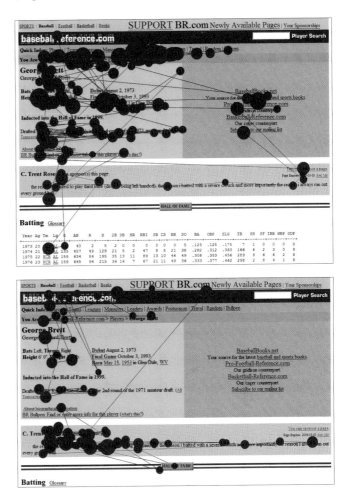

Figure 3.32 During his second visit, Mark looked again at the top three sections but did not look at the table.

On the Baseball Almanac site, people spent more fixations —123—than on any of the first three sites. They were not positive multiple fixations, with the user enjoying the process and making progress—what we call **desired exploration**. Instead they were repeated fruitless looks at items, an example of **exhaustive review**. There were too many sections on this site, and the multiple typefaces, type sizes, and colors made it difficult to determine which were priority spots (**Figure 3.33**).

Figure 3.33 There's a lot of information about George Brett on the Baseball Almanac page but nothing about the position he played.

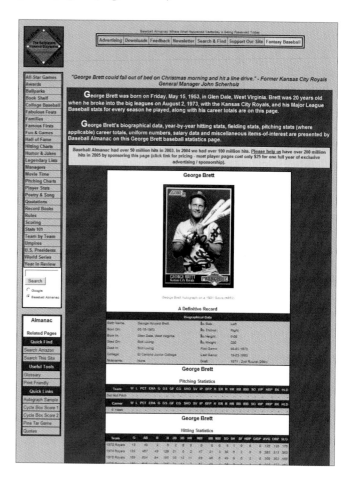

Figure 3.34 The heading *A Definitive Record* coaxed users to look hard for Brett's position there, but it wasn't listed.

Users first scanned the green sections at the top but soon noticed the title *A Definitive Record* below the baseball card (**Figure 3.34**). Thinking this signaled the information they needed, they spent most of their fixations there. But this was a **miscue**—a design element that attracts users' attention at inappropriate times and derails their progress. It coaxed users to spend many fixations on the beige box below the title, even though the needed information was not there.

The fifth site in this sampling was the Baseball Library site, where people spent the most time and fixations—250 on average. This site suffered from serious miscues. First, users expected the information to appear in one of the sections at the top of the page. When it wasn't there, they faced another, and bigger, miscue: a sea of gray text. In the absence of headings and sections, people expect priority content to appear somewhere in the prose. Unlike the Baseball-Reference site's matrix of statistics, which users knew to avoid, this site dragged them into a quicksand of prose with no headings or bold callouts (**Figure 3.35**).

People were attracted to various links, but these usually led to information that was not about George Brett. And some stumbled right over the long-sought answer, which appears like this in the second horizontal box: *3B-DH-1B 1973-93 Royals.* The site does not explain the abbreviation *3B* to mean third base—George Brett's position. Along with the lack of clear priority spots, this caused users to spend five times as many fixations looking for the answer here than they did on the Baseball Hall of Fame site.

Figure 3.35 The unclear priority spots, undefined abbreviations, long section of unbroken text, and links to unimportant information on the Baseball Library site made it difficult for people to find the information they wanted.

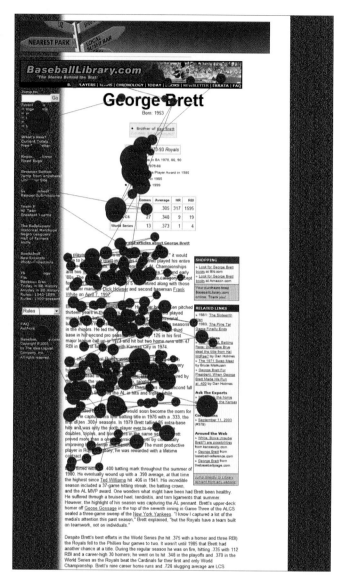

This is another example of mismatched priority, with expected priority information not appearing in a priority spot. In fact, the many examples of mismatched priority on the baseball sites show how common this problem is on the Web today. But our users' experience on these sites also showed that the easiest sites to navigate were those that may seem boring but had clear sections and headings as well as information presented in the places where they expected it.

Figure 3.36 The date of Groundhog Day in 2006 is not listed in the main content area on this site about Groundhog Day.

Priority Spots and Users' Tasks

In another example of mismatched priority, the user Amy was looking for the date of Groundhog Day in 2006. She searched and found the site Groundhog.org (**Figure 3.36**). Amy expected to easily learn the date in the main content area. But it was not there. The site creators seem to have been so focused on the events on and surrounding Groundhog Day (which looks fun, by the way) that they failed to make the date clear.

Amy looked at the bold *General Information* label in the left-side navigation for her first few fixations (two seconds into her page visit). She did not seem to realize that this was a heading for the three links below. To her, it looked like a page heading. She did an exhaustive review, looking for several more fixations at the main content area. Not seeing a date there, she looked toward the left-side menu, probably for a link that would lead to the date. Instead, she found links to two dates (**Figure 3.37**). Still unsure which was *the* day, she clicked the first one, *February 1*.

Figure 3.37 At six seconds into Amy's visit on this page, she fixated on the two dates in the left-side menu and finally clicked the first one to see whether it was, indeed, the date of Groundhog Day.

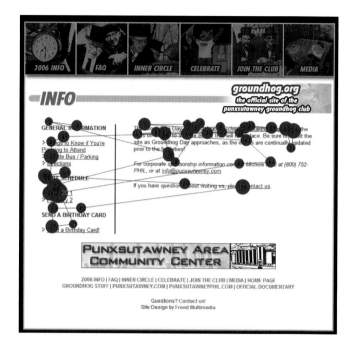

The link took Amy to a page that was of no help, so she returned to the previous page. Her second visit there was just as futile as the first. Again, she scoured the links and content area, especially the places where she didn't look during her first visit. The fact that Amy dedicated another 25 or so fixations to this page after a first round of more than 40 fixations shows that she really believed the information should be here.

Ultimately, Amy clicked the second date link, *February 2*. This did not help her find the answer either. So, she returned to the main page for a third and final time (**Figure 3.38**). Clearly, had this site not been a high hit on the SERP or not been named Groundhog.org, the user probably would not have spent so many fixations here. But she expected the site to do right by her, with fundamental information in a priority spot or main content area. Suprisingly on her third visit, she looked at the links and content. Sadly, even a true Web believer such as Amy has a threshold, and finally she quit and went back to Web search.

Eyetracking Web Usability

Figure 3.38 Not getting help after following the first or second link, Amy returned to this page a third and final time. Again, she looked at the content, though less this time, and fixated on the links. She finally left and returned to searching the Web.

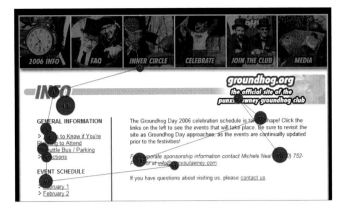

Amy's experience illustrates why sites need to put content that is of high priority to users in the most visually high-priority areas. Considering the different kinds of tasks that people might want to do on a site is not enough. We must focus on their main tasks—their *top tasks*. And we should exhibit discipline and courage by letting some features fall off the site, or at least a few page levels down, to make the information most often sought more visible.

Focus and Unify Your Design Team with Top (Ten) Tasks

Kara was first introduced to the concept of top tasks when she started working in interface design on Lotus Freelance Graphics, a presentation software product, in 1991. The product was losing both market share and design awards, so the user interface lead, MaryKate Foley, and the marketing lead, Betsy Fortin, came up with the concept of "top tasks."

The idea was to do research to determine the ten (give or take a few) things that users wanted and needed to do with presentation software. If they couldn't do them easily with the Freelance Graphics designs, then the designs had failed them. More advanced and innovative features could coexist with the top task features, but the bread-and-butter tasks had to be possible, simple, and quick.

The kinds of things that ultimately made the top tasks list—such as make it easy to add legible

text, have a consistent look across a presentation, make a chart or bulleted list, and add clip art—would not seem groundbreaking by today's standards. But researching the top tasks, stating them, and making them known and always available to the product team helped the group focus on the user and do it with confidence. It also imposed some discipline on the team.

Top tasks proved successful and was the basis for designs such as the first prompt text—"Click here to type text" (spearheaded by the late Scott Davidson)—and the greeting "Welcome… Do you want to create a new presentation or work on an existing one?" Freelance Graphics won multiple design awards for usability and innovation, even beating out presentation packages such as Microsoft PowerPoint and Harvard Graphics. Great designers, usability testing, and top tasks deserve much of the credit.

Census Site Makes Little Sense to Users

Now the unfortunate part: Even designs created with all this in mind can go wrong. We saw this on the U.S. Census Bureau's Web site, where we asked people to find the populations for the United States and the state of Texas.

The site designers did their task-analysis homework and knew that finding the populations of the United States and individual states are top tasks for people who use their site. The designers addressed this quite wholeheartedly in their work. The current U.S. population figure is in large, bold, bright red text in the upper-right corner of the homepage. Huge. All people have to do to find it is to look up and to the right—not scroll, click, or type. And to find the Texas population, they could type in a plain, open field also in the upper right.

Sound ridiculously easy? It wasn't. More than half the people in our study did not look at these features or saw them briefly and ignored them.

William opened the site and did a three-second evaluation of the page (**Figure 3.39**). He was immediately drawn to the search box in the top middle area of the page. Users are often drawn to open fields and drop-down list boxes when they scan pages, but he was not looking at all the open fields on the page. In fact, he ignored the open field in the upper-right quadrant, which would have helped him, and the drop-down fields.

The layout of the page had much to do with William's look pattern, but past experience and expectations were also factors. William knew that he could try searching if he could not find something via browsing. And people tend to search rather than browse for tasks that involve finding specific information. There are also some people who just gravitate toward searching over browsing, at least initially. This is especially true on a page like this, with many choices and a lot of clutter.

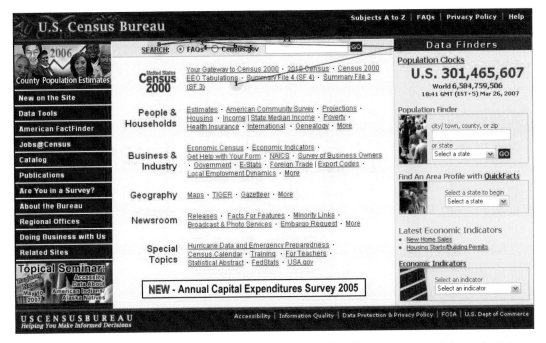

Figure 3.39 William looked first at the search field on the U.S. Census Bureau's Web site, partly because searching was familiar to him but the site's navigation was not. The cluttered page also did not encourage browsing.

Within seven seconds on the page, William had seen enough to act. And nothing on the small portion of the page that he scanned drew him away from searching, which probably felt safe to him on this cluttered page because it is about the same on most Web sites these days. This is not to say that searching will always work—it may in fact be a lifeboat with a gaping hole in it—but William thought that with it, he had a chance of not drowning in data.

Still, William was not completely convinced about searching. As he put it, "OK, I am just going to type in the search box here…. It *might* just give me the answer" (**Figure 3.40**). And as he typed in his search query, somewhere in the United States a baby was born, and the big, red, bold U.S. population number on the upper right flipped from 301,465,607 to 301,465,608. This slight flash did not distract William, however. Within his first 18 seconds on this page, he had typed his search query, "united states population," and put his pointer over the *Go* button.

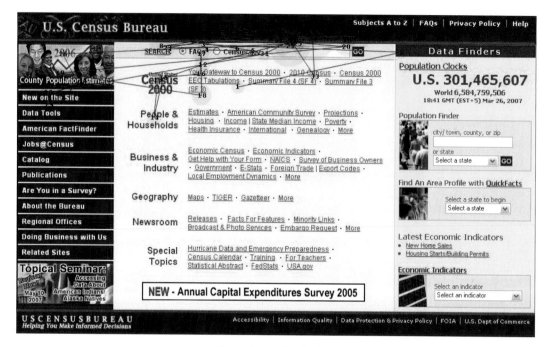

Figure 3.40 After looking at search, William typed in his query and ignored the *Data Finders* feature on the right, which he needed to find the population of Texas.

Note: Images in this book do not show search queries in the search field. At the point of the gaze plots here, the search term was visible in the field.

Before he clicked the *Go* button, however, his eye flicked to the right side of the page for five fixations—directly on the needed *Data Finders* feature. Even though the U.S. population is right there, it simply did not register with him because he was already off and running in a different direction (**Figure 3.41**). William then analyzed the search results page, never to return to the homepage where his answer was in plain site. This scenario—in which a user is on a relentless roll in a certain direction—is known as **momentum behavior**.

Eyetracking Web Usability

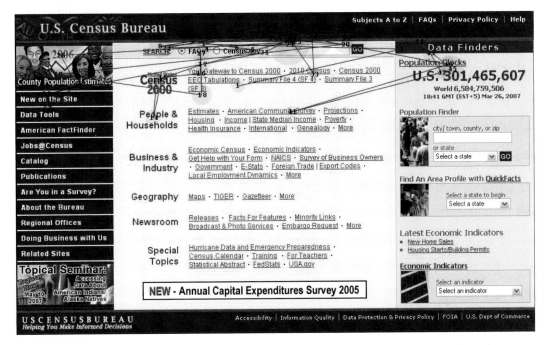

Figure 3.41 As William clicked *Go*, his eyes passed over the information he needed on the right. But it did not fully register with him because he was already on the search path, displaying momentum behavior.

Other users also looked at and ultimately used the Census site's search feature instead of the *Data Finders* feature. Why? One reason is the wording of the labels: *Data Finders* is vague and too branded, and *Population Clocks* is also unclear. Though the latter cheeky label is meant to show that this site stays up to the moment on the nation's changing population, it is tough to make sassy work in a Web interface.

When we encounter features like this, we try to imagine how the design actually came about. We envision designers brainstorming fun names for these features. And maybe they are entertaining names for the design team to use internally. But for users, branding features is usually of no help. So, when naming interface elements, consider the way users are thinking as they hit the page. Asking them to exert any extra brainpower to distinguish what *data* is or what a *clock* has to do with population is enough to make them move on and miss a truly cool feature.

A cryptic or unclear name can repel users' gazes even from the very feature they are looking for. It's better to name features based on how users think and what they are trying to do on the page.

The rule of thumb is that if you find yourself wracking your brain for clever names for Web features, stop. Name features based how users think or what they're likely to be looking for. Labels such as *U.S. Population* or *Find a State's Population* may not be exciting (or win you any branding contests), but they will probably get the job done better. Users are more likely to look at the feature and even give it a click.

The placement and look of the population feature is another bad design call on this page. It is on the far-right column of the homepage—an area usually reserved for related information, advertisements, and promotions. The meatier features tend to be toward the left and top.

Although the label *Data Finders* caught William's attention momentarily, the user Renee never even saw it (**Figure 3.42**). She looked at the menu, the search feature, and the middle of the page extensively, but she completely avoided the area of the page that she needed most. She was probably experiencing banner blindness, with the right side of

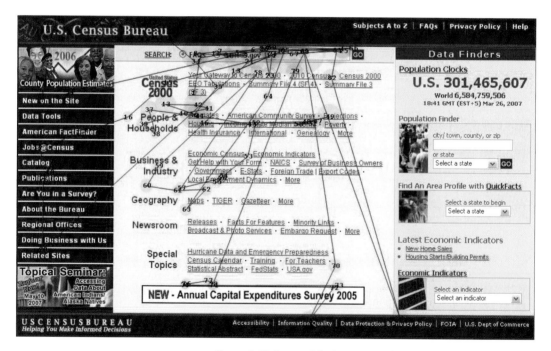

Figure 3.42 Banner blindness at work: Renee looked everywhere but the area on the right side of the page, which housed the features she needed.

Eyetracking Web Usability

the page peripherally resembling a promotion or superfluous information to her. She didn't even give it one look to see whether it might help her, probably because of the visual treatment—it is set off with a border and background. The center section of the page, on the other hand, offers many obvious links to attract the eye.

Tracy also ignored the right column (**Figure 3.43**). Instead, she looked at headings, links, menu on the left, and the search field—items that people are often drawn to when they first hit a Web page.

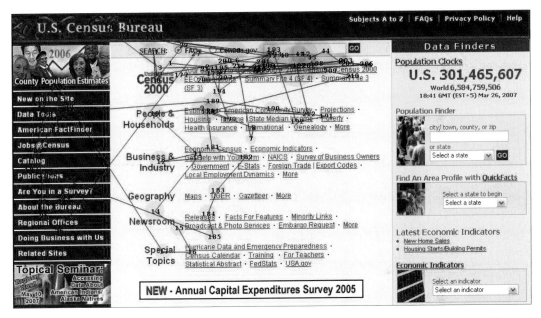

Figure 3.43 Still another user, Tracy, looked at the menu, the search feature, and the main content area, but she ignored the area on the right side of the page.

Red Isn't Always Right

When users don't see an important feature on a site, a desperate designer's knee-jerk reaction is often to change the color to something shocking—usually red—or make it flash.

But resorting to red can be like putting a Band-Aid on a broken arm. In a quagmire of disorder, injecting red or animation in the hopes that they will make items stand out is a mistake. We still encounter many sites that employ the "red and blinking" Band-Aid approach, but the real solution is a well-defined and prioritized layout.

Katherine, after trying pretty hard, actually left to find the answer on another site. She started out ignoring the right column, she searched "population of the U.S." elsewhere on the U.S. Census Bureau's Web site. Many of the results were press releases, and she looked at a few, but they were not well formatted for the Web and were long, with more information than she wanted to read. After spending an unusually long 3 minutes and 47 seconds on the U.S. Census Bureau search results page, she said, "It's not really giving me the answer I want. You have to read a lot to get the answer to just one question. I know how I can probably find this faster: Google." She went to Google and typed "What is the population of the US?" The third hit was the U.S. Census Bureau's population clock, but she did not select it. She found her answer on a different site. That's gotta hurt.

Unlike these users, Nora found and used the population feature on the U.S. Census Bureau site, but it wasn't easy. For a long time, 1 minute and 18 seconds, she did not look to the right on the homepage. In fact, she left the homepage by clicking the *American Fact Finder* link in the left-side navigation. Only when she returned did she see the feature on the right (**Figure 3.44**). For some reason—possibly the credibility of a government organization to her—she stuck with the homepage and found the answer to the first part of the task: finding the size of the U.S. population.

The second part of the task—to find the population of Texas—took even longer. Initially, she did not see the area with the state population finder, below the U.S. population number. She looked all over the page, except on the right. When nothing struck her, she looked to the right of the page and saw the feature she needed. Maybe she intuitively looked to the right again because she had already had some success there.

Like Nora, Aimee ultimately found and used the state population feature—but not until she first looked on the left, middle, and top of the page. After about ten seconds, she looked to the right and found and used the *Population Finder* feature for Texas.

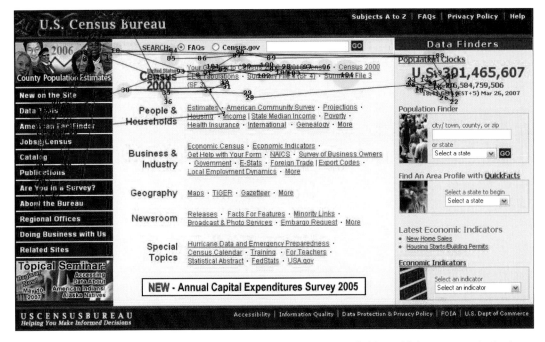

Figure 3.44 On Nora's second visit to this homepage, she had trouble finding the state population feature on the right. She looked away from the feature to the main content area of the page and through the left-side navigation.

Yet even for Aimee, one of the few people who found the feature, it was not smooth moving. After she completed the task, we asked her whether she had any comments. "It's kind of crowded and not that easy to find," she said. "None of the information in the middle really stands out. Maybe it is just too much information, and it's all mushed together."

Users often have difficulty expressing what is right or wrong with a Web interface, except when it comes to clutter. Like Aimee, people notice and say when a page is too full, busy, cluttered, "mushed together," or just too much. This usually means that there are too many items on the page or it is too disorganized.

The user success rate for this task was only 14 percent, far less than the 84 percent average success rate for this round of testing on other sites. And more than half of the users did not look at the needed feature at all or saw it briefly and ignored it.

The factors that contributed to task failure on this site are common on Web sites today:

- **Banner blindness.** For many users, the maroon boxed-off feature, sectioned-off areas, and small images that are almost impossible to make out peripherally resembled promotions. This instance of banner blindness was particularly acute because users who were "protecting" themselves from a potentially unnecessary or unscrupulous advertisement ended up missing a feature they truly needed.

- **Mismatched priority.** Users do not expect a central feature to be in the right-side column. And too many types of interface elements on the page draw users into the wrong places.

- **Too good to be true.** Even though the features users needed were right in front of them, people sometimes have such low expectations for Web site design that they just don't see them. Users don't fathom that an application like this could even exist.

- **Unclear terminology.** Even after some users peeked at the correct feature, the terms *Population Clocks* and *Data Finder* were not clear or enticing enough to make them want to spend more fixations or thought on them.

- **Users' past experience.** Users know they can search. So, when the browsing seemed ineffective, they quickly resorted to searching.

- **The task at hand.** We asked users, "What is the population of the United States and the state of Texas?" The words *search* and *find* were not mentioned, but perhaps the act of searching is intuitive to users for any task involving finding information.

- **Momentum behavior.** Once started in a direction, some users continued moving in that direction, even if a better option was available.

Categorize the priority and importance of content and the physical sections of the page. Match the importance of the information with the priority area and likely viewing order of the page.

Plotting Priority Areas on a Page

When matching high-priority content, the rule of thumb based on where people often look is that the upper left of the content area is the highest-priority section for a general page layout with top and left-side navigation and a right rail (**Figure 3.45** and **Figure 3.46**). This varies depending on the entire page layout.

Figure 3.45 This is a commonly used page layout. Users look to the menus on the top and left side for links and menu commands.

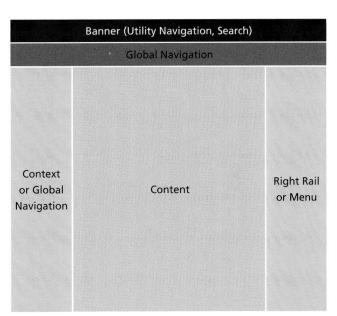

Figure 3.46 Generally users look for high-priority information in the upper left of the content area.

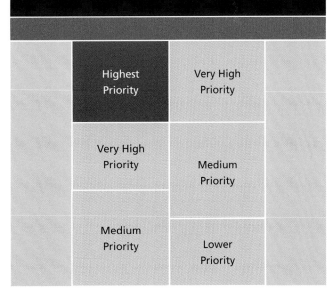

Allocate Screen Real Estate Wisely

When a large percentage of a page is allocated to items that people don't look at or look at only minimally, we call it **misallocation of screen real estate**. This is not an effective or efficient use of space. And it can be a serious problem if it means people skip information they could benefit from.

Homepages that present users with countless banners, bars, and useless graphics are particularly guilty of this. And they are the very pages that should not do it because people visit a Web site's homepage first 25 percent of the time.

The homepage for Agere Systems, an integrated circuit components company, exemplifies this (**Figure 3.47**). A large, generic image of a smiling woman in a blue shirt staring at a laptop takes up much of the page but does not tell us very much about Agere Systems or its offerings. The other images on the page are throwaway items—obviously there as filler because they don't draw the eye or add anything to the text they accompany. If you study them, they might tell a little story, but people don't do that. In some cases, it's difficult even to decipher what the images are. (See Chapter 6, "Images," for more information about what makes good images.)

Our users did not waste their time looking at these images (**Figure 3.48**). They intentionally worked to avoid the black-and-white images that look, at first glance, like turntables and boxes. The page is a classic **obstacle course**—a page area filled with features that people intentionally avoid looking at.

Figure 3.47 The homepage on the Agere Systems Web site uses a good deal of its real estate on images that don't attract the eye or provide useful information.

Figure 3.48 Images take up about 33 percent of this homepage but generate no heat—a serious misallocation of screen space. People looked at only about 67 percent of the page.

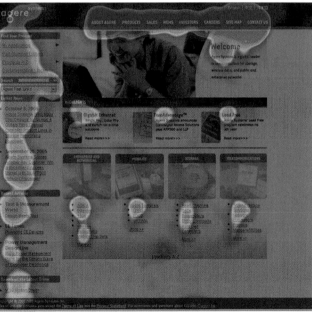

Now let's take a look at the homepage for the BNSF Railway site, which features a large picture of a train at the top (**Figure 3.49**). It's not a bad idea, but the size, location, and treatment of the train image are a problem. The image is just too big, and its color blends in with the orange banner. There is also too much peripheral action. It's not crisp enough to draw the eye. When asked to learn about the company and find its latest news, users did not look at the train at all (**Figure 3.50**).

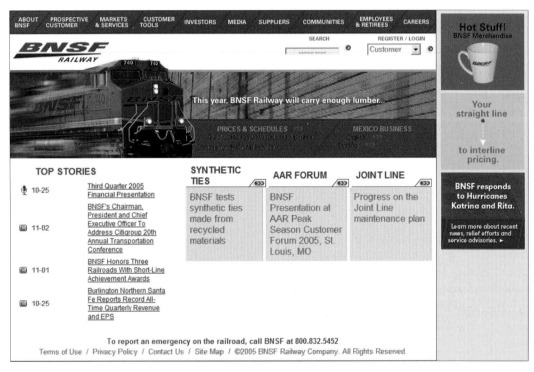

Figure 3.49 Although the picture of a train on this site is a good choice for a railway company, the image is too large, and the orange train blends with the orange banner.

Eyetracking Web Usability

Figure 3.50 Users avoided looking at all at the image of the train on the site.

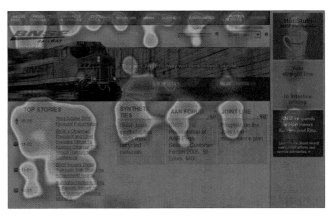

Similarly, on the Web site for Pioneer Electronics, a manufacturer of audio and video products, the user Gloria avoided the main image on the page until her 40th fixation and then looked at it only once (**Figure 3.51**). She also avoided the smaller, hard-to-see images on the page.

Figure 3.51 Gloria avoided looking at most of the images on this page of the Pioneer Electronics site and fixated only once or twice on the others.

We empathize with what the designers were trying to do on these pages: make them more exciting, convey a message or feeling, or at the very least give users a visual break from all the text. Those are all good ideas. But well-placed white space is better than busy, unrelated, low-contrast, or hard-to-decipher images at providing a visual or cognitive break.

At best, poor use of images is nothing more than a missed opportunity. At worst, it consumes valuable space and pushes more worthy messages "below the fold," sends a weak or wrong message, or makes users expend energy avoiding the images.

In some cases, valuable messages are inadvertently hidden within these ignored areas of the page. This was the case on the homepage for the JCPenney Web site (**Figure 3.52**). Most of the page on the retail store's site was allocated to a promotion and accompanying photo for a major sale on bedding and furniture for children and teens. The image is busy, and it veils the promotional text in the bottom right of the picture: *save 10–40% on bedding, furniture and all the cool accessories they want.*

Well-placed white space is better than busy, unrelated, low-contrast, or hard-to-decipher images at providing a visual or cognitive break.

Figure 3.52 A promotion takes up a large part of the homepage real estate on the JCPenney Web site. Important information is hidden in the text in the lower right.

Eyetracking Web Usability

Our users looked around the image at the text above and below it. They did not see the bedding sale information that the store was trying to highlight (**Figure 3.53**). They commented that the page was "loud" and "busy." No kidding! They also did not look much at the large, colored text *kids & teens bedroom blast*. (Even if they did, what is a "bedroom blast"?)

Figure 3.53 JCPenney's large sale promotion on its site was ineffective. People looked around the loud image, not at the items or the text within.

Sometimes a misallocation of screen space occurs because designers are not sure what else to put in the priority spots. Other times they are not aware of the problems associated with misallocating screen space. If you are reading this, you can no longer chalk it up to ignorance. Consider how much space images and banners take up on your site—particularly the homepage. Can you come up with content that communicates, sells, or inspires to put there instead?

The Most Important Elements Should Stand Out

All designers know that their Web page is competing with other Web pages for people's attention. But there is also competition occurring on each page. Menus, images, links, and promotions are competing with one another for people's attention—and not all of them can win.

Menus, images, links, and promotions compete with one another for people's attention, so it's important to know which ones are most likely to win.

In one example from our study, Nancy was looking for a cell phone calling plan on the T-Mobile site. She navigated to a page that asks users to type in their zip code to retrieve the calling plan for their area. There is nothing else on this page in the content area—almost no competition vying for people's attention.

When Nancy first came to the page, she was riveted to the field (**Figure 3.54**). Even the page title couldn't compete. People are often drawn to open fields, especially when they represent a feature they need at the time and the rest of the page is spare.

Nancy continued to look at this field as she typed in it (**Figure 3.55**). Only when she was finished typing did she look elsewhere on the page.

Sometimes users are drawn to a magnetic element first or longer than they are to other elements on a page. But in many cases, they will not look away from a very magnetic element. Every Web page asks users to look at or select one item over another, so it's important for designers to know which elements have the strongest attraction for users and will beat out weaker elements for their attention.

Figure 3.54 Nancy was drawn to the open field on this spare page.

Figure 3.55 Nancy looked up at the page title after she understood all she needed to about the most magnetic element on the page, the open field.

Note: This image does not show text users typed in on a page.

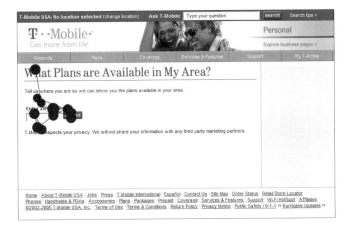

The Price of Miscues

Elements that mislead site visitors are called **miscues**. Even if people get past them and complete their tasks successfully, miscues are a problem. Users should spend their time, thought, and fixations on the right command for their task, not on design elements that are not what they need.

Of course, Web pages can include entertaining elements such as a phrase, article, or image that make users interested or happy. But enticing users with these items at the wrong time can be counterproductive. Generally in Web design, it's not a good idea to mix business with pleasure. If users are trying to get through a serious task—such as purchasing an item or signing up for a bank account—a site should help them get through it. That's what the organization's executive board is probably shooting for—not distracting users from completing these tasks, even if they are having a great time, which is very unlikely. It's more likely that they're exasperated by the distractions.

Now we know you probably think we are being pretty persnickety here with the idea of miscues, and we agree. We are being picky. But it's in the interest of making great designs.

For example, we discovered in one eyetracking exercise that attractive miscues on pages of the Web site for Skype, an Internet telephone service, caused people to miss catch-phrases that would have helped them better understand what was being offered.

One page on the site is called *What is free and what costs you a little money*. That title is pretty straightforward—and necessary to see in order to understand the information presented on the page. But users such Bev completely skipped over it, attracted instead to the orange *free* sticker because it is a priority spot on the page (**Figure 3.56**). Other reasons why the sticker caught people's eye: It fits in with the site style, and the word *free* pops off the orange background. And, of course, the word *free* is magnetic.

Figure 3.56 In the first moments on a page about what is free and what is not free from Skype, Bev focused on the bright orange *free* callout. But she did not look at the page heading.

In her next moments on the page, Bev looked again at the *free* element and read some of the offerings in each section (**Figure 3.57**). But their wording was unclear. The first item in the *Free features* section is *Calling other people on Skype*. Does that mean calling others is free if you use Skype or that it is free to call from one Skype account to another? In fact, it means the latter, but calling people who don't use Skype costs only a little money. The site does not communicate this clearly (**Figure 3.58**).

Figure 3.57 After a few moments, Bev read the words *Calling other people on Skype* but didn't understand that this was free.

Figure 3.58 Then she looked at much of the page and at some miscues about prices. She still did not see the important heading *What is free and what costs you a little money.*

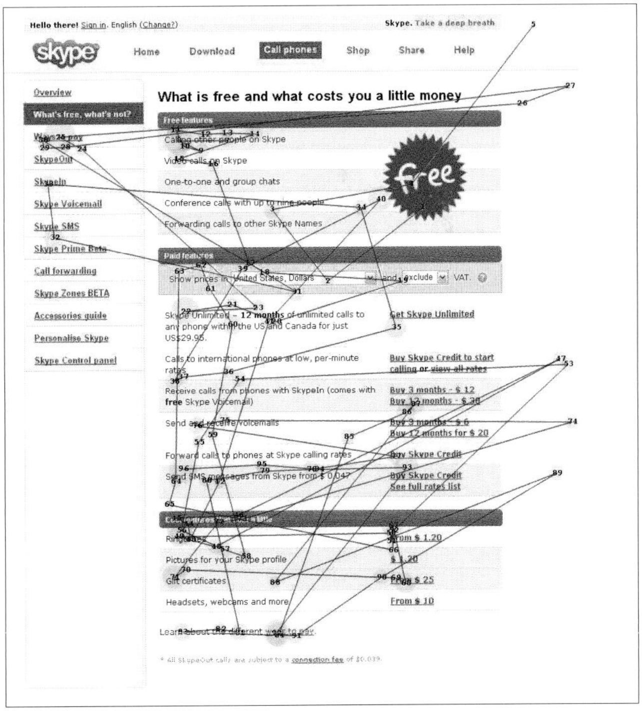

When still trying to learn what Skype costs, Bev landed on a page that displayed the methods of payment accepted on the site (**Figure 3.59**). This clinched it for her, and she said, "The download is free, but there are costs associated with it." She never understood that it was free to download the product and call other people on Skype.

Figure 3.59 Seeing this page of payment options helped convince the user that the product was not free.

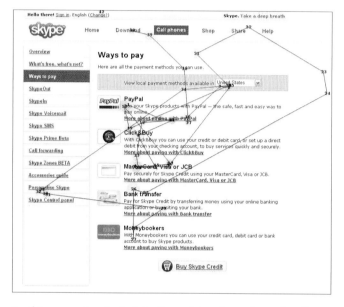

In this example, the bright free sticker is a miscue, leading people to believe that most or all of the features offered on the page are free. The wording of some of the offerings is also a miscue, leading to further user confusion. The take-home message is that highly promoted items or ambiguous phrases can cause users to waste time and fixations or, worse, to misunderstand what a site is offering.

Using Eyetracking to Improve Page Layout

Organizations should consider whether they are using their important and expensive Web site real estate effectively. Even if your layout "tested well" despite diverging from some of the guidelines we've discussed here, what that means depends on how it was tested.

Did someone show people an image and talk about it? Run a focus group? Ask people to rate it? Asking people to take a moment to look at a Web page and give their impressions is very different from behavioral research—the kind of down-and-dirty, guerrilla testing we did for this book. It didn't involve asking or rating; it involved *using*.

If "tested well" means many looks and clicks, your site could be an outlier. There are certainly exceptions to the points we have been making. If your site has a big picture of a puffy neon pink marshmallow and it is working for you, all power to you. But instead, consider whether you are content to leave well enough alone when your site could be better.

If you think you already have a usable design, your next step may be an eyetracking study to see where you *almost* lost (or drew in) people. You can study this somewhat even without eyetracking technology if your users are very "good talkers" and constantly holding the pointer over items as they ponder them. Few users are like this, however.

Eyetracking technology is very good at exposing design miscues, so you can almost get into users' heads and see what they are thinking. You know if they look at something and spend time reading it or if they stare at a link, word, or image. Understanding the miscues in their interfaces can help designers refine a page so that it is perfect.

Of course, many design teams do not have eyetracking technology and cannot conduct a deep study like this. With tight schedules and lean teams, many struggle just to respond to the basic findings from usability testing done *without* eyetracking. So, we recommend that miscues be researched by design teams that have already found and fixed most usability issues pertaining to misclicks (users selecting items that take them down the wrong path) and unsuccessful tasks.

If you want to study miscues but are unsure how they relate to our traditional usability measures, consider our four basic quantitative measures:

- **Task time.** Time that elapses until users say they are finished

- **Success.** How much users actually got done

- **Errors.** Instances when users clicked toward a path that was in the wrong direction

- **User satisfaction.** How users rate their experience with the interface

(Note that of these measures, errors are the most like miscues because both draw users away from what they should be looking at or clicking. But an error is an actual *click* in the wrong direction, not just a *look*. Errors are difficult to measure because today's Web sites are so expansive and there tend to be so many avenues to getting to the "right" answer.)

Miscues affect all the other measures. Even if users are 100 percent successful with a task, what happened on the way to their success is maybe even more important. Maybe they were almost directed away from the right path with miscues. Maybe they took longer to complete the task or questioned their own judgment because of them. In fact, miscues have the most profound effect on task time and user satisfaction. Even if users don't realize that they are spending more time than they should have to on a task, they don't like wasting time and feeling unproductive. These feelings will be reflected in their rating of a site.

Remember, a successful site is one in which the most important features are easy for people to see and use. To create one, designers need to cut through the clutter that politics can cause and the visual noise that too many commands, banners, images, and other items create.

4 Navigation

Menus and links are the crux of the
Web and hypertext media. Designing
links to look like links, and menus
to look like menus, is relatively easy
today on the Web. But organizing
and naming them is one of the most
difficult and time-consuming challenges
for Web designers. In this chapter, we
discuss what attracts users in positive
and negative ways as they attempt to
traverse Web sites. We also provide
advice for making navigational items
visible and explicable.

Understanding people's needs and improving a product to better meet them were central design concepts long before the Web came along. But it's important for designers not to get so caught up in adding dazzling supplementary features that they lose sight of the basic purpose of a device.

Consider the telephone. In the old days, callers just had to pick up the receiver on a wall-mounted phone, and an operator would ask to whom she could connect them. Now that was service. But it was also costly, it was error prone, and it forced introverts to talk to people. Later versions of the telephone allowed people to call just a few numbers with the press of a single button. Rotary-dial phones enabled limitless calling, although they also required people to remember a lot of numbers or carry a phone book. Push-button speed dial made things a lot faster, and so on.

Now handheld phones can be so complicated that people often don't know how to make a simple call on them. A phone that taunts you—now that's not a successful design. Let's see that our Web designs don't do the same.

Menus and Information Architecture

People need to look at Web site menus. And they do look at them when the menus are across the top and down the side of the page. This is true whether the menus look like boxes, tabs, or Mac or Microsoft Windows–like commands.

Global Navigation

Don't make your site's global navigation change when users make sub-navigation selections. Once people are focused on subnavigation, they usually do not recheck the global navigation to see whether it has changed.

Global navigation is the anchor on small and large Web sites. In our study, people looked at horizontal navigation across the top of the page 24 percent of the time (**Figure 4.1**). They looked at the top horizontal subnavigation 54 percent of the time and vertical navigation on the left side 49 percent of the time.

Figure 4.1 People in our study were about twice as likely to look at top horizontal subnavigation and left-side vertical navigation than at horizontal navigation across the top of a page.

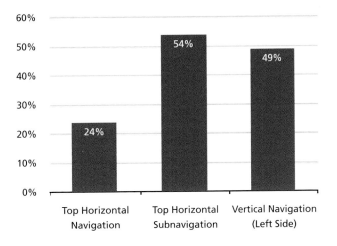

It may seem like people should look at global navigation more than a quarter of the time, but think of it as you would a lifejacket stored under your seat on an airplane. You may confirm its existence during the safety instruction presentation, but you are not going to put it on, inflate it, and wear it just in case you need to evacuate. Nor will you repeatedly look to make sure it's still there during your flight. (As frequent flyers, we have a word of advice for you if you do either of these things: medicate.) But you know where it is if you need it. You ignore it when you don't. That's the way it is with Web site menus.

For this reason, it is usually not a good idea to make the main menu change when people select a submenu. Users almost always miss these discreet changes because they are no longer focused on the main navigation.

Search: The One-Hit Wonder

As design for Web search has advanced, users have come to rely less on site menus. If they are going to a site for one answer, they'll often go through a search engine directly to the page they want.

For example, let's say you're looking for a Best Buy store near you. Type "best buy" into a Web search engine, and links will appear for the retailer's homepage and its most popular departments. Topping the list is the *Store*

Locator link. You may never even go to Best Buy's homepage.

As long as a link takes users where they want to go on a site, they don't need the site's menu. So, for quick, one-hit tasks, menus are becoming less important. However, when people want more than one answer on a site or are loyal site users, they want to see other pages. For this reason, we should always employ usable, persistent global navigation.

Consistent, Persistent, and Simple Navigation

People cannot look at all the things they are bombarded with on most Web pages. So, they develop defenses such as *banner blindness* or what we call **selective disregard**— which means that they ignore items they do not need or do not want to see at that time. This goes beyond not using items to not even looking at them.

Consider the people in our study who used the FreshDirect Web site (**Figure 4.2**). Some users had first used the site to shop for groceries, so they were well aware of what the top horizontal navigation offered when they began looking for ready-made meals.

Figure 4.2 After using the top, horizontal global navigation, users knew they could ignore it as they focused on the choices offered in the center of the page.

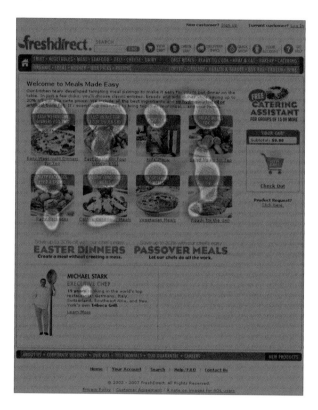

After they selected the *Easy Meals* link, they looked in the main content area on that page, where there are eight categories of meals, such as *Easy Weeknight Dinners for Two* and *Fast Meals for Four Under $30.* The names and headings of the offerings make them attractive and easy to read, and people did read them.

Eyetracking Web Usability

At this point, people did not ponder the top horizontal menus. This does not reflect poorly on the site's menus; it reflects well on its persistent menu structure. Because the menus were consistently designed, placed on every page, and followed the site's defined standard information architecture (IA), people felt confident ignoring them for the time being.

The T-Mobile Web site also does a good job with its navigation and subnavigation. The design helps users by offering obvious global navigation at the top (**Figure 4.3**). Based on what link users select there, a row of tabs appears below. It can be tricky to present rows of navigation, but the space between the rows in this design helps. Users can also locate where they are in the IA because the global nav link changes from dark gray to light yellow, and the tabs change from gray to white, when selected.

Figure 4.3 The obvious global navigation, the space between it and the subnav, and the visual indication of what users have selected in both nav bars all help people acclimate on this site.

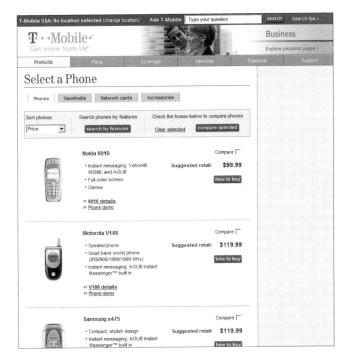

We asked people to look for a mobile phone on this site. One user quickly scrolled to the top of the products page, pausing to fixate only twice as she did. Once at the top, she immediately located the global navigation at the selected area, confirming that she was in the *Products* section. She then scanned to the subnav tabs, looking at the possibilities (**Figure 4.4**). Based on the menu choices, she determined that they were links to related items, not to phones. Having so few simple, visible choices helped her determine that the *Phones* section was where she needed to be. This is an example of persistent global navigation design.

Figure 4.4 One user acclimated to this site by scanning the global navigation and then all the subnav tabs.

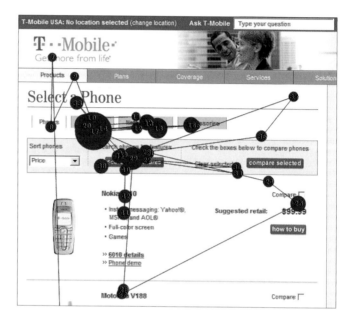

Subpar Subnavigation

Many sites today offer persistent global navigation and visually display the selected category in it, but some fall short with their subnavigation. It is equally important to visually display selected categories in subnav and sub-subnav, however.

Good information architecture can shatter when a site offers many products or when designers must amalgamate different elements into the design. It can be difficult for designers to deal with those few odd choices that don't fit well with the design and to determine how to indicate to users when they are in a category, subcategory, and sub-subcategory. Adding other features—such as one that suggests products to users—also complicates the design challenge.

Eyetracking Web Usability

Figure 4.5 After using the horizontal global navigation at the top of this page, users knew they could ignore it and focus on the left navigation to further refine their search.

For example, the Amazon Web site must accommodate a surfeit of different types of products, yet its global navigation manages to stay consistent and persistent. As we discovered in our study, the site's subnavigation can sometimes go amiss, however.

When we asked people to "shop for a gift for a teenage nephew who likes music," several chose to use the Amazon site. They easily located the link to the *Music* section in the global navigation. Once on the music page (**Figure 4.5**), the left-side navigation offers links such as *Alternative Rock*, *Classic Rock*, *Rock*, *Rap & Hip Hop*, and *Pop* under the heading *Narrow by category in Music*. None of the users looked at the heading for this menu, but they picked up on the idea that these were links to music subcategories just by looking at them. Most assumed their nephew would like pop, rap, and rock, so they looked at those categories. And since they knew the names of these genres, finding them in this long alphabetical list was relatively simple. (Had the users not known the genres, however, they probably would have had a difficult time with this layout.)

Consistent Category Names Help Users

Web site menus are organized in various ways: by types of products, users' tasks, users' background, or whatever makes the most sense for the individual site. Many menus also combine different categories. It's unrealistic to think that all menu categories and choices can be parallel, but designers should still try to make menu choices expected and analogous when possible.

Be consistent in wording when naming categories in menus, on pages, and in tables. For example, don't combine a single-noun link name, such as *Clothing*, with verb-noun name, such as *Buy Bedding*, in the same list. Instead, make it clear in the list heading that these are

products for sale and then use uniform link wording, such as *Bedding* and *Clothing*.

Another example:

Do: *Humidifiers, Humidifier Accessories, Vacuums, Vacuum Accessories*

Don't: *Humidifiers and Accessories, Vacuums, Vacuum Accessories*

Users don't always read every term in a menu choice. Sometimes only the first word catches their eye. And they often scan menus quickly, so words that are expected and easy to digest are most effective.

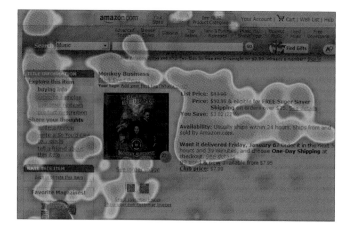

Several people selected *Pop*. The pop page presented them with subcategories of pop music on the left-side menu. The users did not bother looking at the tabs or other horizontal navigation at this point because they had already drilled down to the sections they were interested in and were using the left menu. Again, people knew what the top navigation was and that they could ignore it at this point.

Then things started to get sticky. The left-side menu presents choices such as *Pop Rap*, *Rap*, and *Pop Rock* (**Figure 4.6**). This confused users because they seemed to be the same choices as in the previous menu. This led to exhaustive review: It took some people several fixations to realize that these were not the broad categories from the previous page but rather subcategories of pop music. Some people never did seem to realize this.

People did not look at the title of the menu, so they did not see that it had changed from *Narrow by category in Music* to *Narrow by Category in Pop*. This change was too understated for users. Inserting space or using a different treatment for the text or heading could have helped.

People pressed on, however, and after looking at several CDs (for singing groups that most users stated they knew nothing about), some narrowed down their choice to one (**Figure 4.7**). They looked at the cover art and information about it. A smattering of users was still unsure whether to buy this CD as a gift for a teenager. Some just bought it, and others looked left for the menu for a different CD to buy. But the menu was not there. They looked at the

Figure 4.6 Users who came to the pop music page on Amazon had selected *Pop*, not *Rock* or *Rap*, on the previous page. So, they were somewhat confused when they saw *Rock* and *Rap* listed again on this page.

Figure 4.7 After selecting a Black Eyed Peas CD, some users weren't sure whether to buy it and considered starting over to find a different CD. They looked left for the navigation to find more CDs, but it was not there. So, they looked up to the *Music* tab in the top row of navigation.

Title Information section that had replaced it, and some looked up to the *Music* tab in the global navigation. For them, it was helpful to have this anchor there, of course. But then they had to start over, moving through the sub-nav and sub-subnav and sometimes running into the same issues again.

Vanishing Navigation

In one scenario, we asked users to buy something for themselves on the Web site for Kiehl's, which sells skin and hair products. The Kiehl's site uses traditional top horizontal navigation, a left-side menu, and a less common right-side menu (**Figure 4.8**). So, users must deal with three menus in addition to utility navigation. Despite this, the site's structure works when main product categories appear in the right menu.

Figure 4.8 The Kiehl's Web site offers a top, left, and less-common right-side menu. The side menus change depending on what is selected in other menus.

Upon their first visit to the site, the people in our study typically looked at the top navigation—the only navigation available at that point—and easily selected an item there (**Figure 4.9**).

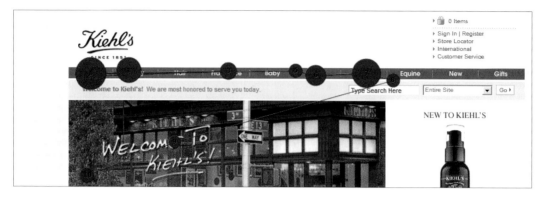

Figure 4.9 An example of what many users did first on the Kiehl's homepage: They looked at the top horizontal menu.

When this took them to a page with both right and left navigation, they tended to look first, for a fixation or two, at the left menu, not the right (**Figure 4.10**). This is most likely because users are more accustomed to seeing and using a left menu, and they expect to find helpful commands there. But people were not very attracted to the choices offered on the left. They did not want to spend time customizing their search based on criteria such as skin type or aging concerns. They just wanted to see the products. Since this categorization of content seems to be of lower priority to users, it should not have been in the left rail—a priority spot.

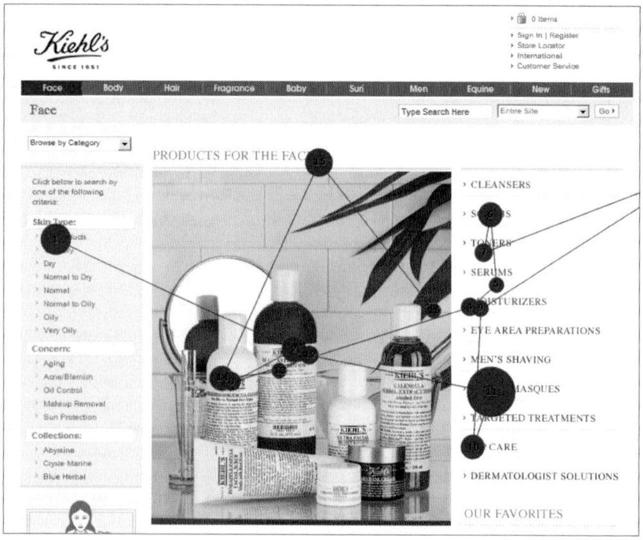

Figure 4.10 The hot potato phenomenon: Betsy looked at the left menu for one fixation and then dropped it and looked right.

The design and content of the right menu also drew their attention away quickly. The large type and white space made the right menu seem more important and workable than the left menu, with its small, more crowded type.

For example, Joe chose *Men* in the global navigation. Upon reaching the page with products for men, he first looked to the left but for just one fixation, and then he beelined to the right menu for several. After he made a selection from the right menu, he continued to examine the page. At one point, he gave two more fixations to the left menu just to see what was there. Three is a very small number of total fixations for the left menu.

Betsy chose to go to the *Face* products section of the site. Like Joe, she looked to the left menu for just one fixation and then at the product picture and right menu. We call this trend, when users quickly look away from what appears to be an unhelpful element (in this case the left menu), the **hot potato** phenomenon.

In a heat map of many users' experiences, we can see that there were fewer fixations on the left menu than on the right, although people saw both (**Figure 4.11**). From our observations of user sessions, we learned that many of the looks on the left simply reflected users doing an initial page survey and could even be considered miscues because the users weren't really looking at desired choices. The left menu was often treated like a hot potato.

Figure 4.11 Coming upon the Kiehl's site's right and left menus, users often looked first, but very briefly, at the left menu. Then they looked at and used the right menu. They ignored the top menu when they did not need it.

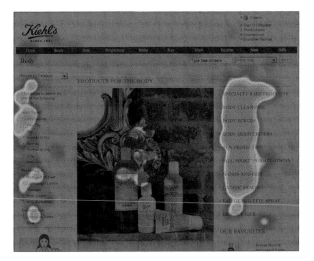

This may not be such a big deal, but eyetracking is about making a page as good as possible. So if we want to get picky about it—and we do—we must note this: People expect the commands they need to be on the left. When the commands aren't there, they must expend extra looks to find them.

The bigger issue on the Kiehl's site is the sometimes-vanishing subnavigation. The top, horizontal global navigation is always present and the same. The selected section always looks selected. This is very helpful. But the right and left menus perform somewhat erratically, and this can cause problems. Both the right and the left are context-sensitive, based on what is selected in the top global navigation and in the subnavigation.

For example, the user Kevin selected *Men* in the global navigation and started to shop for products on the men's page (**Figure 4.12**). He looked at the image of products, the right menu, the left menu, and the right again. Then he selected the *Shave* link in the right menu.

Figure 4.12 Kevin selected *Men* in the global navigation and then looked at the right and left menus, as well as at the product images in the center of the page.

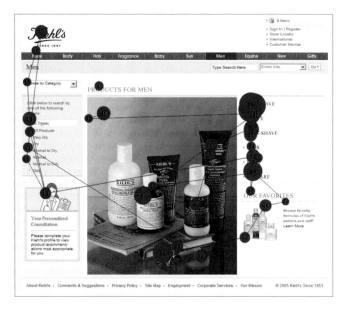

This opened a page with images of shaving products. In his initial moments on the page, Kevin looked at the top two shaving products and then wanted to see more items (**Figure 4.13**). He looked to the right for the menu, but it wasn't there. He looked at the third product and the left menu, but that was not what he wanted. This could make many users start to feel a bit trapped.

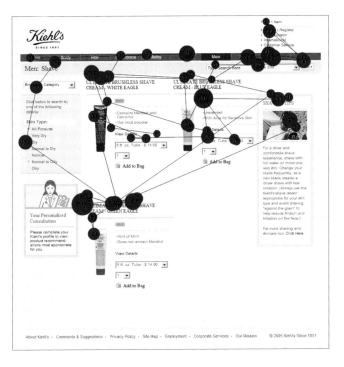

Figure 4.13 Kevin resorted to global navigation when he could no longer find the men's categories he wanted.

Kevin quit looking for the menu he wanted and thoroughly examined the products that were offered to him. Then he started looking at the top global nav and ultimately selected *Men* there again.

This example demonstrates **vanishing navigation**, our term for navigation that should be persistent throughout a site but instead mysteriously disappears at some point.

The Kiehl's site also falls short when there is only one item in a category. In that case, there isn't content for the right and left menus, so the designers needed an alternative approach. They replaced the personal attributes menu on the left with a *Personalized Consultation* offer—it's a nice offer but not the expected menu. Even more jarring, they replaced the right-side menu with a *Related Products* offering.

For example, people can select *Essence Oils* from the *Fragrance* offerings. But instead of seeing what they have come to expect on this site—a sub-submenu and a photo of multiple products—the essential oils product page has just one product (**Figure 4.14**). People can select the oil and then select different scents for it by choosing the drop-down menu that defaults to *Cucumber*. But users didn't expect the scent to be an attribute of the product, as they would with sizes or colors of a product. Therefore, calling the menu *Essential Oils* is misleading because you see only one oil and would have to know to first choose the product and then choose the scent as an attribute of it. On the right side of the page, the site displays a few *Related Products* instead of a menu.

Figure 4.14 A first-level subnavigation page on the Kiehl's site has neither a right- nor a left-side menu.

Part of the design problem is that Kiehl's offers relatively few fragrance items compared to other types of products. But the site adds to the problem by putting related products in the right rail instead of the expected subnavigation.

In one example, the user Geraldine selected the *Essence Oils* link. When the page loaded, she looked at the product, and it did not seem to be what she wanted (**Figure 4.15**). She looked to the right side, probably for more fragrances. But there was only one fragrance item there: a spray version of the featured fragrance. The other items were lotions and a body cleanser—not exactly the stuff you want to dab behind your ears before a hot date.

Figure 4.15 When Geraldine did not see a variety of fragrances to choose from in the *Essence Oils* section of the Kiehl's site, she looked back up at the global navigation, particularly at the *Hair* and *Body* links.

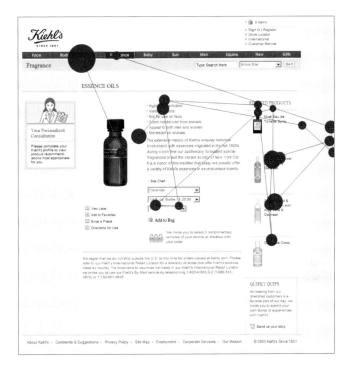

> *When users turn back to the global navigation midtask or use the Back button, it often means they find the subnavigation perplexing.*

The navigation design also ruptures on the *Samples* page. Before we go any further, we should say that offering samples on the Web site is a brilliant move on the part of the Kiehl's design or marketing team. It mimics the experience of shopping at a Kiehl's store, where customers often receive many samples to take home with their purchases. It also promotes loyalty to a store and interest in its products.

On the Kiehl's site, the default set of samples is displayed in the middle content area, which is fine. Users saw them and selected some (**Figure 4.16**). On the left are several categories of products that users can also choose samples from. But this left-side navigation is different than it is elsewhere on the site, housing commands more like those found in the global navigation. And there is no right-side navigation.

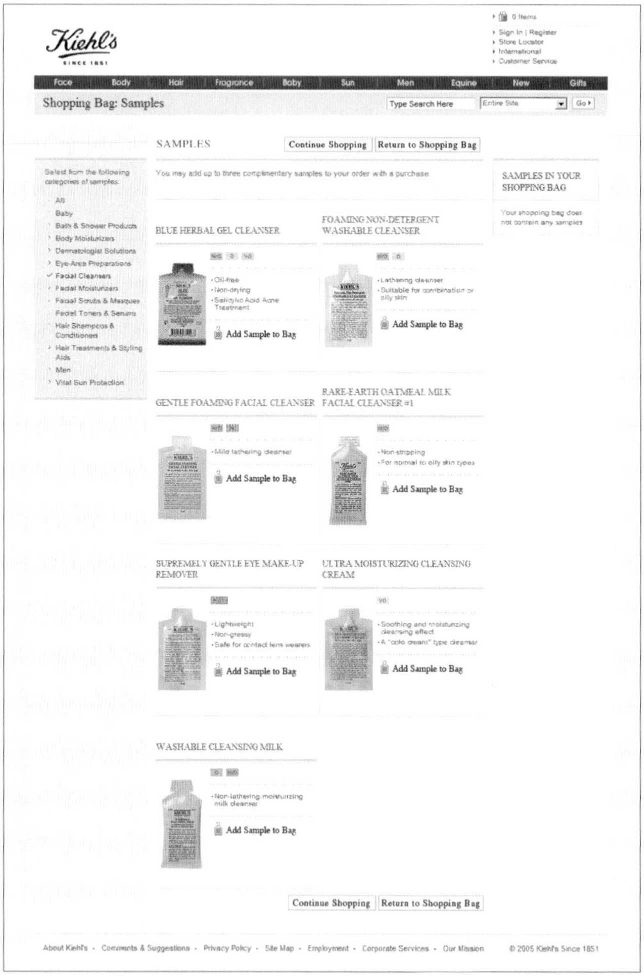

Figure 4.16 Inconsistent IA: The left-side navigation on this *Samples* page is different from elsewhere on the Kiehl's site. And there is no right-side navigation.

Users did not realize that they could choose samples in the left categories (**Figure 4.17**). There are two likely reasons for this. First, some of them may not have thought to look for more kinds of samples. Second, they were used to seeing categories in the global nav or right menu. In the

Eyetracking Web Usability

end, most people looked at the samples and the right rail, but not to the left. And they just selected from the default list of samples.

Figure 4.17 Most of our users looked at the samples in the content area and to the right for the menu. Even when they did not find the menu there, they did not look to the left menu. Instead, they selected from the default list of samples.

Note: The red heat in the upper-right area *Samples In Your Shopping Bag* reflects the fact that users looked there to track their samples as they selected them. The heat map doesn't show this dynamic element.

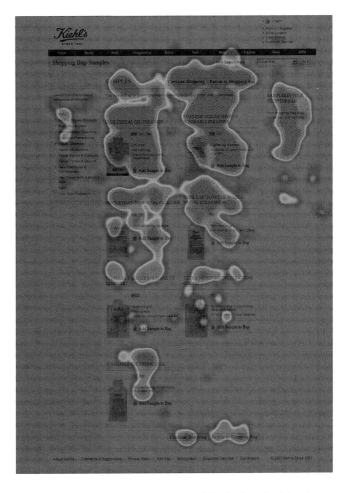

We wonder how the people at Kiehl's deal with this when they study their Web analytics. Let's hope it goes something like this: "Let's move the samples categories on the right or to the top because people aren't seeing them." Not this: "Order more Blue Herbal Gel Cleanser samples. People love 'em!" Or: "We need to rework our Ultra Moisturizing Cleansing Cream formula because 95 percent of our site users take this as a sample, but we don't sell many of them."

Thanks, Kiehl's, for this interesting example of a challenging IA problem.

But before you remove or change it, do thorough usability research. We are not saying that all sites that have subnav and sub-subnav need to always display it. If replacing subnav with other information increases your sales, OK. But make sure you understand whether you are gaining a quick hit or actually increasing customer loyalty and fostering a long-term relationship.

Designers shouldn't underestimate the importance of having basic navigation that people can quickly find, use, and count on. Designs that are too fancy confuse people. For example, when Rhonda was trying to research flat-screen televisions on the Panasonic Web site, she was greeted with an animated global navigation menu, which took up most of the visible page (**Figure 4.18**). She watched and watched the animation. She seemed to think it would stop at some point (**Figure 4.19**). When it didn't, she said, "Pretty Web site, but everything on it is going too fast." As she read one of the small text boxes in the animation, she exclaimed, "Ahhh." She then moved the pointer over a link but soon became discouraged and said, "I am going back. I don't like that." She then left the page.

Figure 4.18 Looking for information about flat-screen TVs on the Panasonic Web site, Rhonda waited for the menu to stop animating.

Eyetracking Web Usability

Figure 4.19 At this point, Rhonda seemed to realize the animation was not going to stop. She looked at the moving images and tried to read the small accompanying text.

There is no reason why users should have to look many times at menu choices or watch a site's basic navigation draw and redraw. Talk about exhausting. And Web sites that require people either to wait for the navigation to stop moving or to catch the correct menu command as it moves are just ridiculous.

How Information Architecture Can Alienate Users

Sticks and stones can break your bones, but word choices on the Web can hurt people's feelings. Surprisingly, people sometimes read things into a poorly named link. Just one menu choice can color how they regard an entire site.

In one example from our study, David, a snappy dresser in his early 30s, was turned off from the entire Neiman Marcus site in about seven fixations because of its menu names and IA organization.

We had asked him to use the site to buy himself a shirt. When he hit the homepage, he looked at the top horizontal menu (**Figure 4.20**). There is a menu link for women's clothing called *Apparel for Her* and two others geared toward women: *Shoes & Handbags* and *Jewelry & Accessories*. He looked at these links, plus those for *Designer Index* and *Beauty & Fragrance*, before he saw *Men's & Electronics*. Even after seeing this, he continued to look for another option, but then it sunk in, it seems, that *Men's & Electronics* was his only choice.

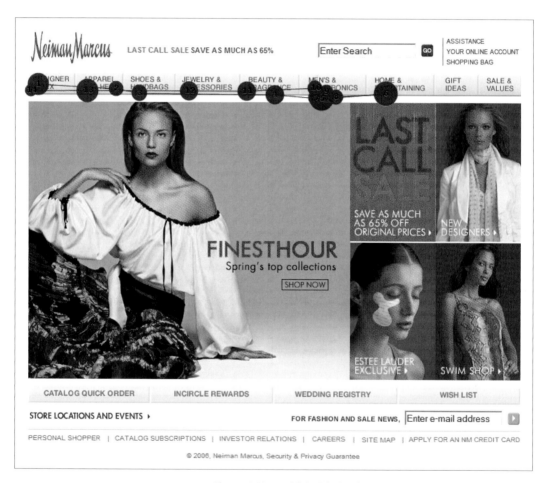

Figure 4.20 David decided in less than five seconds that this site was not targeted toward men because men's products were lumped together with electronics, while women had several product options from which to choose.

In less than five seconds into his visit, he asked in a rather sassy tone, "Why do they have *Men's* with *Electronics*? They have *Apparel for Her*, and they separate by *Shoes & Handbags*, *Jewelry & Accessories*, and *Beauty & Fragrance*. But then the *Men's* is with...," he trailed off but then added, "obviously, their target is not men, right?"

Jim had a similar reaction, although he professed very little interest in fashion or clothes shopping. When he hit the homepage, he looked all across the menu. He looked at *Men's & Electronics* a few times, but he did not seem to make the connection that this was the link he needed (**Figure 4.21**). After all, the link was not named *Apparel for Men*, like its counterpart, *Apparel for Women*. Within eight seconds, he asked, "Do they *have* apparel for men?" He then looked toward the bottom of the page to see whether there was a link there.

> *Menu wording or IA arrangements can make people feel included or estranged on a site.*

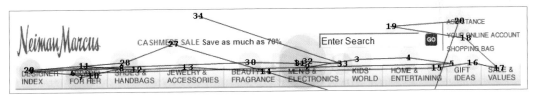

Figure 4.21 Jim's exhaustive review when searching for men's clothing on this site shows how a simple link name can throw off users. In this case, it also alienated him from the site.

After some futile looks at the bottom of the page, Jim reverted to the top global navigation. He looked further at the *Men's & Electronics* link, which he had already passed over previously, and said sarcastically, "Men's and electronics. It figures."

Although Jim found the menu choice he was looking for, the strange lumping of unlike products required him to take more time and looks to do so—an example of exhaustive review. Also, he found the name *Men's & Electronics* disagreeable—all this within his first ten seconds on the page. In a real-life situation, he probably would not have continued on the site.

We sympathize with the designers of this site because we know how difficult it can be to sort and present menu commands. With ten choices across the top, adding one more button for electronics might have pushed the top-level menu over the edge—literally. So, the designers may have thought they needed to combine two areas to fit everything in.

This is a common dilemma with horizontal menus, which is why we see horrible designs such as rows of horizontal tabs. Generally, designers in this situation just have four choices:

- Shrink the text or space between commands to fit more. This is usually a bad idea because people can't read tiny text and the graphics are not scalable fonts that users can magnify, if needed.

- Demote an item from the top-level menu to another menu or make a new category name for multiple items. Of course, this works only if the items are highly related and the category name represents all the items under the new category.

- Create new and scalable information architecture. Admittedly, this is time-consuming, expensive, and intricate.

- Marry two pretty unrelated categories together, as the Neiman Marcus site does. This last option is probably the least expensive and least painful for the design team. But it was painful for some users.

Branding and Marketing in Menus Confuses People

Branding is an integral part of good business. But using branding terms as interface elements is not.

In one scenario, we asked people to look on the Sony Web site for the address of the nearest Sony store in Manhattan. The user Tim tried a search but was not successful. He then looked at the top horizontal menu—first at *Register* and then over to *Music, Movies & TV*. As he looked at the links, he said, "If there was a subdivision up here that basically gave store locations, that would make it much easier."

So, from the start, this user had trouble. Organizations that have stores usually include a *Store Locator* feature on their sites. But the Sony site has store locations listed under *Shop*—something that our users didn't expect.

Tim started to move the pointer over the top horizontal menus from right to left, beginning in the middle. As he did, the menu items opened, and he looked at the title and one or two links under each category. When he got to *Shop*, he did not look at the links under the expanded menu (**Figure 4.22**). Instead, he immediately moved on to *Register* and a few of the commands there. He continued, "The store listings and addresses do not seem to be available here."

Figure 4.22 After first discounting it, Tim fixated on the *Shop* menu on the Sony site.

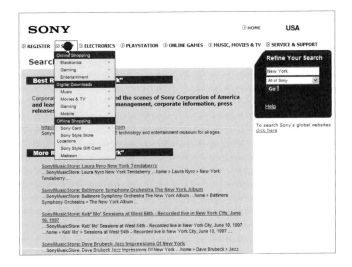

Tim then backtracked to the *Shop* menu. He stared at the word *Shop*, looked away, and looked at it again for a longer fixation. He looked at *Online Shopping* and then *Offline Shopping* in the *Shop* menu (**Figure 4.23** and **Figure 4.24**).

Figure 4.23 (left) Tim fixated longer on the *Shop* menu the third time he looked at it, after he had exhausted most of the other possibilities on the site.

Figure 4.24 (right) Tim paused on the *Digital Downloads* category as his eye moved down to the *Offline Shopping* category on the site.

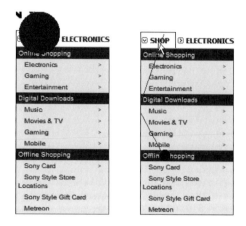

It is not very common to have category names under menu commands, and it is not something we recommend. And although *Offline Shopping* may have sounded like an obvious label to the designers, in practice this user and others did not understand it to mean that store locations would be listed there.

Tim did look at those categories, but at this point he was already deep in exhaustive review of the menus. He fixated on the link *Sony Style Gift Card*, focusing especially on the words *Sony Style*. He then looked up at the link he needed, *Sony Style Store Locations*. But he didn't select it (**Figure 4.25**).

This is where the branding issue comes in. Tim was confused by the term *Sony Style*. He just wanted to find a Sony store location and didn't know that *Sony Style* is a brand for the company's stores.

So, he looked again at the categories for *Offline Shopping* and *Online Shopping* and once again at the main *Shop* link, among others (**Figure 4.26**). He looked again at the *Sony Style Store Locations* link and said, "Actually, under *Shop*, I am finding a category here for *Sony Style Store Locations*. I am going to click on that, and hopefully it will give me the Manhattan address." He was not very confident about where the link would go, but he was hopeful.

Figure 4.25 (left) Tim looked at the *Shop* menu and its *Sony Style Store Locations* link. He was looking for Sony stores but did not choose this link because the term *Sony Style* confused him.

Figure 4.26 (right) Yet again, Tim looked at the *Offline Shopping* category, clearly still puzzled by the term *Offline*. This is not how people think of a physical store.

Even after he said this, Tim continued to look for several more fixations at various areas, including the *Online Shopping* category, the *Sony Style Store Locations* link, the *Shop* main menu yet again, and the *Sony Style Store Locations* link (**Figure 4.27**). He continued to ponder the *Sony Style Store Locations* link even as he clicked it.

Figure 4.27 Tim continues to ponder the *Sony Style Store Locations* link as he moves his pointer over it.

After much exhaustive review of the menu, Tim finally landed on the *Sony Style Retail Stores* page, only to be greeted with a *Sony Style* logo in the upper left. He looked at it a few times before the rest of the page loaded. As a large image of a store with the heading *Sony Style Retail Stores* loaded in the center of the page, he focused several times on the words *Style* and *Retail* and said, "Now these are Sony-style retail stores" (**Figure 4.28**). He looked at the image of the store and said, "I don't know if this is exactly what's being asked for because it seems to be a proper name: Sony *Style* stores as opposed to just a generic Sony store."

Figure 4.28 In the first moments of his visit to this page, Tim looked quite a lot at the words *Sony Style Retail Stores* in the image. He was trying to figure out whether the Sony Style store was different from a regular Sony store.

He then looked at a few of the store addresses and the rest of the page (**Figure 4.29**). He focused on the *Sony Outlet Stores* link on the lower right. After finding a Manhattan address, he said, "Although I am familiar with Sony products, I am not familiar enough with the corporate infrastructure to know if *Sony Style* just means your regular all-in-one Sony store or if this is a particular specialty." He reexamined the image of the store and added, "It looks to be more of a specialty store."

This was not a good user experience, and one of the main reasons why was bad branding placement. We ask you— OK, we *beg* you—to stop branding menus, buttons, links, features, and headings. Name things simply, describing what they are. There is only one exception to this: when a branded name or slogan is so much a part of the public consciousness that using another name would be confusing. For example, if McDonald's called a link to information about the Big Mac something like "burger with double beef patties, three buns, and sauce," it would confuse people rather than help them. "Big Mac" is better in this case.

It takes deep research to know where to draw that line. The Sony designers may be so close to the Sony Style brand that they believe it is well known enough to use it as a navigable link on the site. But just a few usability studies showed us that this is not the case.

Figure 4.29 Tim looked quite a lot at the logo, the *Sony Style* text in the image, the *Sony Outlet Stores* box beneath the blue color box, and the addresses of store locations. He still assumed that the Sony Style store was "more of a specialty store," not the brand for Sony stores.

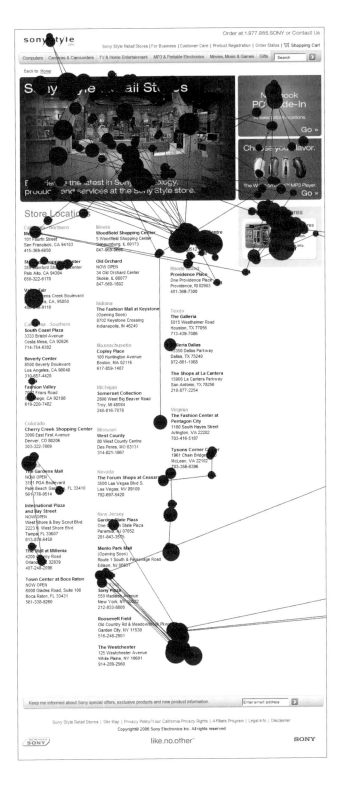

In most cases, strip all signs of branding and marketing from menus and link names.

Why does this happen so often? There is the occasional renegade designer who feels compelled to bestow a name like "zesty travel wizard" in a menu when "book travel" will do quite well. But more often, this kind of decision comes from a far-off land called Marketing. We mean no disrespect to marketing, because it has a big, important place in this world and should influence a multitude of decisions—just not decisions in Web interface design.

Utility Navigation

Let's face it: Utility navigation is not the glamour girl of Web pages. Even main site navigation gets more looks. People look at top utility navigation 9 percent of the time and bottom utility navigation only 4 percent of the time, probably because it is "below the fold."

We believe people have learned that utility menus hold administrative, or operational, information about the organization: jobs, locations, contact info, privacy policy, help, and the site map. When people in our study needed this kind of information, they looked toward the very top and very bottom of pages.

Utility navigation typically has small text that is lighter than the rest of the page text but still easy to see and is located at the very top (above main navigation and banners) and very bottom of pages. The location and look of utility navigation helps people differentiate it from the global nav. So, for the most part, it is a positive thing that people do not always look at it. This is selective disregard.

The Skype Web site's utility navigation has some typical and atypical traits (**Figure 4.30**). It has many more links than is common. The design is also unusually large, with columns of links and a border around it. The gray shade of the text is a bit too ghosted, making it difficult to read, even for utility navigation.

Figure 4.30 Even though the utility navigation on this site is unusual in size and design, a user still realized what it was, partly because it is located at the very bottom of pages.

On the traditional side, it is located at the bottom of the page, which is probably the most important identifying factor. Most of the text is smaller than the text on the rest of the site and is light, also common traits. These characteristics made it traditional enough that people in our study looked at it when they needed to find information about the company, its privacy policy, and how to contact it. Because the pages on this site are generally very spare, it was also easier for users to scan all parts of the pages (**Figure 4.31**).

Figure 4.31 A user scanned an entire page on the spare Skype Web site. Scanning feels effortless when there are not too many choices.

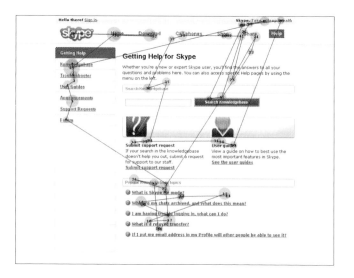

In sum, utility navigation should not compete for attention with other elements on a page. It should look faded and less significant than the site's main navigation. This look and placement will help people recognize utility navigation easily.

Navigational Elements

In our usability sessions, we often see Web users select items that are not actually clickable—and sometimes multiple times. Some people get annoyed. More get embarrassed or blame themselves for not knowing what's clickable. But it's not their fault. Web site aesthetics should reveal what is clickable and not clickable. And sites should make users confident that they are taking the right path by providing language on links and buttons that is specific and understandable.

Links and Headings

People have a special relationship with links. A link is more than an item on a Web page; it is a promise. A link is a vow to users that it will take them where they want to go. Every time a link's promise is kept, the user advances. But broken promises confuse users, require that they fixate on the words too much, and chip away at their trust.

Let's look at this dynamic in action. Aimee wanted to buy some cookies on the Girl Scouts Web site. When the homepage loaded, she looked on the left of the content area at the blue box with pictures of cookies and the words *Find Cookies Now* (**Figure 4.32**). She said, "*Find Cookies Now.* I am going to click that to see what choices there are."

Figure 4.32 Aimee's eye was quickly drawn to the image of cookies and the words *Find Cookies Now* in the blue box on the left side of this homepage. Note that this figure shows only one fixation on the page, but she looked for about seven fixations before she selected the link.

A link is a promise. The link name sets the user's expectations for what is to come.

When the page loaded, Aimee decided after only two fixations that this was not the page she needed or expected (**Figure 4.33**). If there was a way to order cookies on the page, it was not apparent. There were no cookies; there was no order form. There was just an image of girls—possibly Scouts—and some text about the cookies being an "icon of American culture." She said, "Wait. I have to do that again." She went back and selected the same link again.

Figure 4.33 The page that appeared after Aimee selected *Find Cookies Now* was unexpected and confusing.

This is a case of link wording making a promise it does not keep. The user ended up confused and disappointed (and maybe even a little hungry).

Use Information-Bearing Words

People usually scan headings and links before they scan the normal text on pages. A good link or heading is understandable and meets their needs. After reading even one link or heading, users may be able to eliminate further scanning or reading, thus expediting their tasks.

Turn information-bearing words within text into direct links, rather than creating additional links and buttons for a topic.

Use information-bearing words for links, headings, and section titles. Better yet, make a title or word or phrase in the body text an inline link rather than adding separate, generic links such as *more, click here,* or *go,* which only add unnecessary visual clutter. Section headings make for acceptable links as long as the affordance is good—in other words, as long as they appear to be clickable.

Use the most specific words you can for links. Here are some good examples: *plants discovered on the moon, new director of operations, edit your profile.* When naming non–information-bearing links, use the most specific word possible, such as *search* and *submit,* rather than *more* or *read more.*

Buttons

Buttons invoke an action when clicked. They are typically used more than links within applications, forms, and other processes and flows. Buttons on the Web sometimes take visual cues from buttons in operating systems, but they don't need to do so. Just about any button style can work as long as it looks clickable, is not distracting, and matches the site design.

Looking Clickable

Buttons on the T-Mobile site look clickable (**Figure 4.34**). When people in our study were looking for a mobile phone on this site, Ruthie determined that she needed to be in the *Phones* subnavigation area to conduct her search. But she wanted to sort and view the phone offerings in different ways. The green *search by features* button was waiting for her like a vacant taxicab during a rainstorm. It is just under the subnav on the site—visible but not so distracting that she was drawn to it before she scanned the menu (**Figure 4.35**). The text is understandable. And the button's appearance—a rectangular box with a green background and subtle shadowing—looks 3D, like a button. It stands on its own and cannot be mistaken for a heading, advertisement, or other element. After looking at the global navigation and subnav, she looked at and selected it.

Figure 4.34 The *search by features* command on this site is legible, is understandable, is well placed, and looks like a button.

Figure 4.35 Ruthie looked at the button and selected it because of these features.

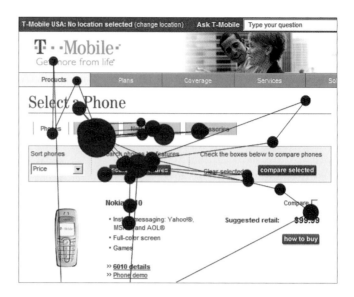

Similarly, on the Dansk site, Nora was instantly drawn to the *Add to basket* button (**Figure 4.36**). Its shape, placement, and orange color make it stand out on the page. Users are drawn to buttons when they are small, contain one or a few words, and have some kind of border, shadow, or beveling effect.

Figure 4.36 Nora was drawn to the orange, beveled button, which stands out against the white background on this site.

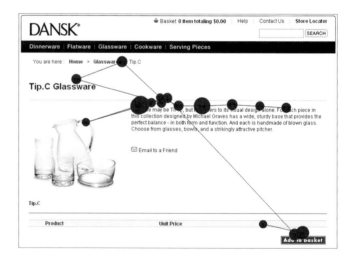

This was not the case with the buttons on the Comedy Central Web site. On the site, there is a joke area in the middle of the page under the heading *Joke of the Day* (**Figure 4.37**). Although there is no text saying that there is more than one joke a day, the buttons in the form of arrows above and below the joke area are for this purpose. But our users were hard-pressed to see this.

Figure 4.37 The green arrow button on a green background camouflaged a good feature on the Comedy Central site.

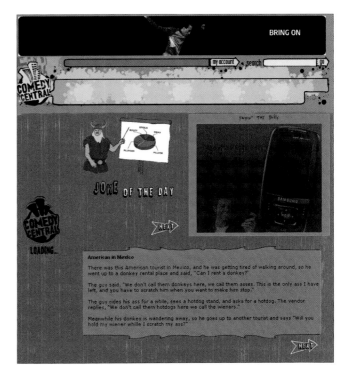

Renee read and laughed out loud at the joke of the day. Then she wanted to read more jokes. She looked at the page but did not see the *Next* buttons (**Figure 4.38**). They blend in too much with the page to lure users to look at them. The typeface is not readable. And the unsystematic way that they and other items are strewn on the page does not help.

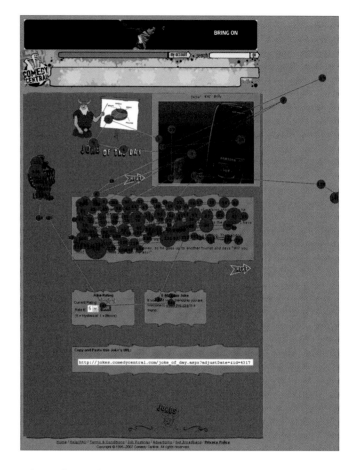

Figure 4.38 Renee looked almost everywhere on the page except at the faint *Next* buttons when looking for another joke.

The Web site for the Benjamin Moore paint company offers a splash page with language choices (**Figure 4.39**). Language pages are far less common than they were even a few years ago, so people are not always accustomed to choosing a language when they hit a site. So, the buttons in a case like this should really look like buttons to help indicate to users that they must perform an action at the start.

The two boxes, too large to be buttons, have language choices featured in arrows within them. Large boxes and graphics are usually used to signify sections or are callouts, and people have come to expect them to be informational, not actionable elements. So adding a smaller element within the boxes that looks clickable in the boxes was a good idea. However, these arrows with text inside don't exude clickability.

Eyetracking Web Usability

Figure 4.39 People must read and pay close attention to understand what is being asked of them on this page.

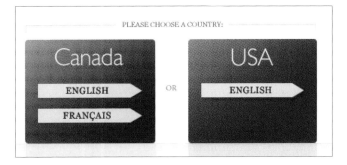

Featuring two buttons for English is also somewhat confusing, and the buttons do not stand alone. People must read the words above them to know that one box is for Canada and one is for the United States. And the helpful text *Please choose a country* is incredibly hard to read; it's light gray and tiny above the huge button area. Users such as Katherine eventually selected these buttons but not before giving them several fixations as she tried to understand their meaning and reason for being there (**Figure 4.40**).

Figure 4.40 Katherine looked several times at the buttons before clicking any of them. Even though there was nothing else to select on this page, the buttons did not give off a strong button scent because of the way they looked, their text, and the elements around them.

Buttons That Look like Links

If there are already many buttons on a page or the usual button design seems too blocky or heavy for the page, designers sometimes opt to make buttons look like links. Of course, these really are just simple links that look like links (their text is different from other text on the page), with no or few accompanying graphics. While we typically recommend using buttons for action commands, link-looking buttons do get looked at and clicked on. These can work quite well as long as they are placed effectively and have descriptive action text.

For example, the JCPenney site features an *add to bag* button (or link) on its product pages (**Figure 4.41**). There is plenty of white space around it, so it is clear and visible. A small icon that looks as if it is supposed to be a bag accompanies it. The user Carlos looked at and selected the *add to bag* button as needed (**Figure 4.42**). But he did need to fixate about four times to be sure this was the right. A button would have been easier to recognize in this context.

Figure 4.41 The button to add items to a shopping bag is understated on this site but looks like a clickable link and is well placed at the end of the page, above the fold, and near the *quantity* field.

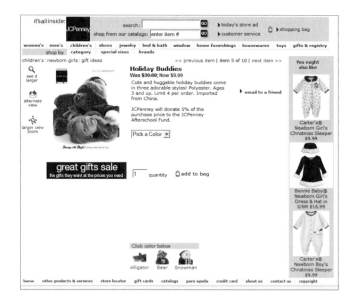

Figure 4.42 Carlos looked at and used the *add to bag* button on the site.

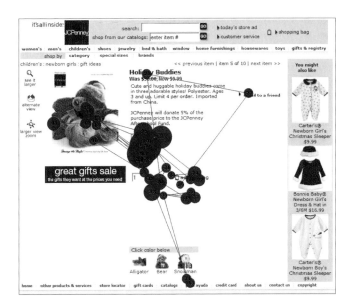

The Kiehl's site also uses links with a small graphic as buttons. The *Add to Bag* button appears just below the fields for type, size, and quantity on the product pages. The button itself is not a big visual standout, but in context, users saw it and selected it as needed. The small gray bag icon may have helped, as did the colored type. But one of our users, Betsy, did not even fixate on the icon. She just read the text, even though it was not strongly bolded or underlined (**Figure 4.43**).

Figure 4.43 Users looked at the "button" on this page even though it didn't look like a button mainly because of its placement, color, and action, and the words *Add to Bag*.

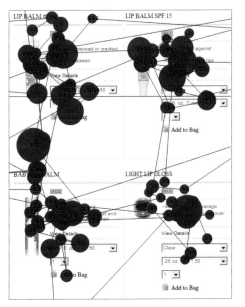

What can we deduce from this? The strength of the words told users that this was a clickable button. *Add to Bag* is an action phrase, and it is very commonly used and expected.

Links That Look like Buttons

A close cousin to the link-looking button is the button-looking link—a hypertext link that looks a lot like a button. These are commonly used as headings for sections of Web pages or as page headings.

When Rob was completing a task to plan a ski trip in our study, he looked at the button *Resort Information* on the Colorado Ski Country USA site (**Figure 4.44**). The box shape, the absence of anything clickable near it, and the arrow icon help make it look like a clickable item. But the words *Resort Information* are the best clickability indicator. Rob looked at and clicked it.

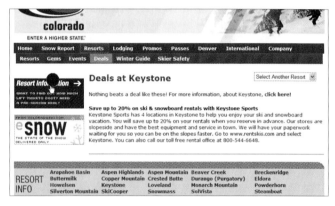

Figure 4.44 The words *Resort Information* in the box under the top menus told Rob it was clickable. But you must be careful if presenting links in this way as the affordance of the button's visual design is weak.

Faux Buttons

Some elements that are designed to be status indicators look like buttons. Users waste looks and clicks on these faux buttons, which let them down and make them feel stupid. The idea of affordance goes both ways. Items that are clickable should not look like informational status text. And items that are not buttons shouldn't look like clickable buttons.

In an example from our study, the user Fred was looking for a product that would prevent his car windshield from fogging up. He found Rain-X on the Aum Auto Web site. On the product page, there are a few button-looking items: a set of icons under the top global navigation, an *Add to Cart* button at the bottom of the page, and two *Secure Shopping* boxes—one in the upper-right banner and the other, in yellow, on the bottom right (**Figure 4.45**). The last item looks the most like a button because of its coloring, stylized graphic, and placement on the lower right of the page. But neither of the *Secure Shopping* items is what the user Fred needs to buy the product. He looked at all of these elements and was most drawn to the ones that looked like buttons (**Figure 4.46**).

Figure 4.45 The *Secure Shopping* faux buttons on this site look more like buttons than the actual button, *Add to Cart*.

Figure 4.46 The user mistook the yellow *Secure Shopping* box to be a button for adding items to his shopping cart.

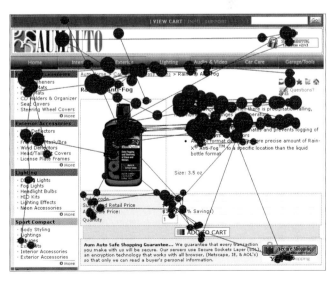

In another example, users who were buying a headset on the Headset Zone site consistently selected the progress status images during the checkout process (**Figure 4.47**). The yellow and gray arrows are the size and shape of many buttons on the Web. The white frame on these images can easily be mistaken for button beveling. The terms on the images—*Shipping*, *Payment*, *Review*—connote the steps our users wanted to take to complete their purchase. Compounding these problems, the form for entering shipping information and the *Continue* button is "below the fold."

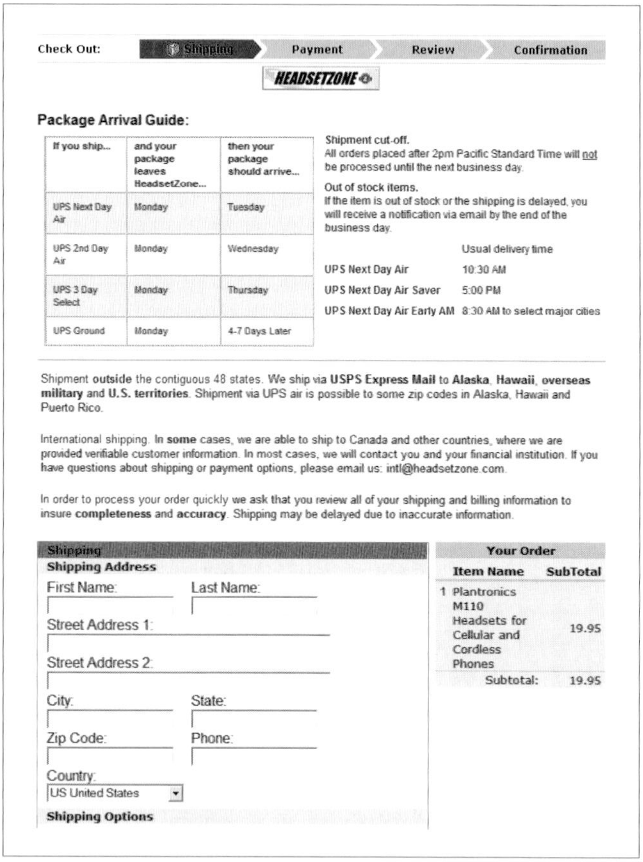

Figure 4.47 The images at the top of the page denoting users' progress in completing an order look like clickable buttons on this site. The form for shipping information is "below the fold."

Eyetracking Web Usability

One user, Valerie, read through the shipping options, which did not indicate that she should scroll down to enter her shipping information (**Figure 4.48**). She looked several times at the *Payment Information* graphic, the next step in the checkout process. With no fields in sight, it seemed even more like a button. She clicked it once and, when nothing happened, clicked it a second time. She then realized this faux button was not a link and began looking toward the bottom of the visible page.

Figure 4.48 Valerie did not scroll the page because there was a poor information scent. She clicked one of the progress indicators twice because she thought it was a button. Imagine if you saw only this much of the page. Would you do what she did?

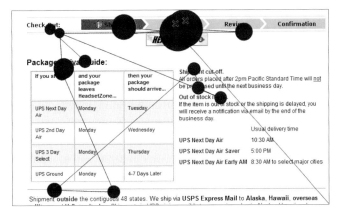

Progress, status, or informational elements should not be designed to look like clickable buttons.

A Comedy of Interface Errors

When a site has a usability problem, developers often like to argue about which user interface element is to blame. But the truth is that there can be many design issues that cause a usability problem. Keep your mind open to the idea that usability issues can result from a whole comedy of interface errors, not just one. Find and fix all of them.

As this example illustrates, many times there is more than one design issue that can cause usability problems. In this case, there were several:

- **Miscues.** The wrong elements attracting attention
- **Poor affordance.** Lack of clarity about what is clickable
- **The illusion of completeness.** Elements at the "fold" of a page that seem to indicate the end of the page when there is really more below
- **Weak information scent.** Poor prioritization of information giving few or no clues about what to do next.

Some users proceeded as Valerie did. Others did something similar. Gina, for example, was drawn to the progress image. She looked at the *Payment* image for a long fixation and then clicked it. When nothing happened, she scrolled and looked at the rest of the page.

To summarize, users selected faux buttons on the Headset Zone site because of the following:

- The size and background of the images, as well as the appearance of beveling around the edges, make them look like clickable buttons.

- The terms on the images connote actions in the check-out process.

- The clickable buttons they needed appear below the page's natural "fold."

Breadcrumbs

Breadcrumbs—the navigation trails that show people where they are on a Web site—are godsends on sites that have convoluted information architecture. As they were meant to do for Hansel and Gretel, breadcrumbs show people—in this case, users lost in a quagmire of menus—the way back out of woods. (And fortunately for Web users, forest animals cannot eat them.)

People look at breadcrumbs 31 percent of the time. When you consider the many other places where users can also navigate or find their place in IA—menus, search, the site map, and even page titles—and the number of other design elements competing for their eyes, that is quite a bit. And most people use breadcrumbs only for what they are really good for: backtracking.

Breadcrumbs deserve a place in Web interfaces because they typically are simple and contextual. When users want to cut through all the design noise, they can look to these helpful little morsels. *Viva las breadcrumbs!*

Search Front-End

People look at the search feature—usually an open field in the upper two quadrants of a page—a measly 16 percent of the time. This is because, in most cases, they scan, read, use menus, or do other things that don't involve searching on Web sites. But when they do try to search, the function should be there for them.

People do fixate on the search box on certain occasions—when they need it or because open fields are magnetic elements. But when search features are buried in menus or are links instead of open fields, people's eyes are not drawn to them.

We found that 56 percent of our users looked for the search function first in the upper-right quadrant of pages, and 44 percent looked first in the upper-left quadrant (**Figure 4.49**). Some of those who looked in the upper-left quadrant were probably confirming the site name, however—not necessarily looking for the search function. And many people—62 percent—who first looked left quickly migrated right, while 38 percent looked in the upper-left quadrant also on their second fixation.

Figure 4.49 People usually look for the search function in the upper-right quadrant of pages and, to a lesser degree, in the upper-left quadrant.

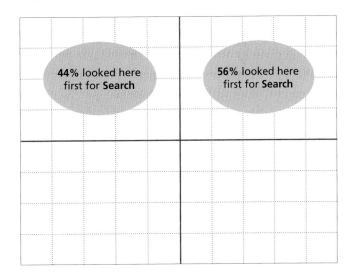

44% looked here first for **Search**

56% looked here first for **Search**

Remember, navigation and IA present the most difficult challenges for Web designers. But mastering the challenges is very important because navigation represents so many things to users. It can be safe like a Volvo, fast like a Maserati, or simple like a Bugaboo stroller. The words used in links, buttons, and menus can affect people's movement on and overall feeling about a site. Ensuring that the wording and look and feel of navigational elements are expected—even common—may not be exciting to designers, but it certainly makes users happy and productive.

5 Fundamental Web Design Elements

We're often asked what specific elements people look at most on a Web page. The answer: Each site's design, along with users' goals and experiences on that site and others, dictates where they look. Still, we can shed some light on how people generally look at various elements on a page. Read about our findings to see the common ways people look at fundamental elements on the Web.

To see where people gravitate when they are looking for a specific Web command, we asked users to find common page items such as search, the shopping cart, open job listings, and contact information on various sites. This task enabled us to see how people find a function they are familiar with. In effect, it was kind of like an Easter egg hunt. (This wouldn't be the case if the users had known what they wanted to do but had to figure out the correct link. In most cases users knew the name of the link they were looking for.) Still, there was variability in how people looked at pages because of different site designs.

On the Homepage

Once the participants were told the task, we opened a site on the homepage. We asked people to select a function as soon as they found it. Of course, through eyetracking, we could see whether their eyes rested on a command, but we wanted them to indicate that they chose it. This confirmed that users not only looked at but also registered an element and believed it to be the one they needed. (Imagine the misleading results we could have gotten otherwise—for example, if users fixated on a hard-to-read word to make it out, not because it was the correct element.)

In these rapid-fire situations, we discovered some patterns. People most often gravitate first to the upper-right quadrant of homepages—about 50 percent of the time (**Figure 5.1**). They go to the upper-left quadrant first about 44 percent of the time and, far less frequently, to the lower-right (3 percent) and lower-left (2 percent) quadrants.

People's second fixation is often in the same quadrant as the first, so it is in the upper-right quadrant about 51 percent of the time (**Figure 5.2**). But they look second in the upper-left quadrant almost as often—about 46 percent of the time. They rarely look in the lower-right (2 percent) and lower-left (1 percent) quadrants on their second fixation.

First Fixation for Rapid-Fire Tasks

- ■ 50% Upper Right
- ■ 44% Upper Left
- ■ 3% Lower Right ("Above Fold")
- ■ 2% Lower Left ("Above Fold")

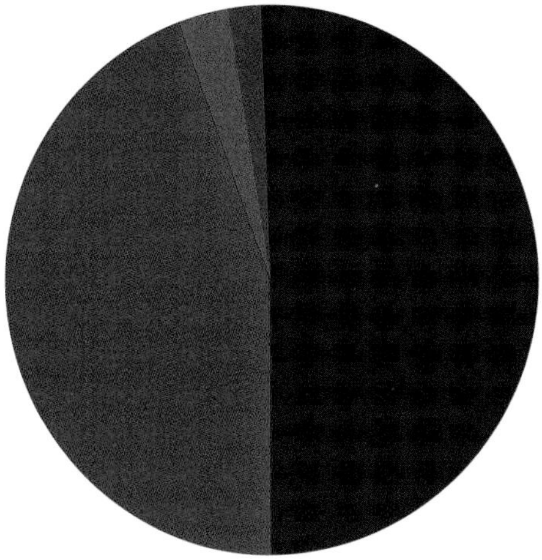

Figure 5.1 People more often look first in the upper-right quadrant of a homepage. They rarely look first in the lower-right or lower-left quadrant.

NOTE: Numbers don't sum to 100 due to rounding.

Second Fixation for Rapid-Fire Tasks

- ■ 51% Upper Right
- ■ 46% Upper Left
- ■ 2% Lower Right ("Above Fold")
- ■ 1% Lower Left ("Above Fold")

Figure 5.2 On their second fixations, people again look mostly in the upper-right quadrant and, slightly less often, in the upper left. Even fewer people look the lower-right and lower-left quadrants on their second fixation than on their first.

About one-third of the time, our users found basic Web elements in five or fewer fixations. Five fixations go by very fast—usually in less than three seconds depending on how long each fixation is. In about one-fifth of cases, they found the elements in six to ten fixations—also very fast. And in another fifth of cases, they found them in 11 to 20 fixations, possibly looking at several areas and scrolling the page. Finally, about one-quarter of the time, it took users more than 20 fixations to find the element, and in some of those cases, it took them more than 100 fixations.

People did not find the interface element at all and gave up looking in 2 percent of cases. That's a fine rate for users given a somewhat difficult task. But since people were not given a complex task and usually did not even need to scroll to find the element, nobody should have had to give up. After all, they were just looking for a command on the homepage.

People look in the patterns they do because many common user interface (UI) elements are often placed in the upper-right and upper-left quadrants. Thus, these elements are easiest to locate when positioned in familiar places free of clutter.

Usually people can find basic Web design elements —such as search and the shopping cart—in ten or fewer fixations.

Login

People look at open fields toward the top of a page even when they don't need them because open fields are magnetic. Login features are often open fields, and people look at them in 26 percent of cases (**Figure 5.3**).

Figure 5.3 How often people look at various elements.

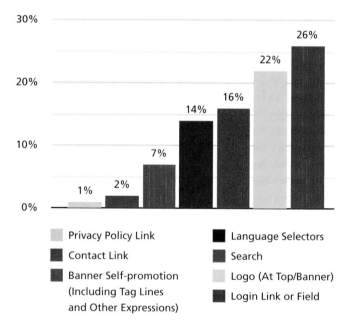

Legend:
- Privacy Policy Link
- Contact Link
- Banner Self-promotion (Including Tag Lines and Other Expressions)
- Language Selectors
- Search
- Logo (At Top/Banner)
- Login Link or Field

When going about various other tasks, many of our users undoubtedly confused login fields with the search feature. Site designers sometimes try to make the login field or link

> *Even when people don't necessarily want to search or log in, they often scan these fields. Open fields are magnetic UI elements.*

very attractive, so users can easily log in and reap the benefits of a relationship with the organization (and vice versa). The *Sign In* link is also frequently the first or last one in the utility navigation, so as users scan the site, they may happen upon it more often.

Privacy Policy

People look at *Privacy Policy* links only 1 percent of the time. There are several reasons for this:

- Links to privacy policies often appear in utility navigation, which users generally tune out unless they are looking for administrative information.

- People look at privacy policies rarely, such as when they are entering very personal information about themselves and are concerned about who might have access to it.

- When people want to look at a site's privacy policy, it is usually during a specific process during which which the site furnishes a link, so they do not go to it through utility navigation.

- Many users just don't care to see a site's privacy policy.

This is not to suggest that sites drop privacy policy information because it is looked at so seldom. Privacy policies keep a site's credibility high and increase trust, so we recommend that you offer a link to yours in the site navigation.

Contact

People look at the contact information link, commonly presented as *Contact Us*, very infrequently, in 2 percent of cases. Contact links often appear in global navigation, in utility navigation, in banners, and as inline links with related information. Although these links add credibility to an organization, users don't go looking for them unless they need them or want to confirm that a Web site is somehow connected to the physical world. As one user said of not finding a contact phone number, "It's scary. You don't know who you're dealing with." As with the privacy policy, we highly recommend that all Web sites have a contact link in the navigation, and ideally on the homepage, so users can call, e-mail, or chat with someone at the organization.

Language Selectors

Participants look at language selectors, which are not offered on most sites, in 14 percent of cases. Do people really need to change languages that often? Probably not. Most likely users look at them because they are presented as drop-down lists toward the top of the page. Like open fields, applications and UI components are magnetic elements that draw the user's eye.

Logos and Tag Lines

Logos have two functions. They are a navigational feature, linking people to the homepage on most sites. And they confirm what site users are on.

Post the logo in the upper left of every page on your Web site. It gets fixated on enough, about a quarter of the time, to warrant the space allocation.

People look at the site logo as it appears on all pages in about one-quarter of cases—22 percent of the time. Because logos generally appear in the upper-left corner of every page on most Web sites today, people do not need to look at them much. Often they look at the logo only once. But the site logo should still be on every page because it's like an insurance policy—if people need to go to the homepage, it's there.

People look at the logo after they hit a site from a search engine and want to confirm where they are. (Our fundamental usability research shows that people access a site via a search in 89 percent of cases.) Finally, people look at the logo if a site's style changes drastically and unexpectedly and they are wondering, "Am I still on the same site?"

People look at tag lines and other self-promotional information much less than logos—in just 7 percent of cases. These items are usually in banners that users ignore. Also, the tag-line text is often written over an image or watermark, which decreases contrast and makes it more difficult to read.

People most often look at tag lines and promotions when they first hit a Web site and want to confirm where they are or learn something about the organization. Taglines are especially helpful for people who hit a site after conducting a search or following an unidentified link from another site. In other words, when users are not quite sure where they just landed, tag lines can help orient them.

Shopping Carts

The shopping cart has become intrinsic to today's
e-commerce site. People look for it first in the upper-right
quadrant of the homepage (**Figure 5.4**).

Figure 5.4 More than half of users
looked for a site's shopping cart first
in the upper-right quadrant of the
page. Less than half looked for it the
upper-left quadrant.

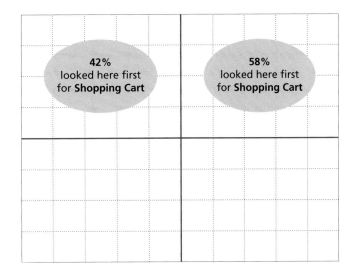

*Most people look to the
upper right of pages for
the shopping cart icon.*

On the Web site of the jewelry store Zales, a *Shopping Bag*
link and bag icon appear in the upper right of the page as
part of the topmost horizontal navigation menu. They are
above another row of navigation and a small promotional
banner (**Figure 5.5**).

Figure 5.5 The Zales *Shopping Bag*
link and bag icon appear in the
upper right of pages.

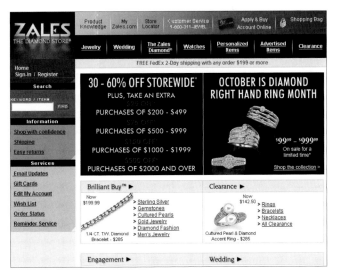

On this site, 67 percent of our users looked in the upper-right quadrant, and 33 percent looked in the upper-left quadrant, for both their first and second fixations (**Figure 5.6**). And in 40 percent of cases, people who looked at the upper right of the page found the shopping cart almost instantly, in five or fewer fixations.

Figure 5.6 Many people easily located the shopping bag in the upper right.

The users found the shopping bag easily in the upper right. It was the first area they gravitated toward when looking for the shopping bag. They looked at the simple words *Shopping Bag* combined with the relatively standard little icon of a bag. (Whether it's a bag, basket, or cart is not important.)

What about the other 60 percent of people who needed more than five fixations to locate the shopping bag?

In John's first 15 or so seconds, he looked at the second row of navigation at the top and at the left navigation (**Figure 5.7**). He did not look much in the content area of the page because he knew from past experience that a shopping cart would probably be in a menu area. Still, he did look there a little and even scrolled the page, but he snubbed the top level of navigation. It is possible he was experiencing banner blindness.

Figure 5.7 Navigation snubbing: During his first moments looking for the shopping cart on this site, John looked at the second row of horizontal navigation and the left side, and then he scrolled the page.

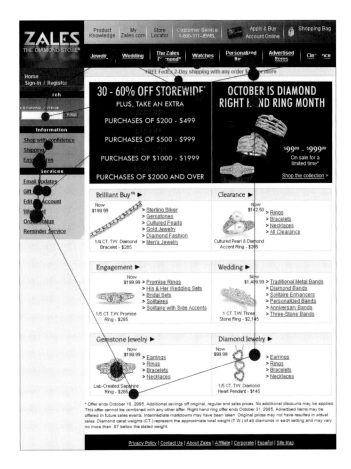

After a thorough examination of the other menus, John looked at the top navigation, where the shopping bag is located. He found the *Shopping Bag* link there after about 40 fixations on the page.

Another user, Borris, seemed to be distracted by the many choices on the homepage (**Figure 5.8**). He spent many fixations on the left-side menu, some in the middle of the page, and a few at the top of the page, before settling on the shopping cart.

Figure 5.8 Borris was distracted by the other elements on the homepage and did not immediately see the shopping cart.

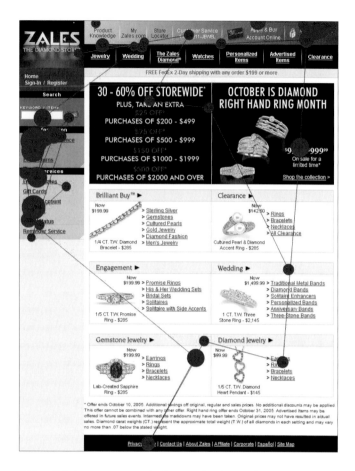

Why did these users snub the top horizontal navigation, which housed the *Shopping Bag* link? These are the most likely reasons:

- The navigation area resembles a wide banner.

- Two rows of horizontal navigation, plus the row for the promotion, are too many elements for users to deal with quickly.

- The text does not stand out against the light gray background as much as the page's text on the black background.

The Web site for Baskits, which sells gift baskets, features a few rows of top horizontal navigation, with the shopping cart at the right in the uppermost row (**Figure 5.9**). But in this design, the uppermost navigation does not look like a banner. Instead, it resembles traditional utility navigation.

Figure 5.9 The row of navigation where the shopping cart appears on this site resembles utility navigation.

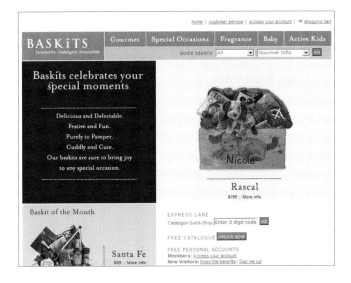

On this site, 36 percent of people found the shopping cart in five or fewer fixations, and another 36 percent found it in ten or fewer fixations. Eighteen percent found it in 20 or fewer fixations, and 9 percent needed more than 20 fixations to find it.

Because the Baskits page is not too cluttered, users could tell where the menus are fairly easily. Some people, such as Heather, immediately looked to the upper right for the shopping cart (**Figure 5.10**). Once she found it, she continued to look around on the page.

Denell was fist drawn to the image in the center of the page, especially the dog's face (**Figure 5.11**). His gaze quickly gravitated up the page toward the shopping cart icon in the upper right. In other words, this user inventoried the page before he looked where he thought the shopping cart icon would be.

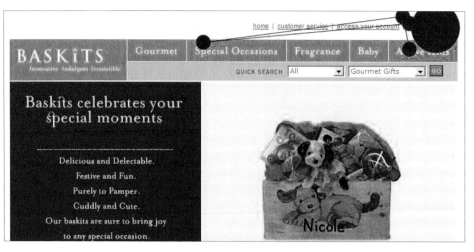

Figure 5.10 Heather looked directly to the upper right for the shopping cart, which was in the expected location. The sparse page also helped her find it easily.

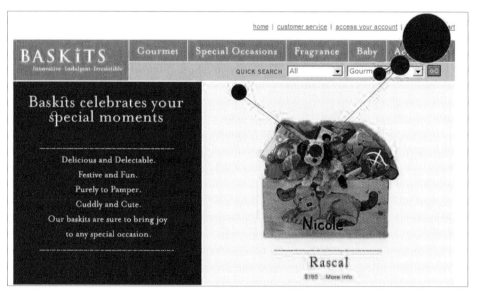

Figure 5.11 Denell very briefly inventoried the page before locating the shopping cart.

Rob took a longer look at the page, particularly the menu area, before he located the shopping cart (**Figure 5.12**). It's likely that the three levels of navigation at the top of the page made it difficult for him to locate the right one and the shopping cart. If so, this was a case of exhaustive review—looking several times at the same areas because he was not seeing what he wanted.

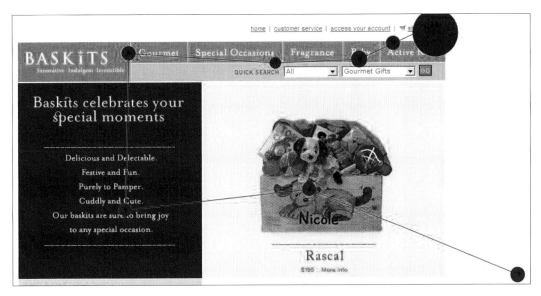

Figure 5.12 Rob looked at the image, the dog's face, and other menus briefly before locating the shopping cart.

Multiple rows of navigation and borders at the top of a page—as well as overly stylized designs—can make it difficult for people to quickly find elements that are typically located there, such as the shopping basket, login, or search function.

When users cannot quickly find a shopping cart or another element that is typically at the top of a page, the culprit is often multiple rows of navigation and borders. Although the top of the Baskits page is not particularly dense, users must still scan three rows of navigation when looking for the cart. And because there is no real Web standard for where a shopping cart (or login or search function) should appear, people must scan them all, as these users did.

The following chart shows the relative visibility of the shopping carts on the Zales and Baskits Web sites and the amount of time it took users to find them. We scored each site on the attributes that helped or hindered its shopping cart's visibility, and we compared the total with the number of user fixations needed to find the cart. The higher the visibility score, the faster people saw it.

What makes people see shopping carts	Zales	Baskits
Rows of top horizontal menus/banners, -1 for each	-2	-3
Bag or cart icon as well as text, +1	+1	+1
Shopping cart is the rightmost command, +1	+1	+1
Well-contrasted background, +1	+1	+1
Location in upper right, +1	+1	+1
Shopping Cart Visibility Score	**2**	**1**

How long it took users to find the shopping cart	Zales	Baskits
Within 5 fixations	40% of users	36% of users
Within 10 fixations	40% of users	36% of users
Within 20 fixations	0% of users	18% of users
More than 20 fixations	20% of users	9% of users

When to Feature Exposed Shopping Carts

Many Web sites show a running tally of items in the shopping cart as they are added. This can be very helpful on sites where people tend to buy several items. We observed that users consult the exposed shopping cart to make sure items have been added and keep track of the amount they are adding up to. But exposed shopping carts also use a fair amount of page real estate that could, on some sites, be better filled with other content.

During our testing, people who used the Amazon site consulted the shopping cart even when they had only one item in it. While shopping for a gift for a fictional nephew, they often added a popular CD to the cart while they continued to shop for other options, comparing as they went along.

Notice the yellow gaze on the products in the content area (**Figure 5.13**). It connotes fewer gazes than the red heat on the shopping cart. At this point, users had made their decision to buy the item in the cart and were looking for the *Checkout* button. As they did, they looked at *Your Shopping Cart*.

Eyetracking Web Usability

Figure 5.13 People looked at the shopping cart area on this site, which was quite busy. But they wasted looks on the *Edit shopping cart* and two *Proceed to Checkout* buttons.

Users gave many looks to both the top and bottom *Proceed to Checkout* buttons. Repeating buttons is overkill when users can easily see both without scrolling, and it causes them to fixate more than is necessary.

They also looked at the *Edit shopping cart* button. Those who were not interested in editing their cart at this point still wasted quite a few fixations on this attractive button, which resembles the *Proceed to Checkout* button. Making the edit button look slightly weaker might have eliminated some of these unnecessary looks. (Or perhaps Amazon has data showing that people often want to first edit their selections before they check out. In that case, the placement and boldness of the button here is warranted.)

There were no fixations on the item's price, which is not typical user behavior. The reason, we believe, is that users had already seen the price of the CD several times and didn't feel the need to confirm it again. Users did see the *Subtotal* label, however.

Exposed shopping carts (with the list of items added to the cart appearing usually in the right rail) can help people stay appraised in their shopping experience.

People looked at the note for free shipping if they bought $14.04 more worth of items and at the *Show gift options during checkout* check box. They also fixated on the word *save* in the tiny note, just under the gift options check box, specifically about "A9.com users." *Save*, like *free*, is a magnetic word in e-commerce.

Amazon had the right impulse in featuring an exposed shopping cart, but the organization loses points for including too many features and elements. The FreshDirect site's shopping cart presentation is more successful (**Figure 5.14**). While shopping for groceries, our users referred to it frequently, keeping track of how much they were spending and scanning for items in it. And often, just before checkout, they reviewed the items in the cart for several fixations.

Figure 5.14 Like other users on the FreshDirect site, this one reviewed the shopping cart before checking out.

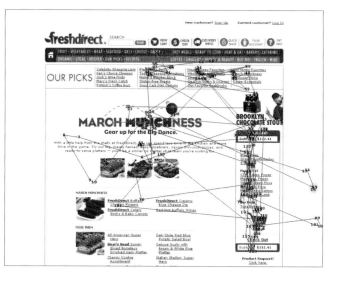

The take-home message: When it's likely that users will add multiple items to a shopping cart or shop for an extensive time on a site, an exposed shopping cart can be a very helpful feature.

When a feature is very important or frequently used—such as a recipe finder on a cooking site—sometimes it is a good idea to present it, instead of a link to it, directly on a page. Search is a good example. Good search design has an open field and a search button on every page, not just a link to the search feature. But that's easy to figure out. Search is one of the most important navigational elements on most sites. With features that are less commonly used or take up a large amount of space, it can be more difficult to decide when to display the entire feature and when to link to it.

These are two pros of putting the full feature on the homepage or all pages:

- It may be more visible than a link would be.
- It may be more accessible than a simple link.

These are two pros of putting just a link to the feature on the homepage or all pages:

- It takes up less space.
- A simple link adds less clutter to the overall page design.

Consider the importance of the feature and whether it deserves real estate on the homepage or all pages. Does it stand out on the page or add a dimension of clutter that will repel users from the page altogether?

For example, on some sites that customize or personalize content, the login feature is an open field rather than a link. On some travel sites, the tools for booking tickets are right on the homepage rather than linked to from the homepage. The shopping cart is yet another item that may be worth displaying as a running tally of items.

When trying to decide whether to put a feature directly on a page, use this chart as a guideline:

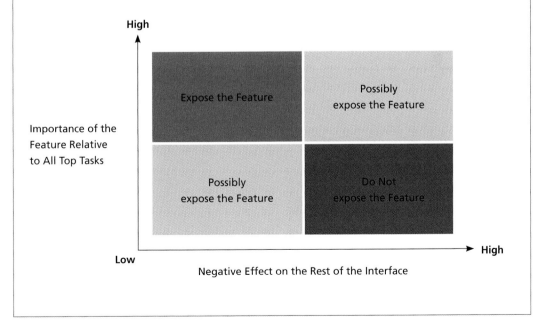

Forms, Fields, and Applications

Eyetracking allows us to get very picky in our usability recommendations. But we have to admit that a design change that will save users a fixation or two on a regular page may not be something to turn your development team upside down over. In UI elements such as forms, however, it's important to save any fixations because it reduces both users' time and the effort of having to look and relook at fields and text as they enter information.

Saccades—the eye's movements between fixations—contribute to the taxing feeling people get from that kind of effort. Although we often count people's fixations and how long they last, we think less about the additional effort involved in long saccades. Reducing necessary fixations also reduces necessary saccades.

Although usability testing has shown us that poor presentation is confusing, eyetracking shows us the wasted looks and over-thinking that it causes. The following sections give some examples.

Grouping Sections and Placing Field Labels

The order in which interface elements are presented is important for any Web page, including those with forms or applications. It should be easy for users to quickly look at, register, and deal with all parts of a form.

For example, Corry was booking a hotel room in Aspen, Colorado, on hotels.com (**Figure 5.15**). He was using the site's search function, which is basically a form that asks users to type in a city or choose from the *Most popular cities* area, which has radio buttons. There are also fields for adding other travel information. This form is fraught with eyetracking issues.

Foremost, a radio button is meant to present a choice between two or more elements. The visual layout alone should demonstrate to users that they are to choose just one item from the radio button options, but in this application, it is difficult to tell that you are to select between typing a city or choosing a city from the list. Also, when choosing a city it appears as if users can choose one item from each column of cities. To confuse matters further, the cities are not in alphabetical order.

Figure 5.15 The search form on this site is somewhat confusing because of the thoughtlessly conceived radio buttons and sections, among other things.

What is the point of this arrangement? From the perspective of hotels.com, perhaps it is to nudge potential travelers to consider traveling to another city. And for users, having choices readily visible to select from (instead of having to open a drop-down list or type them in, for example) has some merit. But what good are these benefits when the layout is so bad that users must fixate many times just to understand the options? Really, waste is waste—whether it's a wasted click or fixations.

In addition, the page's two kinds of visual separators—thin blue lines and a thick white banner—provide no sense of hierarchy in content.

The poor layout of the page made Corry waste many fixations here (**Figure 5.16** and **Figure 5.17**). All he needed to do was type *Aspen* into the open field. But he first looked for the city of Aspen in the popular cities area—and had to look through all the cities for it because there seemed to be no rhyme or reason to the order. Zooming in on this interaction, we can see that Corry spent about 30 unnecessary fixations on the radio buttons related to the cities alone only to find that Aspen was not even in the list.

Figure 5.16 Corry needed to look at the application more than he should have had to because of its poor presentation.

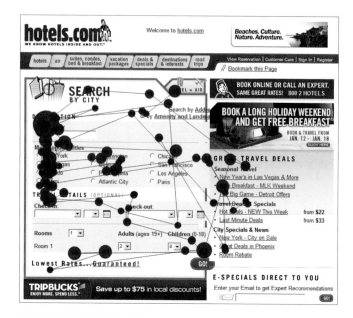

Figure 5.17 Wasted: Corry spent about 30 unnecessary fixations in the *Most popular cities* area because of the confusing radio buttons and because it was the most attractive area.

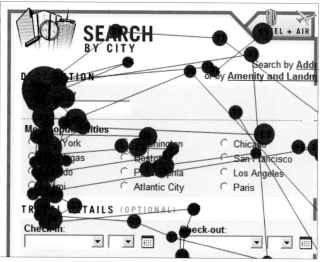

Putting field labels above the fields helps users fixate less when the vertical spacing is implemented well. Poor stacking can cause users to question whether the label is associated with the field above or below it.

Comparing the Usability of Three Forms

The design of an entire form or application influences where people decide to look. Putting field labels on top of the fields is a good rule of thumb, but we should consider the interface as a whole unit, as the user sees it. Let's look at some examples.

Eyetracking Web Usability

On the Kiehl's Web site, there are two columns of fields in the *Billing and Shipping* section of the checkout process: one labeled *Billing Address* and one labeled *Shipping Address* (**Figure 5.18**). Placing two columns for addresses side-by-side in one form is not a good idea. It makes users have to fixate extra on the column headings and the fields themselves to understand what the form is asking for. There are several better alternatives to this layout. One is to ask for different addresses on different pages. Another is to have one column follow the other, instead of putting them next to each other.

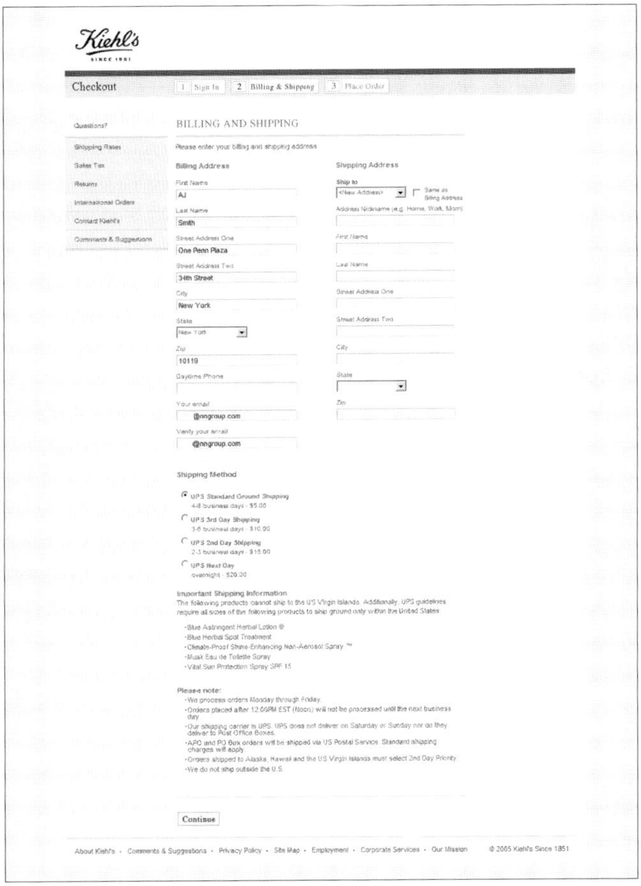

Figure 5.18 The billing form in the checkout process on this site offers two columns of left-aligned fields and labels, with the labels for fields just above each.

All fields and labels are left aligned, and labels appear just above the corresponding field. This arrangement helps users scan easily, sometimes in the same fixation. But there are two hiccups in this aspect of this design. The field labels are slightly too close to the preceding field. As people work down the columns, they have to confirm which field a label accompanies. Also, the label text is very small and light gray on a white background, so it is not as visible as it should be.

Our users fixated more than they should have had to on the form in order to feel confident filling in basic elements such as their names. They fixated on the form title early on when they were trying to determine what it was asking for. They fixated on the *Billing Address* and *Shipping Address* titles (**Figure 5.19**).

Figure 5.19 This user looked at the column titles and several fields in the second column in order to understand the field labels in the first column.

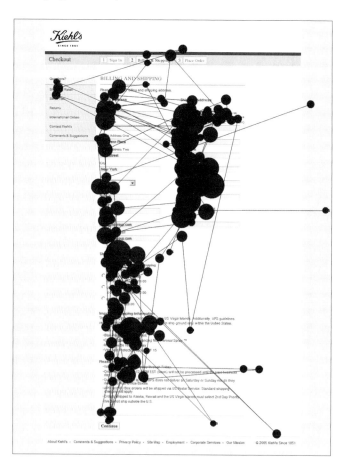

They also looked at the fields in the right column for *First Name*, *Last Name*, and *Street Address*. The first two items in the column on the right—the address book feature, *Ship to*, and the *Address Nickname* label—were perplexing to them and received several fixations. Compounding the issue, their placement at the top of the list shifted the field labels in that column down, so they were not parallel with those on the left.

Finally, the labels *Street Address One* and *Street Address Two* were slightly confusing. It is more common to offer one field for the street address and one for an apartment number. So, the *Address Two* label garnered more looks (on both sides) than the more common label *Apartment Number* would have. Notice some of the larger fixations—represented by huge dots—in the second column. This sometimes occurs after people's eyes need to move a long distance to reach a point. The eyes need to fixate a little longer than they normally would before they register the image they have stopped at.

What does this example tell us? The many labels, two different types of addresses called for, and some missteps in field and label layout meant that users wasted unnecessary fixations on this form.

On the JCPenney Web site, the billing section of the checkout process is organized in one wide column, which is then subdivided into two side-by-side columns: one for field labels and one for the fields themselves (**Figure 5.20**). The field labels are right aligned, and the fields are left aligned. This approach attempts to eliminate any ambiguity between which labels and fields are related.

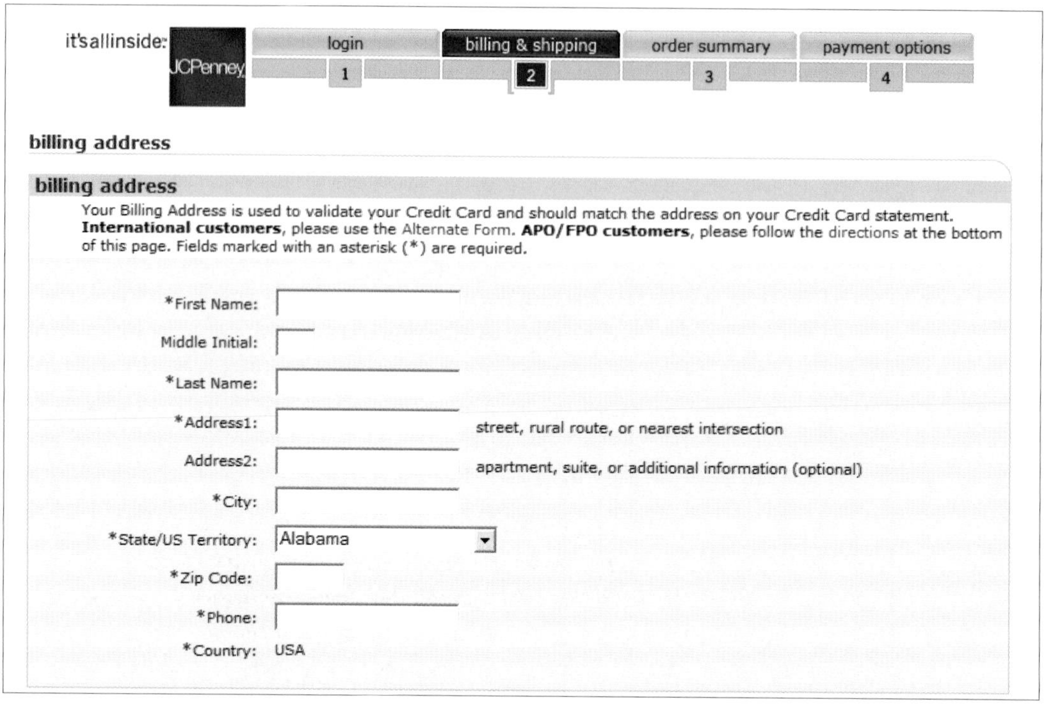

Figure 5.20 In this billing form, fields and labels are in two columns, which join together to form one big column.

When filling in his address, Jeff initially looked three times at the label to the left of the *First Name* field (**Figure 5.21**). Then he looked at the field itself for a longer fixation as he was typing. As he continued filling out the form, he looked several more times at the fields. He dedicated five fixations (including one long one) to the *First Name* label and five more fixations to its field, four fixations (including two long ones) to the *Middle Name* label and none to its field, and two fixations to the *Last Name* label and three to its field. (Fixations on the fields are common when a user is typing into them.)

Eyetracking Web Usability

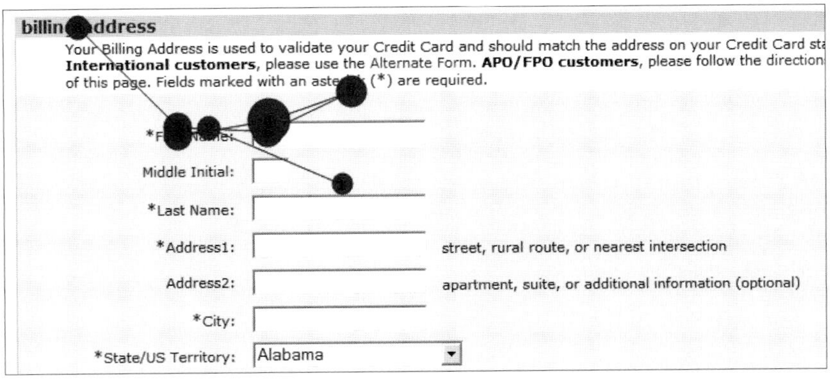

billing address
Your Billing Address is used to validate your Credit Card and should match the address on your Credit Card sta
International customers, please use the Alternate Form. **APO/FPO customers**, please follow the direction
of this page. Fields marked with an asterisk (*) are required.

*First Name:
Middle Initial:
*Last Name:
*Address1:   street, rural route, or nearest intersection
Address2:   apartment, suite, or additional information (optional)
*City:
*State/US Territory: Alabama

Figure 5.21 When he began filling out this shipping information form, Jeff looked three times at the *First Name* label to the left of the field and two times at the field.

It's not surprising that Jeff gave three fewer fixations the *Last Name* label than he did to the *First Name* label (**Figure 5.22**). By the time he reached it, he had already deduced that the form was asking for his name in parts, first to last. But he spent four fixations on the *Middle Initial* field, probably for two reasons:

- Web forms are inconsistent in asking for middle names.
- Forms may ask for the full middle name or just for the first initial.

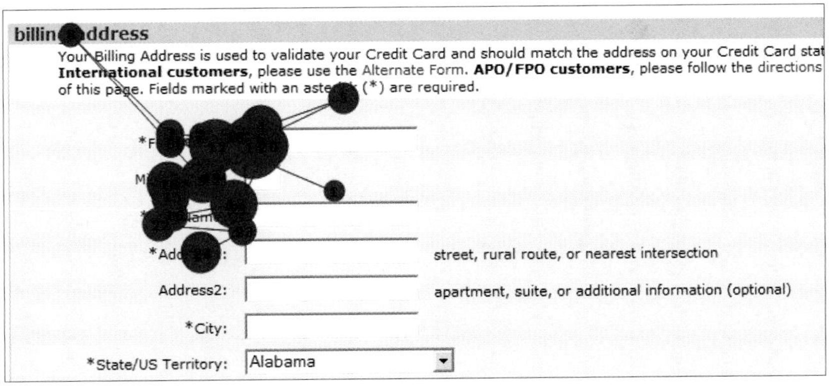

billing address
Your Billing Address is used to validate your Credit Card and should match the address on your Credit Card stat
International customers, please use the Alternate Form. **APO/FPO customers**, please follow the directions
of this page. Fields marked with an asterisk (*) are required.

*F
M
ame
*Add :   street, rural route, or nearest intersection
Address2:   apartment, suite, or additional information (optional)
*City:
*State/US Territory: Alabama

Figure 5.22 Jeff fixated on the ragged-left field labels and fields of this form—and sometimes on the text as he typed it in.

Note: Gaze plots do not show text being entered.

The T-Mobile Web site presents one major column consisting of two left-aligned subcolumns of labels and fields (**Figure 5.23**). In a few places, the layout deviates a bit, with fields for *Middle Initial* and *Zip Code* unaligned.

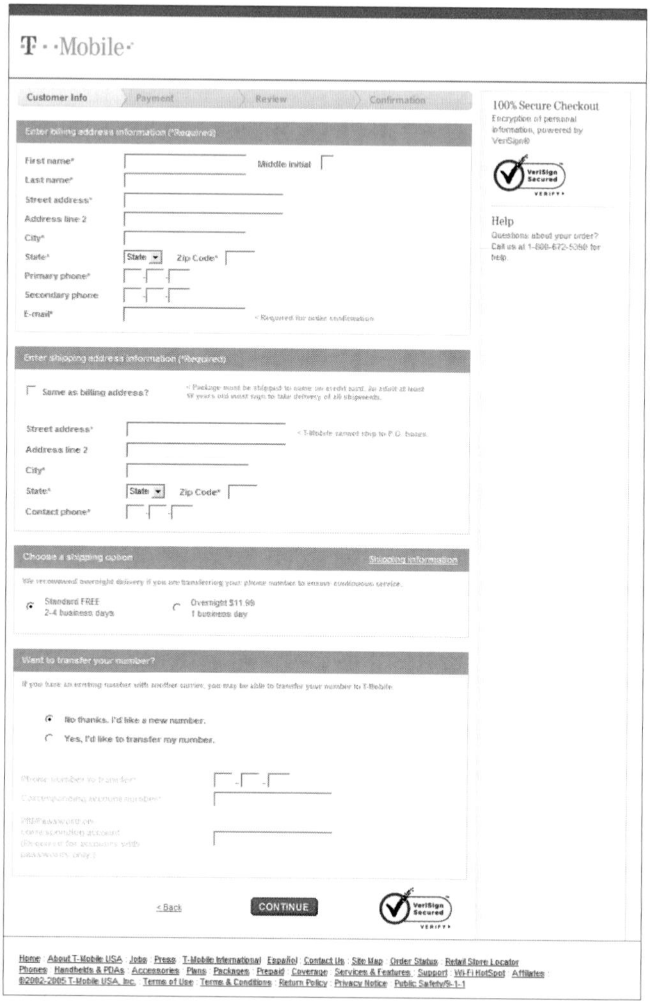

Figure 5.23 The form on this site offers visible sections for like information and typically aligns both field labels and fields on the left.

One user did not even look at the first field label but automatically typed his first name in the first field (**Figure 5.24**). Now that's trust (or carelessness, possibly). He looked at the field as he typed.

He had to fixate three times on the *Middle Initial* field label, after his eye traveled rather far to get to it in its own "special" column. He didn't type a middle initial, so those long saccades and three fixations were wasted—and probably annoying to him. When the eye gets into a groove, people either have to look more for an unaligned field or they miss it completely.

Then his eye traveled a distance back to the *Last Name* field, and he looked at the word *Last* for three fixations (**Figure 5.25** and **Figure 5.26**). During one of these, he also caught a glimpse at the next field label, *Street Address.*

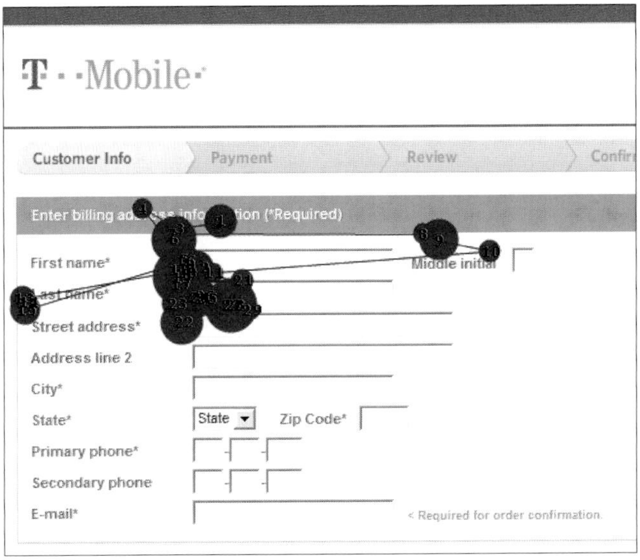

Figure 5.24 A user fixated three times on the *Middle Initial* field, which is used inconsistently on Web sites. The placement of this field also breaks from the typical, left-aligned fields in this form.

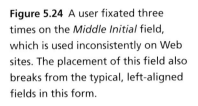

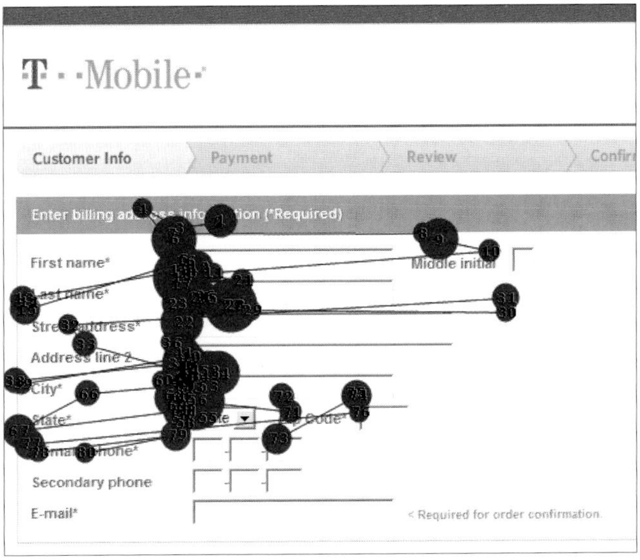

Figure 5.25 The predictability of the left-aligned labels makes them easy to scan and feel comfortable with in just a short fixation. But these fields are too far away from their associated labels, causing users to have long saccades.

This user did not need to spend many fixations on most of the left–aligned labels, which are in an expected place and order. He did need to spend energy jumping from the label to the field, however. He also did not fixate on the asterisks denoting required fields or on the legend at the top of the form explaining what the asterisks mean (**Figure 5.26**).

Figure 5.26 The user didn't look at any of the asterisks or the legend about them on this T-Mobile page.

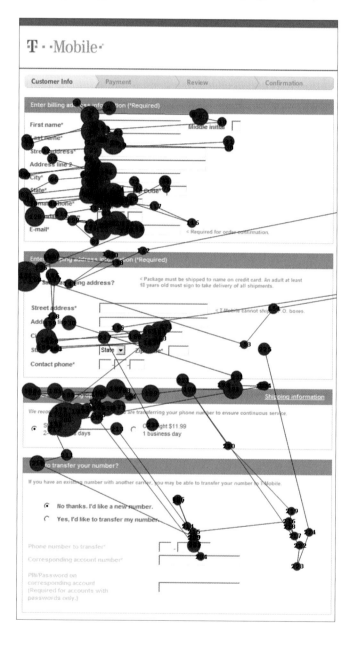

Left-aligned labels make it easy for users to scan them. But if you use them, ensure that the fields they describe are very close by.

Eyetracking Web Usability

How the Forms Scored with Users

There are positive and negative UI elements in each of the forms we've discussed. Now let's tally them up and see how easy they were to use.

The Kiehl's form is cluttered with both billing and shipping address fields "above the fold." T-Mobile tries not to inundate the user by instead offering the shipping fields lower in the form. While the user must scroll to see them this requires minimal effort, and the fields are expected. The JCPenney form practices "progressive disclosure": It hides the shipping address fields under a drop-down toward the end of the form. The layout elements of the latter two sites are positive but are simply no match (in terms of saving fixations) for better label and field layout.

The Kiehl's form has the most positive element for keeping fixations to a minimum: stacking field labels just over the corresponding fields, with both left aligned. (Eliminating the middle initial field also helps.) The T-Mobile form aligns labels and fields to the left in two separate columns, making it difficult for users to associate the field labels with the fields. Though the field labels in the form are usually in one column, they are sometimes in an additional column, and the spacing is inconsistent. JCPenney right-aligns the labels and left-aligns the fields, making their association obvious, although the ragged left alignment of the field labels makes them more difficult to scan.

As a result of these different designs, users looked far fewer times, eight on average, at the fields and their labels on the Kiehl's site, despite its two-column layout. They looked 17 and 19 times at fields and labels on the T-Mobile and JCPenney forms, respectively.

Left-align fields and labels and stack the label just over the associated field.

	Kiehl's	JCPenny	T-Mobile
First Name	6	10	4
Middle Initial	n/a	4	3
Last Name	2	5	10
Total	**8**	**19**	**17**

Don't Break Up Phone Number Fields

Eyetracking shows that breaking a phone number field into shorter fields forces users to look harder and think harder. For example, the Expedia travel site asks users to type into three (and sometimes four) fields: *Country, Area, Phone #,* and, for businesses, *Ext. #* (**Figure 5.27**). Our users looked for several fixations at the labels for these telephone fields. One user, Maria, referred to the field labels at least ten times (not to mention the left-side labels for different types of phone numbers) when entering her phone numbers (**Figure 5.28**).

For ease of use and accessibility, we advise offering just one field per telephone number requested. Of course, prefixes and exchanges are important to include, but people usually do very well with one field, a simple field label, and a visible example of a phone number.

Users have to fixate less when entering phone numbers when forms offer just one input field (and a good example and field label).

Figure 5.27 A form on this site asks users to type each of their phone numbers into three or four fields.

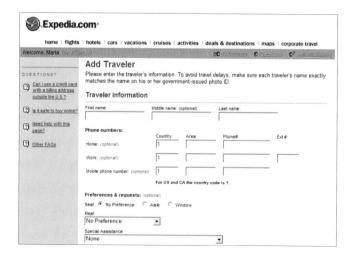

Eyetracking Web Usability

Figure 5.28 Maria referred to the three field labels at least ten times when entering phone numbers on this form.

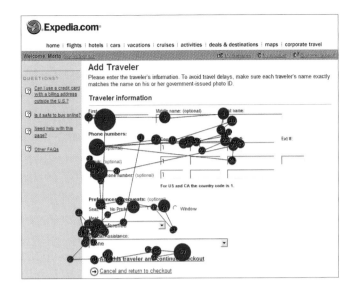

Short Forms Make for Easy Scanning

Ski.com asks users to identify the number of adults and children in a travel party before quoting a resort price. The page displays drop-down fields for each of the travelers, which default to *Adult* (**Figure 5.29**).

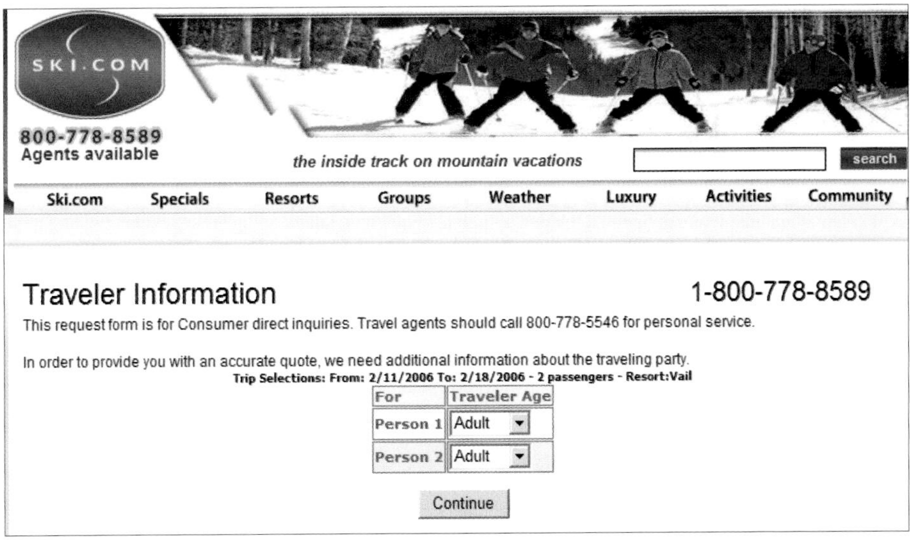

Figure 5.29 When booking resorts on this site, users are asked to select the ages of the travelers from a drop-down menu.

Rob was instantly drawn to the drop-down boxes when he hit the page, and he easily reviewed the corresponding labels in a few fixations (**Figure 5.30**). We know that people often do not read lead-in instructions in forms. But they are more likely to read them if the text is short and sweet, as it was on this page. Rob read part of the note just above the fields.

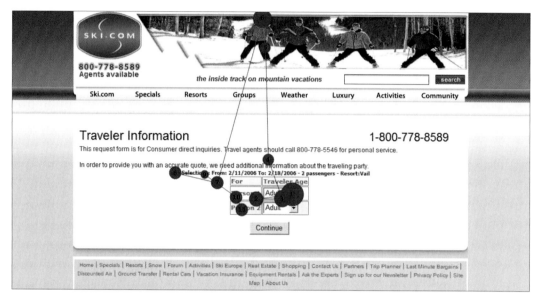

Figure 5.30 Rob was instantly drawn to the drop-down fields on this page.

The *Continue* button was well placed at the bottom of the form. With adequate space between it and the fields above, it was well visible (**Figure 5.31**).

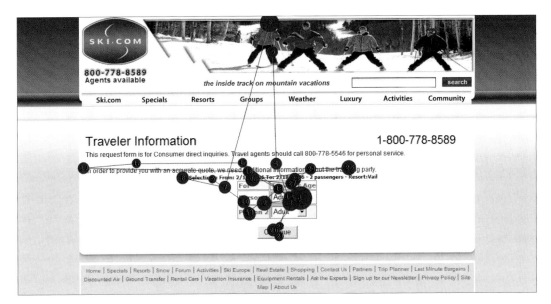

Figure 5.31 The short, simple form on this page was easy to scan and digest. Rob reviewed the traveler drop-down boxes, scanned the note before them, and easily located the button to continue.

Disclosing only what people need as they need it is a long-known UI guideline, one that form designers should heed. Make labels easy to scan and understand so users don't need to over-fixate. Present fields in a consistent layout throughout a form, and eliminate those that are unnecessary.

Avoid Prompt Text in Fields (At Least for Now)

People scan prompt text in fields, such as *Click Here* or *Type Name Here*, but often they mistake the field to be full. Or they may have already read the label for the field, so the additional prompt text requires them to read more than they need to, wasting time and sometimes causing frustration. Perhaps in the future, it will become standard to use prompt text instead of field labels. Until that day, however, prompt text is less efficient than field labels.

Users mistake fields that have prompt text to be already filled in. And when there is both a label and a prompt, they must read the same or similar information twice.

For example, on the Expedia Web site, a *Trip Preferences* form features prompt text in drop-down lists (**Figure 5.32**). The prompt *Select from the list* is superfluous. Users know what they are supposed to do from a drop-down list. It's like putting *Read Me* before every label on the site.

Figure 5.32 The drop-down lists on the *Trip Preferences* page of this site supply prompt text. It is meant to be instructional. Instead, it is useless.

Maria focused on the prompt text in the *Adult* fields (**Figure 5.33**). She probably expected to see a default value there. In fact, it would have been better to display a default value than the words *Select from the list*.

Figure 5.33 Maria wasted multiple fixations on the outmoded prompt text.

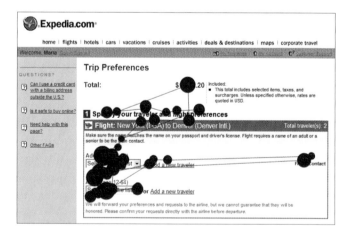

Guidelines for Reducing Fixations in Forms

You can help prevent users from dedicating unnecessary fixations (and long saccades) on field labels and fields in several ways:

Eyetracking Web Usability

- Place a field label just above the field to which it relates.

- Left-align both the field label and the field.

- Provide a small amount of white space between the field label and its field. Provide more white space between the field and the next field label so users can quickly see which field label corresponds with which field.

- Present forms as one column. Scrolling a bit is preferable to trying to differentiate which way a form runs.

- Never lay out a form going zigzag left to right. This requires needless fixations because it is unexpected and takes more skill to move between long horizontal fixations. It's like reading back and forth between facing pages in a book.

- Stick with one format. For example, if you are using a single column, stay with a single column.

- Eliminate all superfluous fields. For example, do not offer a middle initial field unless necessary.

- Display fields based on users' previous selections. Try not to present them with fields they do not need.

- If offering more than one field that may glean the same information from a user, make it visible and simple for the person to determine this, and enter the information only one time. For example, display fields for only the shipping or billing address, and then offer a "same as billing" or "ship to a different address" option (another form or a drop-down). When the latter is selected, the form should expand to accommodate the additional information.

- Use clear names for fields to prevent users from having to determine their meaning.

- Present similar information, such as shipping and billing details, in the same format and order. (For example, present the name first and the address second.)

Remember, don't let additional features get in the way of the basics. For example, the address book feature should be presented only to people who are logged in and have addresses saved in their address book. It should not hinder others from finding the *Same as billing* check box or ask them to use features that are irrelevant to them, such as giving a "nickname" to an address they are typing in.

6 Images

Images are a powerful part of Web design. Good images explain a concept, conjure a feeling, convey information, and enhance people's overall experience on a site. Bad images waste space, are ignored by users, and, even worse, are confusing. In this chapter, we examine what specific attributes attract people or repel them from images on the Web.

There are basically four forms of media for communicating to users on the Web: text, graphics, moving images (such as animation and video), and sound. Graphics are probably the most powerful of these because people respond to them instantly and in a matter of just a few fixations.

There are some very creative, captivating images on the Web today—graphics that evoke emotion, graphics that relay a message far better and faster than words, and graphics that illustrate a process or instructions. People look at and respond positively to these graphics. But generic and pointless images are about as compelling as a garden slug. Our eyetracking research shows that these are even a bigger waste of time than we previously thought because people simply do not look at them.

It's almost as though people have a finite bank of looks to give to Web pages. When they scan a page, they rapidly make decisions about what they are going to view. They are constantly calculating how many looks they have used and have left and whether it is worth allotting them to the image at hand. It's a tough world on the Web, and users are downright miserly with their fixations.

People ignore more images than they look at on the Web, and they look at images for just a fraction of a second.

Just how miserly? Depending on the context and types of images, people look at less than half of the images presented to them on average—only 42 percent. And in general, they look at those images for less than two-tenths of a second.

What Does and Doesn't Draw Attention to an Image

Images that people really look at vary greatly in style and quality.

We have found in our eyetracking research that people determine an image to be worth looking at during their first, peripheral glimpse of it. In general, they decide it is worthwhile if it seems substantive and of benefit to them.

The images people look at most have the following characteristics:

- Are high contrast and high quality (crisp and colorful)
- Are cropped, rather than overly reduced, when necessary to fit a small space
- Are not excessively detailed: easy to interpret, almost iconic
- Are highly related to the content on the page
- Possess magnetic features

Features that make images magnetic include the following:

- Smiling and approachable faces
- People looking at (or at least facing) the camera
- Sexual anatomy (and sexy bodies)
- Appetizing food
- Clear instructions or information

People ignore images that have the following characteristics:

- Are low contrast and low quality
- Are too busy for the space
- Look like advertisements
- Are not related to content on the page or only slightly related to it
- Are boring
- Include people or objects that are generic or obvious stock art
- Are cold, fake, or too polished

Images as Obstacles

People often treat Web pages as obstacle courses and the images they perceive to be unhelpful as obstacles they must go around. This was the case when our users went to the Adelphia cable company's homepage to learn about digital video recording.

The page offers horizontal navigation and text, buttons, and links in the content area. It includes several images that are not very magnetic. They are low contrast or too small for the space allocated to them, and the people in the images are not looking at the camera (**Figure 6.1**). Amazingly, almost all our users looked everywhere on the page but at the images (**Figure 6.2**).

Figure 6.1 Adelphia's homepage tries to entice with images of people happily using the company's cable products or services.

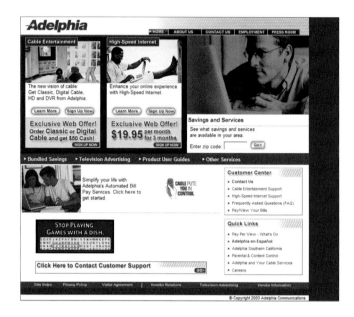

Figure 6.2 Most people went out of their way to avoid the generic-looking images on the page.

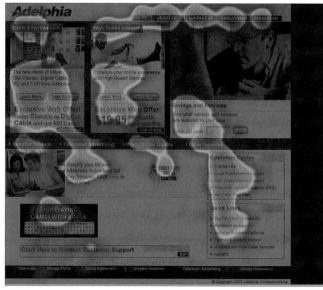

On Web pages with multiple superfluous images, people treat the entire page as an obstacle course they must navigate. They look at the text around images, but not at the images.

Eyetracking Web Usability

Why do designers include lackluster images like these? One reason is simply to give people's eyes a break from the text. But this can also have the opposite effect. When users' cognitive load is taxed from trying to avoid the images, they're not getting a break.

On the Gateway computer company's homepage, people also avoided the images that they believed were of no help to them: the PC monitors, the cow-skin patterned box, the hill and trees (**Figure 6.3**). Of course, what constitutes a "pointless" image is subjective. Presumably, Gateway included the image of computer monitors to draw attention to the text about its new 21-inch monitor. But the image is so small that it does not do a good job of showing that the monitor rotates and swivels. And at first glance, it appears that there are two monitors, not one in different modes. Users didn't even get that far, however, because the image seemed too generic to even merit a look.

Figure 6.3 People looked anywhere but at the boring images on the Gateway homepage.

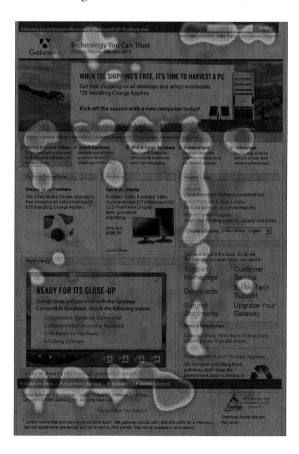

Part of the reason people ignored the smaller images is because the large, irrelevant background farm image at the top of the page hardened them to other images. The small pictures may have a bit more relevance, but by the time users got to them, they were already using an image-skipping strategy to work down the page.

Obstacle-course behavior is not exclusive to homepages, which are known for being "prettied up." It certainly occurs with interior pages too. For example, we asked people to use *New York Magazine*'s Web site to find restaurants in New York City where they might like to dine. Many people looked at the *Food and Restaurant* pages with reviews of big-name restaurants and several images of different sizes.

One image was of celebrity chef Anthony Bourdain, star of the TV show *No Reservations* and author of the best-seller *Kitchen Confidential*. Users looked around the photo of Bourdain, not at it. They also avoided the photo of prolific chef and TV personality Mario Batali (**Figure 6.4** and **Figure 6.5**). They ignored pictures of restaurants and other small photos on the page. Why?

Above all, as a closer look at the images shows, the contrast in almost all of these images is pitiable. Bourdain—a colorful, adventurous guy—is as gray as the backdrop behind him. And a photo of him is not highly related to the page content. It accompanies an article about celebrity chefs' opinions, not about Bourdain himself. Although this is commonly done for this type of magazine article, it is not necessarily effective on the Web.

The photos of restaurant interiors are also too dark and too detailed to be of much use. The illustrations of the woman's head and the chef's hat look like filler images, while the larger-than-life Batali is squeezed into a postage stamp–sized space. Can't a premier chef get a few more pixels? As a result, users did all they could to avoid these images as they negotiated the page.

Figure 6.4 Web page as obstacle course: Users searching for restaurants read the text on *New York Magazine*'s restaurant page but avoided the small and low-contrast images—even of high-profile chefs.

Figure 6.5 A closer look at the images on the page. They were meant to draw people's attention, not turn them off.

While still looking for restaurants on the same site, several users also hit a page with a blurb under the headline *Founding Fathers*. The text and two photos were about the history of two seminal restaurants in Manhattan (**Figure 6.6**). Again, people read much of the text related to the photos but avoided the low-contrast images (**Figure 6.7**). They would have needed to give several fixations and a few seconds to figuring out what the images are of, and people aren't willing to do that.

Figure 6.6 The images of two Manhattan restaurants have poor contrast.

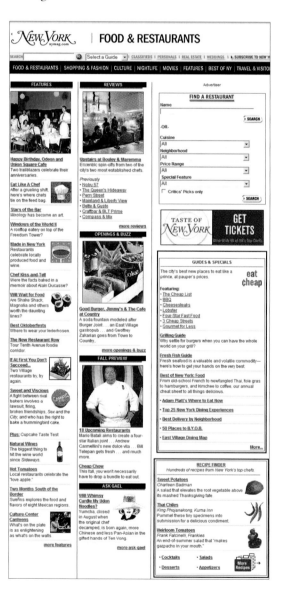

Eyetracking Web Usability

Figure 6.7 Even images that are highly related to the content on the page will be ignored if they are too dark and have poor contrast like these.

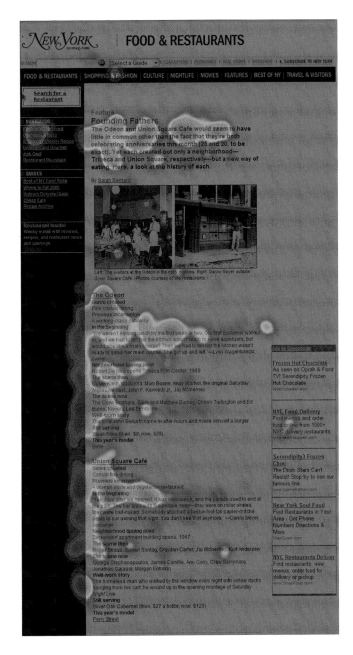

Omit Filler Images

Designers should beware of using images that accompany text but don't do anything to enhance it. We believe that these images should not be on a page. They are a waste of pixels, of the designer's work, and of users' time. We also argue that you should always use great images, although we understand that realistically you may need to run some that are medium quality. If that's the case, at least avoid big irrelevant ones.

A designer might ask, "Well then, what would we put in that empty space?"

Our recommendation: nothing. Use white space. Alternatively, decrease the page length or increase the default size of the text on the rest of the page.

Most important, economize. Spend resources on one image that is meaningful instead of a few that are not. For example, the Gateway homepage could have had a more dynamic illustration or photo of the new monitor converting from the horizontal to vertical view—or maybe even a small animation. And to really showcase the new product, the site designers should have given it more space on the homepage and an eye-catching headline. Similarly, *New York Magazine* could have displayed one clear image of a restaurant instead of two small, unclear images. Of course, this would involve prioritizing and discipline because the article was about two restaurants.

Attributes That Draw Attention

There are images that you can't help but look at and images you can't stop looking at. A crisp silhouette draws attention on the Web. A strong relationship to content, interesting subjects, and base appeal keep attention on an image.

Contrast, Quality, and Detail

High contrast between the subject and background of an image may be the main factor that determines whether people look at the image. Users are more likely to grant a fixation to an image if they can tell from a peripheral look that they will be able to decipher it.

For example, one of our users was seeking information about the feeding habits of mallard ducks on the Ducks Unlimited Canada Web site. She looked at quite a lot of the text and text links on the page but not at the image on the right (**Figure 6.8**). It did not have peripherally attractive properties: It is a landscape in a small space without a main element as the subject—the pond, grass, trees, and sky all compete.

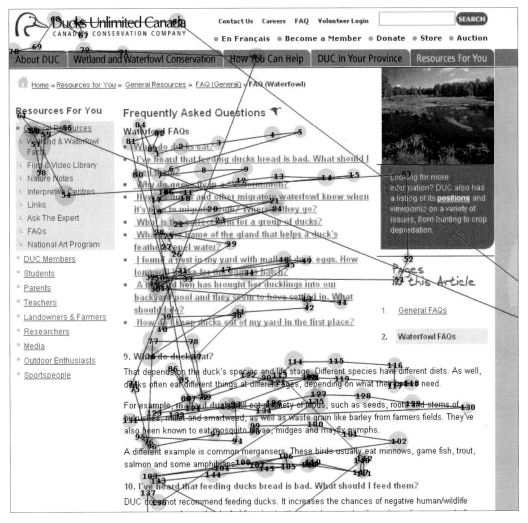

Figure 6.8 A user looking for information about mallard ducks avoided the rather useless image of a pond in the upper-right corner of this site. Peripherally, the image is just a lot of blue and green spots with no real clear subject.

In another task, a user looking to invest $10,000 in retirement did the same thing. On the CityFeet Web site, he looked at a few of the links and headings but gave no fixations to the low-contrast, unrelated images of the map and woman (**Figure 6.9**). He also ignored the rest of the images on the page, which are far too difficult to make out quickly (even if he had looked at them) and too detailed for the small space allocated to them.

Figure 6.9 A user's few fixations on this page were reserved for headings, links, and text—not for the low-contrast and small images.

Motivation and Expectations Can Help Even Bad Images Get Looks

Sometimes people look at an image despite its flaws if they specifically selected a link to images and are interested in the topic to which they relate. For example, on the Travelocity site, the participants in our study who were interested in bike tours looked at a very scenic, though small, image of a mountain biking trip (**Figure 6.10** and **Figure 6.11**). Why? They had expressly chosen the *Photos* tab to view photos of the trip. So, a combination of interest, expectations, and photo quality drew their attention to the image despite its size.

Figure 6.10 This image of a mountain biking trip is small, but people who had selected a link to see photos still looked at it.

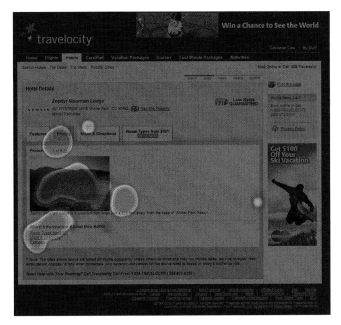

Figure 6.11 The large amount of red in this heat map indicates that there were still usability problems with the biking trip photo.

Still, a larger image would have been better for users. The cyclists are scaled down so small that people need to stare at the photo for a long time to understand what it is. If the image absolutely needs to be this small, it should have been cropped in on the cyclists. But since the landscape is part of the story, why not allocate more space for the photo? Why is it getting less than 4 percent of the available pixels?

Similarly, users on the 1900 Storm Web site chose to look at a slide show of photos from the aftermath of a devastating storm that hit Galveston, Texas, in 1900. The old black-and-white photos are not high quality, but people stuck with them because they had selected the slide show option and wanted to see the wreckage of the storm (**Figure 6.12**). The photo subjects are also captivating, and the quality of the photos adds a historical feel.

Figure 6.12 Even though the slide show images of a storm in 1900 had poor contrast, people were so interested in the subject that they continued to look at them.

When users select a link to a photo section, they usually expect some value-add in that area, such as larger photos or ways to zoom in. Our users who were researching information about vacationing in Shanghai on the Lonely Planet travel site did not look at the small accent images in the upper-left corner of pages about the city (**Figure 6.13**). When they selected the *Image Gallery* page, the same images in the same size appeared, but here they looked at them because they had specifically selected to do that (**Figure 6.14**).

Figure 6.13 People looked at the text and menus on this travel page about Shanghai but did not look at the small image with poor contrast in an upper corner, even though it was related to the content.

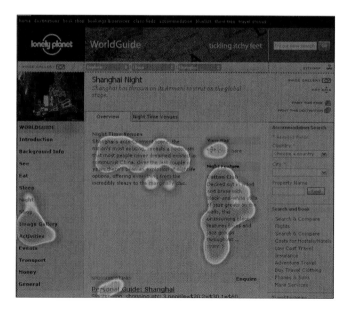

Figure 6.14 When people chose to view images on this site, they looked at images they had ignored on other pages.

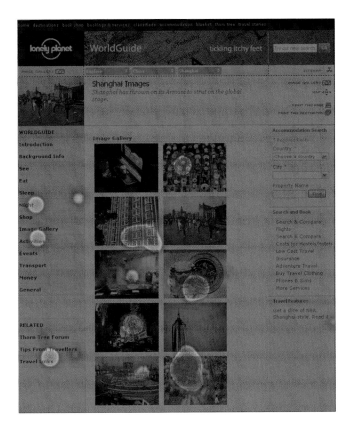

Icons

Iconic images are ones that instantly convey what they are: a printer, a trash can, a bolded letter. They have clear lines, high contrast, and messages that are easily understood. If users wonder even for a moment what an image is, it is not iconic. Contrary to their name, iconic images do not necessarily have an icon in them, nor do they need to be buttons of any sort.

Iconic images do not get looked at if they are difficult to make sense of quickly. The Colorado Fishing Network homepage is full of icons. One of our users who was planning a fly-fishing trip in Colorado gave a fixation to the homepage photo of a man fishing but ignored the icons on the page (**Figure 6.15**). Why? Although the image of the fisherman is small, it is also decipherable and related to the content of the page. But most of the icons are far too small to make out and not even remotely helpful. Does the binoculars icon add anything to the text *Search CFN*? How does the image that appears to be a pond represent *Shopping*? These images clutter the page without providing something of value for users. If this were our Web site, we'd drop the icons, get a better fly-fishing photo, and allot it the space it deserves.

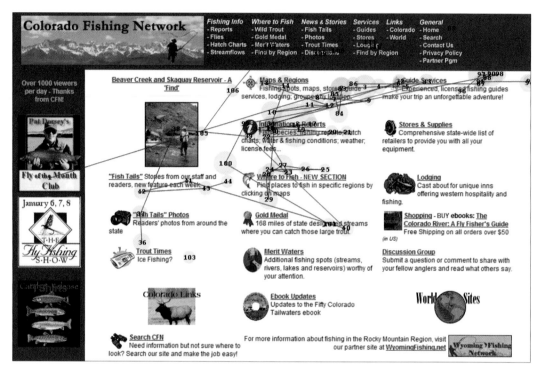

Figure 6.15 A user looked all around this homepage except at the tiny, useless icons.

Consider whether it's beneficial to use small graphics as signposts or bullets. Most tiny images are too difficult to decipher even if users spend time trying to figure out what they are. And most users don't bother.

In contrast, the graphics on File Forum, a site with software downloads and reviews, are simple, clear, and useful. One graphic employs blocks of color to depict consumer ratings on a scale of one to five. A single teal block indicates a score of one, two fuchsia blocks indicate a score of two, and so on. A user who was researching the product Skype went to the site in search of less than favorable reviews of the product. Once he understood the graphic's simple color scheme, it made it easy for him to quickly scan for them (**Figure 6.16**).

FileForum **BetaNews**

Login: _____ Password: _____ [Sign In] Lost Password? **Become a Member**

Search: _____ [Windows Only ▾] [Search] Advanced Search [☰] **List a Program** [?] **Help** [✓] **Preferences**

You proposed the new RFID infrastructure to track assets in real time _

Dice The Career Hub for Tech Insiders™ [FIND TECH JOBS]

Ads by Google   Skype Out   Skype Business   Skype Adapter   Skype to Landline   Download Skype

Write a Review of Skype   **Back to Program Detail**

Reviewer	Date Reviewed	Version	Rating	Review
veeoh	Mar 21, 2007	3.1.0.147	5 out of 5	stisev - get a grip
Paul Skinner	Mar 21, 2007	3.1.0.147	3 out of 5	Hmm. It's still quite good, but does it really need to be 20MB?
stisev	Mar 17, 2007	3.1.0.144	1 out of 5	I've been a long time Skype user, but given their recent history extracting BIOS information (mobo #) and creating hardware hashes, I am not running this software any longer. Pretty sad, actually.
pjb	Mar 14, 2007	3.1.0.144	5 out of 5	Works well for me. Fast at load and good call quality. No problems running it on Vista. I have manually uninstalled the plug-ins (personal choice) as I have no use for them.
harmlessdrudge	Mar 14, 2007	3.1.0.144	1 out of 5	Agreed. Skype is all washed up. I have switched to SIP telephony. It's still a bit like email in the early 90s with walled gardens here and there however. Check out voxalot.com for a way of pulling several services together nicely. Get a number from ipkall.com and a copy of X-Lite for a software phone and FORGET SKYPE! Or rather... forget about giving Skype any money!
sudbury	Mar 8, 2007	3.1.0.134 Beta	1 out of 5	Well. I tried to subscribed to their 50% deal in January. Then I get an email rejection saying my credit card was a fraud???? and I need to contact their customer service to release this on my account . So far I've unable to contact customer service. I've tried calling and email.... no respond by them. My theory is, I guess they don't want my business.
GS5	Mar 7, 2007	3.1.0.134 Beta	2 out of 5	I haven't really used Skype for the last 6 months or so. Not just because they go around collecting hardware info but their voice quality became really poor. If a replacement is needed for skype, Project

Figure 6.16 The rating icons helped one user quickly scan to one of the worst reviews of Skype on this site.

211

The Impact of Background

We've found that people are more likely to look at images of an object set against a very simple background than against a crowded one. People look at 28 percent of objects in a vacant setting and at only 14 percent of images in a busier setting. For Web users, a picture of a tree on a plain white background is more iconic and easier to decipher than a picture of a tree in front of other trees or bushes.

However, people spend slightly more time and fixations on images with more complicated settings—an average of 2.5 seconds and 8.19 fixations on these, and 2.05 seconds and 7.6 fixations on those with plainer settings. This seems logical because busier backgrounds have more detail to decipher. But we can't say that this is necessarily good. We *can* say that people sometimes seem to look longer at an image out of interest and sometimes because they are using *exhaustive review* to try to decipher the image.

People also look slightly more at images of a single object—26 percent—than at images with multiple objects—20 percent. This difference is not particularly great, but it does reinforce the idea that people are more attracted, at least peripherally, to simpler images. People also look slightly more and longer—for 2.13 seconds and 7.74 fixations—at images of one object than at images of multiple objects—1.61 seconds and 6.33 fixations. The lesson? Less is more with images.

Image Attributes	Amount Viewed (Avg.)	Seconds Viewed (Avg.)	Number of Fixations(Avg.)
Single object	26%	2.13	7.74
Multiple objects	20%	1.61	6.33
Simple background	28%	2.05	7.60
Crowded background	14%	2.50	8.19

Originality

With so many creative Web designers, one must wonder why basic stock-art images keep finding their way onto sites. Although some designers must make the dubious decision to use boring images that have appeared on countless other sites, we believe that many designers don't. They snub generic "computer on desk" and "calm forest scene" images that could be on any site and that convey nothing unique or specific about an organization or its products, services, or values.

Take the ubiquitous "smiling woman wearing headset" image. Really, just about any company could boast customer support people who are happy to serve you. Does the woman wearing a headset (who obviously doesn't work for your company because she is too polished and made up to be answering support calls in a big Skinner Box of a room with 50 other people for 8 hours a day) really convey to your users that you are there for them?

The Adelphia Web site is one of many that has succumbed to the "smiling woman wearing headset" syndrome. And sure enough, no fixations (**Figure 6.17**).

We asked Web designers why these images keep popping up. Many of them say that a manager or other person with branding responsibilities often tells designers that they need to "punch up" a page because it is "too boring."

People ignore stock images 85 percent of the time.

What's a designer to do? They can refuse to use a useless image and then risk being reprimanded or earning a reputation as "difficult." They can do the easy thing and use stock art—a choice that's often hastened by schedule and resource constraints. And maybe stock art will appease the people who wanted the page to be more exciting. But in

85 percent of cases, users do not give these images the time of day. Not even one fixation. So, why not punch things up with something more original?

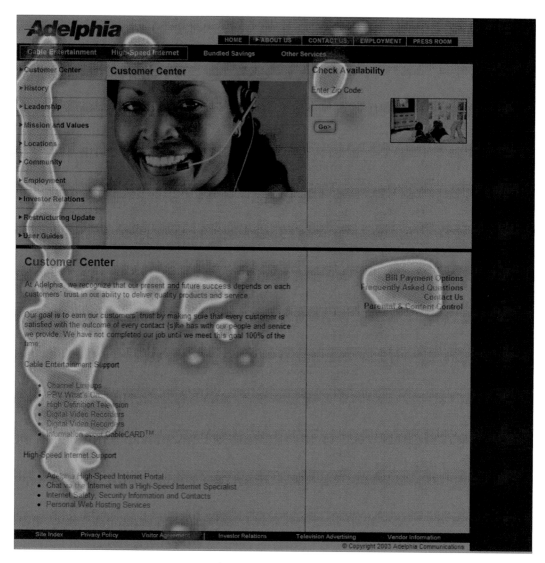

Figure 6.17 Users avoided looking at the ubiquitous "woman wearing headset" image on this site.

The site for Hansen's Natural beverages offers a humorous send-up of the "smiling woman wearing a headset": a deranged-looking man in a suit holding a tin can to his ear. This has visual interest, and our users looked at it (**Figure 6.18**).

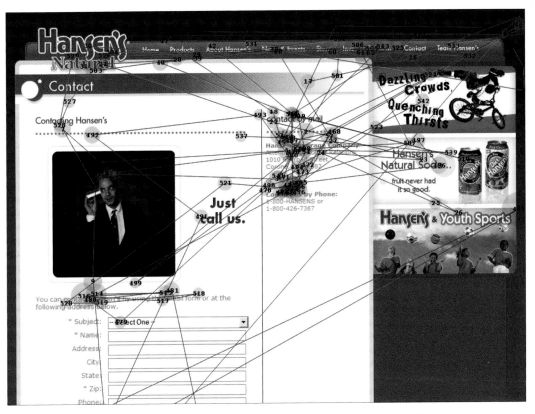

Figure 6.18 A user looked at the image of the atypical customer support representative at the Hansen's Natural Web site.

FreshDirect's twist is to have a small image of a person who looks like one of the grocery service's knowledgeable and friendly employees plugging featured food and drink items in the upper-right edge of pages. The idea of having a little chef (or a little deli bar man, little fishmonger, little produce worker, and so on) giving an OK sign to a featured item may seem as if it would add credibility, interest, and fun. But it loses its charm rather quickly (**Figure 6.19**).

Figure 6.19 People usually ignored the little man in the upper right of pages on this site after seeing him once, but they looked at images of food such as tuna burgers, pastas, and ice cream.

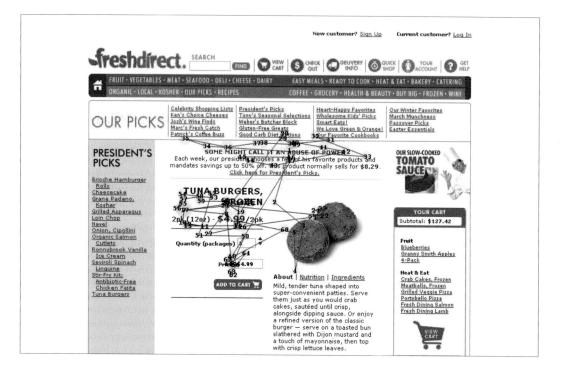

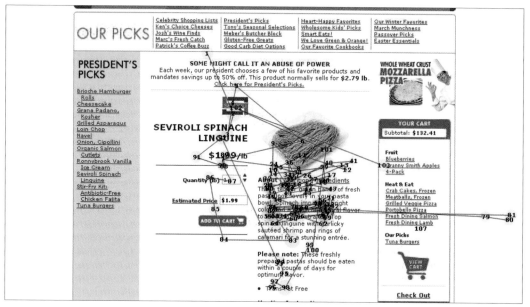

Eyetracking Web Usability

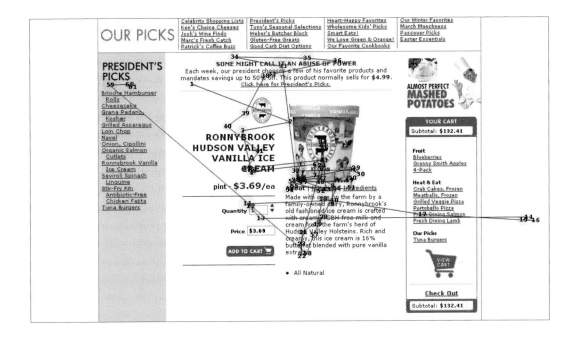

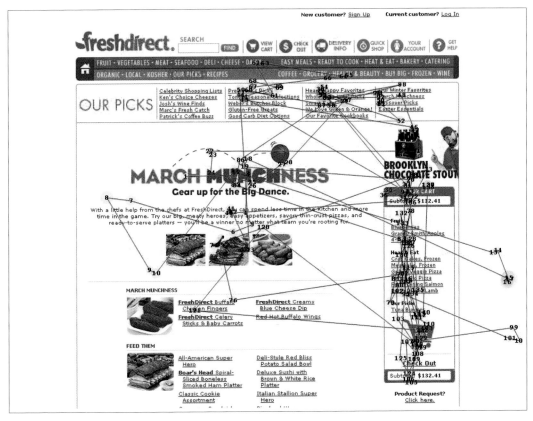

In fact, users rarely looked at these images. So, does this mean they should not be there? It's unlikely that the images increase users' page load time, and because the images have similar shapes and appear on the edges of the page, people may even learn to tune them out peripherally at the right times, selective disregard. And a few users might like them—at least the first one they see. So, they are pretty harmless. But knowing that people look at them very rarely, the site designers might want to come up with a better image or more effective use of the space instead.

Relationship to Content

Many images that appear on pages are simply not related to the main ideas the page is trying to convey, and users ignore or barely look at them. People look at unrelated or somewhat related images just 14 percent of the time. Sadly, all those images of blue skies and oceans, sunny flower meadows, and smiling customer support people are probably not getting the time of day.

People look far more at images that are highly related to the written content on a page than they do at unrelated images.

Images that are only marginally related and not very helpful don't get much response from users either. On the Gerd Institute Web site, for example, people barely looked at the image of pills spilling out of a bottle on a page about drug therapy (**Figure 6.20**).

Figure 6.20 Users looked minimally at the somewhat related image of pills in a bottle on this page about drug therapy.

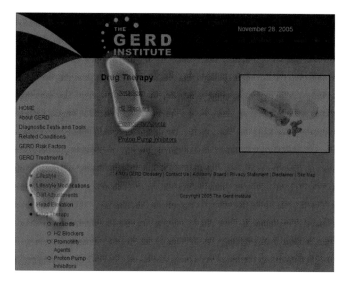

People already know what pills look like, so there is not much added value from this photo. If this were a site that educates patients about how to tell real Viagra pills from the fakes sold by spammers, many people would have looked closely at the pills. Users also didn't look much at the generic image of a woman carrying groceries on the site's page about diet (**Figure 6.21**). It is too obviously stock art.

Figure 6.21 Most people didn't bother looking at a generic image of the woman holding groceries on the site's diet page.

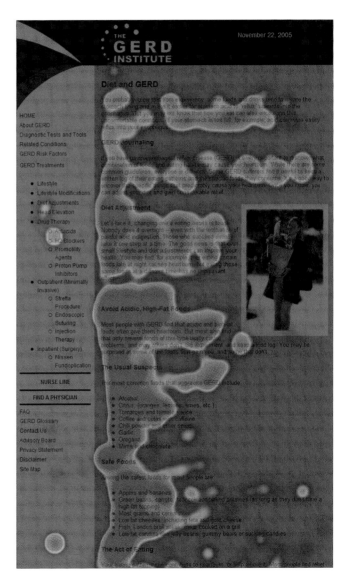

Exciting Images Related to Content

Users look at images that are related to content about twice as often—29 percent of the time. Even peripherally, people seem to sense when images surrounded by written text are stock art or relate to content. It may be that certain characteristics signal this. For example, people may be more likely to interpret an image as relevant if it has high contrast or seems related from a peripheral view.

For example, users looking for the fastest swimming speed of a mako shark looked at the simple, but gripping, photo of the shark (**Figure 6.22**).

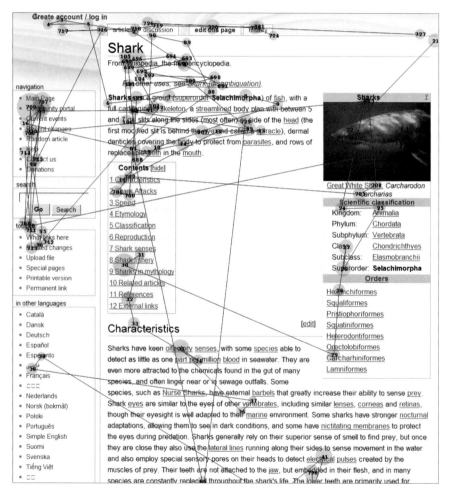

Figure 6.22 A user scanning a Wikipedia page for information about mako sharks was drawn to the photo of one.

Users researching the 1900 storm in Texas were very interested in the text, but they were also drawn to the accompanying images (**Figure 6.23** and **Figure 6.24**). Everyone looked at the photo of a house turned on its side.

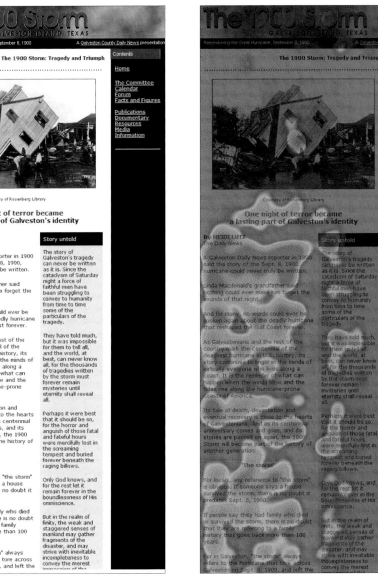

Figure 6.23 The 1900 Storm site runs relevant—and compelling—photos of a storm in Texas at the turn of the century.

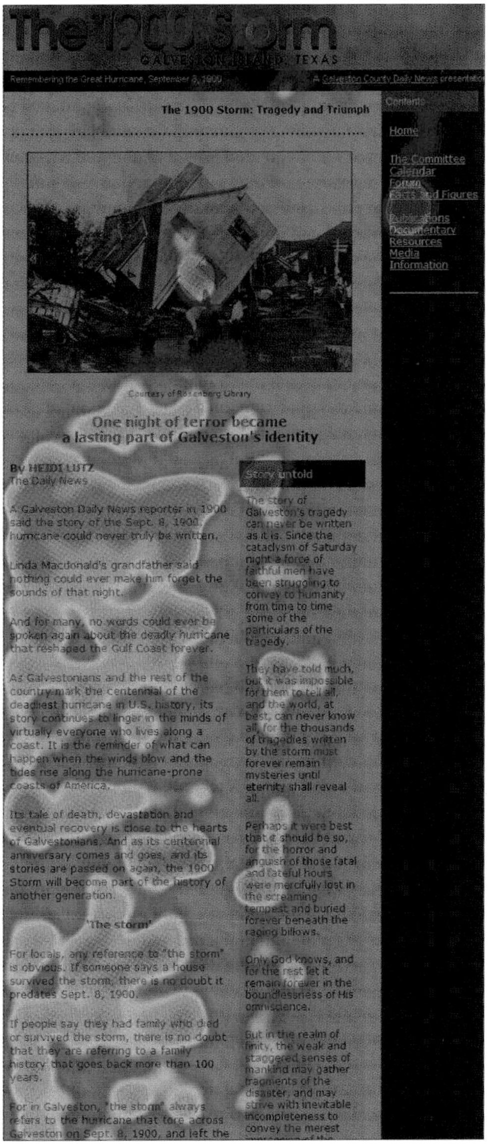

Figure 6.24 All of our users who read about the storm looked at the related image of the house on its side. People commonly look in the windows of buildings in photos.

When reading a CNN article about smugglers who forced Somali refugees from their boats into shark-infested waters, people looked at the image of the boats that accompanied the article (**Figure 6.25**). Some looked at the boats a few times.

Figure 6.25 A user read the beginning of an article about smugglers mistreating refugees and looked at the related image on the CNN site.

Unexciting Images Related to Content

Smugglers, sharks, and storms are pretty thrilling topics, so it's not surprising that people look at related images. But they look at images related to less-exciting topics as well.

When researching whether mallard ducks dive for food, users looked at several good images of ducks on a page of NYSite. Although most of the photos did not relate directly to their task, people looked at them because they related to the subject of the text, mallard ducks, and some of the images did show the ducks feeding. One person looked at all seven duck photos on the page (**Figure 6.26**).

Figure 6.26 A user looking for information about the feeding habits of mallard ducks was drawn to all the photos of the ducks on this page.

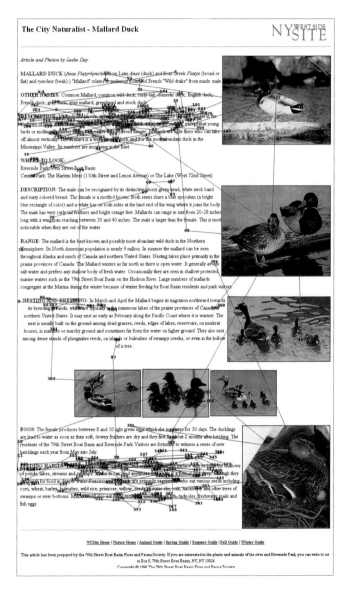

Similarly, users reading about the Bedford-Stuyvesant neighborhood in New York looked at images of the neighborhood on a page of the Living Cities site (**Figure 6.27**).

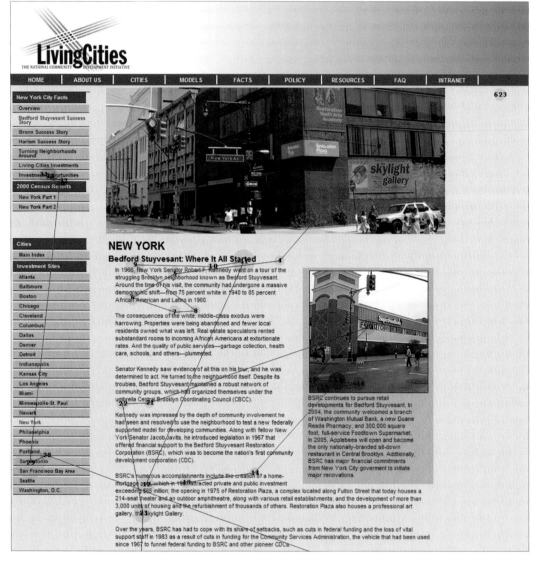

Figure 6.27 A user reading about Bedford-Stuyvesant looked at photos of buildings in the neighborhood. He looked in the window of the top image.

When learning about the John F. Kennedy Presidential Library and Museum, people looked at a relevant photo of the past president, even though they hardly needed to be reminded of what JFK looked like. One user also looked at the photo of Kennedy's mother, Rose, who was the subject of an exhibit (**Figure 6.28**).

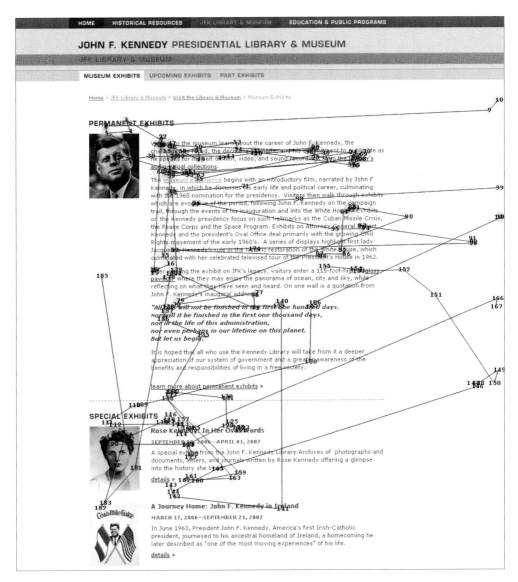

Figure 6.28 A user read the text and was attracted to the clear, relevant images of John F. Kennedy and Rose Kennedy on the JFK Library Web site.

Even a washed-out grayscale photo that is visually interesting and highly related to content can get looks. Users researching onetime New York mayor Fiorello La Guardia looked at the image of him on Answers.com (**Figure 6.29**). The grimace on La Guardia's face was probably part of the draw.

Figure 6.29 La Guardia's grimace helped attract users to an otherwise washed-out photo on this site.

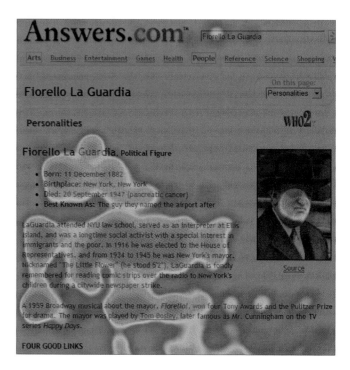

Magnetic Elements

Some images are downright captivating, and users are drawn to them. Many magnetic images exhibit several of the attributes that generally attract people's attention. They are crisp, are the right size, have good contrast, and highly relate to the accompanying text.

It may seem somewhat unrealistic to think that every image can be magnetic. But why can't most of them be? Rather than spending money and resources on several pieces of stock art or having your designers make stock art–like images to pepper all over your site, why not let these talented artists use their talent to create just a few potent images? Think about what you want to convey with

Dump watered-down stock art, and instead use your resources to create a few high-quality, strategically placed magnetic images.

the images. Consider the message, the quality of the images, and their strategic placement on your site.

When users who were asked to find out which sport and position George Brett played wound up on the Baseball Almanac site, they were greeted with information about the third (and sometimes first) baseman and an image of his Topps baseball card (**Figure 6.30**).

Figure 6.30 Irresistible: This image of George Brett has everything a good image should.

People could not help but look at the picture of Brett (**Figure 6.31** and **Figure 6.32**). This image really has it all. It is highly related to the page content. It is clear, has good contrast, and is the right size for the amount of detail. It has visual interest: The handsome slugger is smiling at the camera, with three baseball bats resting on his shoulder. He is identified clearly under the image. Who wouldn't look at this photo?

Figure 6.31 People read the menus, table text, headings, and small chunks of text on the Baseball Almanac Web site. They also looked heavily at the slugger's face, the baseball bats he is holding, and his name in the bottom-left corner of the baseball card.

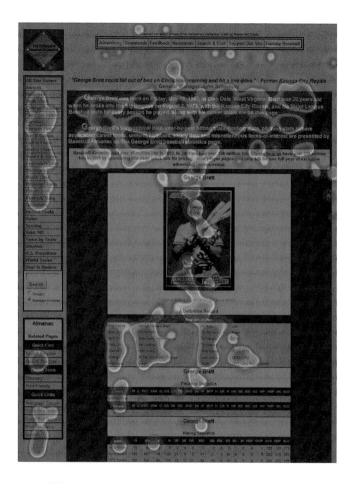

Figure 6.32 A close-up shows much heat on the Brett baseball card.

Eyetracking Web Usability

Another example of magnetism is a photo of about 17 very leggy ladies high-kicking in tandem on the NYtheatre.com site. For obvious reasons, users were drawn to this leggy lineup from the Broadway show *A Chorus Line* (**Figure 6.33**) more than they might have been to a group shot of the cast seated. The dancers' skin contrasts well against the dark background of the photo. And the picture highly relates to the content on the page.

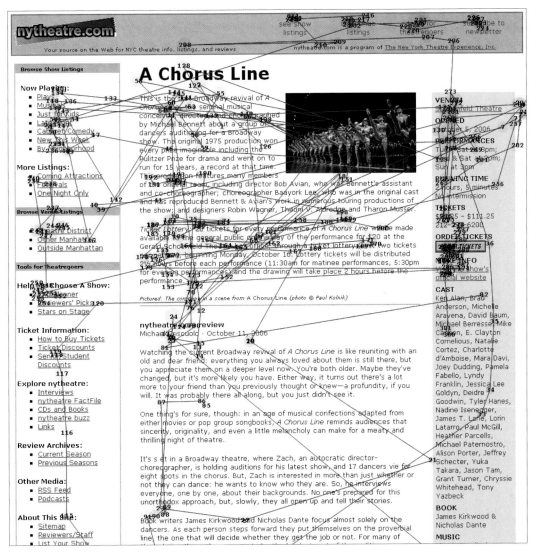

Figure 6.33 A user read the text about *A Chorus Line* and looked at the miles of legs in the image on this site.

Faces

Psychologists have long studied what elements make some human faces more attractive to look at than others. For example, symmetry is often cited as an important factor. Our research shows that people are generally drawn to faces on the Web that are the following:

- **Smiling.** Many of us learned in first-year psych that babies are attracted to their mother's smiling, close-up faces. Perhaps as adults, we are still conditioned to respond to a close-up, smiling face.

- **Facing the camera.** Users look more at images of people who are looking directly at the camera or at least facing the camera.

- **Authentic.** People look at beautiful models on the Web, as they do everywhere else. But attractive people who also look real and have imperfections actually get more looks than stock art or perfect faces.

- **Set in a very simple background.** People seem to be deterred from busy portrait photos, such as those with very detailed backgrounds. They are more likely to look at an image of a face with a plain or very simple backdrop.

Plain Background vs. Detailed Background

As they do with objects, people look slightly more at images of a person set in a plain background (22 percent) that doesn't compete with the person's face than at those of a person in a more detailed background, such as a cityscape (18 percent). They spend slightly less time on images of people in a plain setting, on average gazing for .79 of a second on these compared with 1.5 seconds on a person in a more elaborate setting. Likewise, they spend fewer fixations on the person in a plain background, 3.49, than on the person in a busy background, 5.51.

With people averaging far less than two seconds on a photo, it's good to remind ourselves how little time we have to get our point across. Make sure that what you are trying to convey can register with users instantly.

People

We have found that users look slightly more at images of a single person—20 percent—than at images of more people—17 percent. This is probably because images of a single person often have less detail. In general, the more detail in the image, the lower the contrast and the less crisp it will be.

Certainly, photos that contain several people can be crisp and attractive. But Web designers must often crop very good photos to fit the space allotted to them on the page. Usually there's simply less detail to worry about with an image of a single person.

Once people have chosen to look at an image, they glance slightly longer at those of one person (1.13 seconds) than at those of multiple people (1.01 seconds). But they give many more fixations to images of more than one person—11.47, compared to just 4.3 for those of one person.

Of course, how long people look at an image of several people depends on why they're looking at it. For example, the user Aimee went to the *Management* page on the site for Genentech, a biotechnology firm, to learn about the company's management team and mission. Her first few fixations were on the executive committee member links on the left, not on the image of the management team (**Figure 6.34**). But when she started to really read the names and titles of the managers, she also looked at their faces (**Figure 6.35** and **Figure 6.36**). Before she left the page, she had looked at almost every person in the image, some more than once (**Figure 6.37**).

Photos of one person often have less detail than those of several people. As images get more detailed, contrast diminishes, and people are less likely to look at them.

Figure 6.34 At first, the user Aimee didn't look at the image of the management team on this page of the Genentech site.

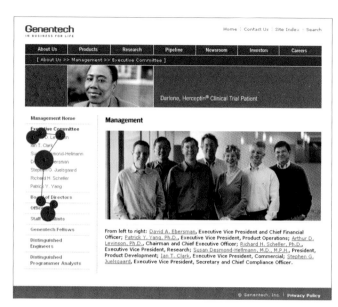

Figure 6.35 Within a few moments, after she had begun to read the names and titles of the people in the photo, she gave a fixation to the image.

Figure 6.36 After a few more moments, Aimee reviewed the names and titles of the people in the photo quite thoroughly and had fixated once on most of them.

Figure 6.37 During Aimee's entire visit on the page, she looked at the names under the *Executive Committee* heading, at all of the names and job titles under the photo, and at most of the faces in it. She fixated most on the face of the chairman and CEO.

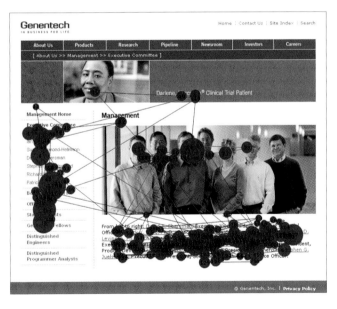

People are most likely to study the people in a photo when they think it will be helpful to do so. When some of our users were seeking information about fishing for bass weighing more than 30 pounds off the coast of Montauk, New York, they went to a site about the charter boat Mistress Too. They fixated on the images of the boat, the captain, and the big catch. The images helped answer questions they might have had about booking a charter fishing trip on this boat: Does the vessel look seaworthy? Does the captain look competent? Are they catching big fish?

People also looked at photos of the guests on the trips (**Figure 6.38** and **Figure 6.39**). These images could shed light on other concerns: Do they look inexperienced? Are they mostly men? Do they look like they are having a good time?

Figure 6.38 (left) The user Tracy looked at the boat, the fish, and the faces of some of the fishermen on the site of the charter fishing boat Mistress Too.

Figure 6.39 (right) She continued to look at more fish and faces on another page of the site.

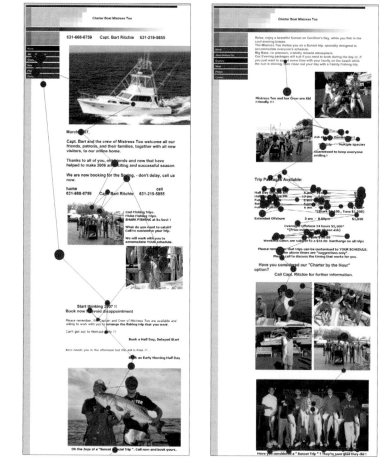

Eyetracking Web Usability

When a photo of many people is less relevant to the topic of the page or users' tasks, people spend less time with it, but that doesn't mean it is ineffective. For example, photos of people are sometimes used to put a "human face" on an organization or Web site.

Kiehl's, which sells grooming products, is pretty well known in New York City, in particular for their wholesome, natural products and helpful sales staff. (And their flagship store in the East Village has some cool motorcycles in it.) There is a photo of this store and eight of the people who work there on the Web site's homepage (**Figure 6.40**).

Figure 6.40 The Kiehl's homepage shows smiling sales staff in front of the company's flagship retail store.

When our users hit this page, they had a task in mind: to buy something of their choice. One would expect people on this mission to look quite a bit at the horizontal navigation bar to browse what is available and at the search field if they have a particular product in mind. Our users did both and looked at the image and text associated with the featured product on the right (**Figure 6.41**). But surprisingly, they also gave a good number of fixations to the main image on the page. In particular, they were drawn to the green tree and the one-way street sign. The street sign is bright, and the tree stands out against the lit-up store. Users looked less at the *Welcome* text (although they probably would have looked at it more if it was on a plain background) and finally at the waving employees. They did not stare at the faces in the photo, but they saw enough to get a sense of a group of people in lab coats smiling and waving.

Figure 6.41 People attempting to buy products on this site looked mostly at the menus on the homepage. But they also looked at the low-contrast but real-looking people in the image.

Without really knowing the designer's intent, we cannot say whether this is a successful image. But we think that, for the most part, it is. If people want to glean the ages of the Kiehl's salespeople or get a sense of whether they can trust them, the faces in this image are not large enough or clear enough. But if they want to know whether the staff is friendly and professional, then the image is probably successful. And users looked just enough at the staff to get this sense. But they also knew that giving more looks and time to the image would not yield more information, so they did not waste time trying to make out details.

Attractive and Real-Looking People

Not surprisingly, people are more drawn to images of good-looking people than to images of average-looking or unattractive people. Of course, what makes a person "attractive" is subjective: Individuals are drawn to very different physical traits. (Hallelujah!) But if we sat in an airport in New Hampshire or New Delhi and asked people which passersby are attractive, a number of common traits would emerge. So, when determining which people in images are attractive, we factored in less subjective measures such as whether they look healthy, their body is well proportioned, and their face is symmetrical.

People look at 33 percent of the images of attractive people on the pages they visit, but at only 9 percent of the images of unattractive people. And they look more and longer at attractive people.

We found that people look at 33 percent of images of attractive people on the pages they visit, but at only 9 percent of images of unattractive people. And not surprisingly, they look longer at attractive people. On average, people look at images of them for 1.12 seconds and at those of less-attractive people for .97 of a second. They also give attractive people 4.48 fixations on average and plain people 3.98 fixations.

This pattern was clear in our research. Users seeking information about digital video recording on the Adelphia Web site read the text and looked quite a bit at the woman holding the remote and smiling at the camera (**Figure 6.42**). She is pretty—possibly even a model—but not ultraglamorous. This type of photo—of a happy person who seems like someone you could know—may subtly make people feel more comfortable with an organization or product.

Figure 6.42 In an image on the Adelphia site, a woman smiling directly at the camera is attractive but also has a "girl next door" appeal. Users looked at her.

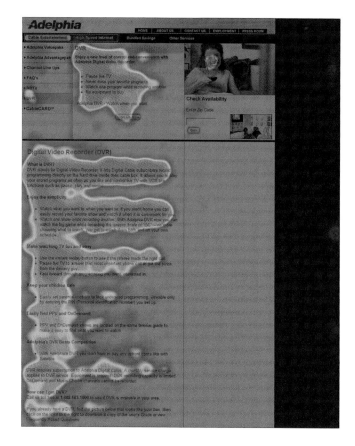

The Fidelity Web site displays an image with two attractive people. The image is clear and has the right amount of detail for its size. Both people are smiling, and at least one person is looking directly at the camera. Users looked at this image too (**Figure 6.43**).

The two photos of the investment specialists at Stringfellow, on the company's site, are good examples of effective group shots. While the background of the main photo is busy, the people are still obviously the subject, and the photo is very crisp. The five people are smiling and looking at the camera, and their black T-shirts make their faces stand out. The T-shirts also play off the rest of the black page.

The same people are in the image at the top of page. It's smaller and not in the center of the page, but our users still looked at it for the same reasons that they looked at the larger image (**Figure 6.44**).

Figure 6.43 Smiling faces: A user was drawn to the laughing, good-looking people in a photo on the Fidelity site.

Figure 6.44 People looked at the menu links and the smiling, attractive faces on the Stringfellow Investments Web site. This user looked directly at all four people in the foreground.

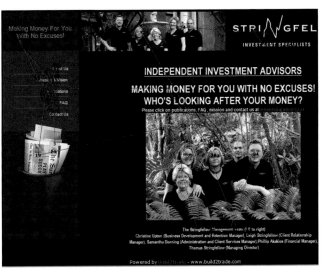

As you saw earlier in this chapter, Hansen's Natural is interested in conveying an offbeat, humorous image on its Web site. Like the site's photo of an atypical customer service representative, the image on the company's *Investor Relations* page is quirky. It shows six men doing the "wave," smiling, and having a good time, though they are clearly not at a sporting event. They are dressed like businessmen but behaving like guys at a Patriots game. Some are looking at the camera, some are not—depending on the stage of the wave they are in. Still, they all face the camera and are pretty decipherable because the photo is high quality. No man is standing up, in the full-wave position, but they are clearly in various wave stages because their silhouettes stand out on the super-white background. None is wearing a white shirt, which helps them stand out—and adds to their casual image. All of these points come together to make a compelling photo that got looked at by almost every user who saw this page (**Figure 6.45**).

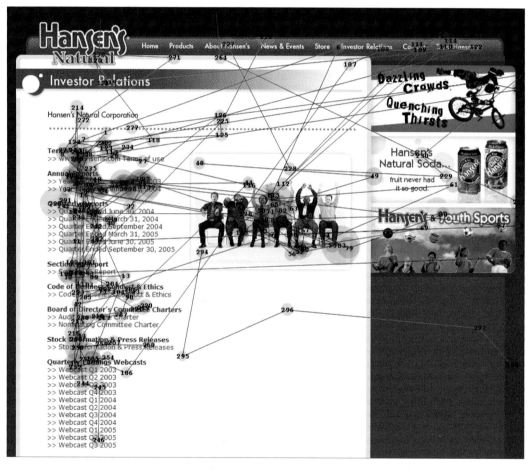

Figure 6.45 A user looked at this image of a bunch of men in chairs doing the wave—an atypical image for an investor relations page.

Figure 6.46 (below, left) The images on this page of the Good Dog Foundation Web site are highly related to the content.

Figure 6.47 (below, right) A user was drawn to the photos of people and good dogs.

People like images of people who look genuine. A user researching what the Good Dog Foundation does hit the site's information page, where there were text and images of dogs and their owners (**Figure 6.46**). The user read the text about the organization's mission to train and place therapy dogs and looked at the images (**Figure 6.47** and **Figure 6.48**). The people in the photos are magnetic because they are not models or actors. Many of them are smiling. The photo quality is not stellar, but the images illustrate the work the foundation does very well.

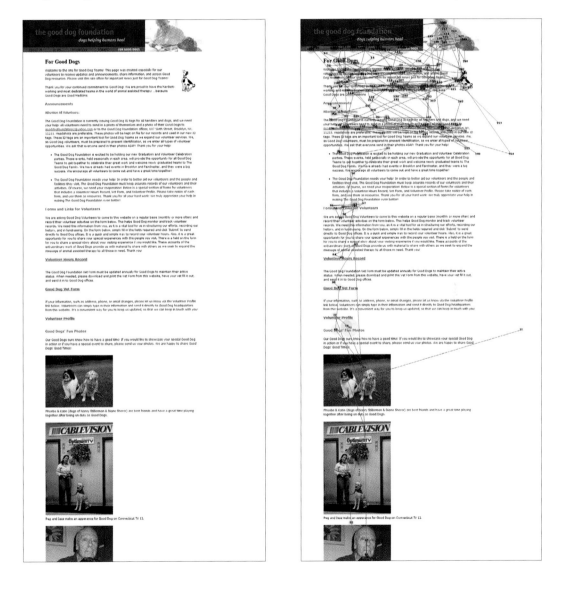

Figure 6.48 A user looked at the headings, text, and images on the site—specifically the woman's face in one photo and the dog's face in the other.

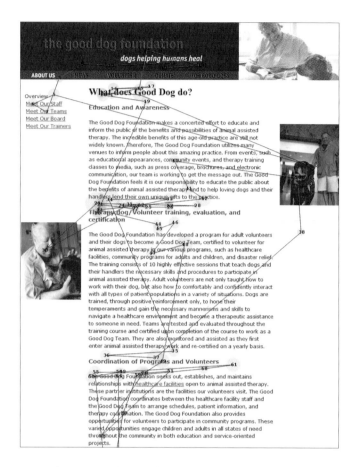

Now the potentially confusing part: Images don't always need to relate to content if the people in them are in some way highly compelling. When researching the Internet telephone service Skype, for example, a user's gaze went almost instantly to the cute smiling girls on the company's homepage (**Figure 6.49**). And she returned to it several times during the course of her visit (**Figure 6.50**).

Figure 6.49 In her first moments on the Skype homepage, a user was drawn to the smiling faces of the children in the image.

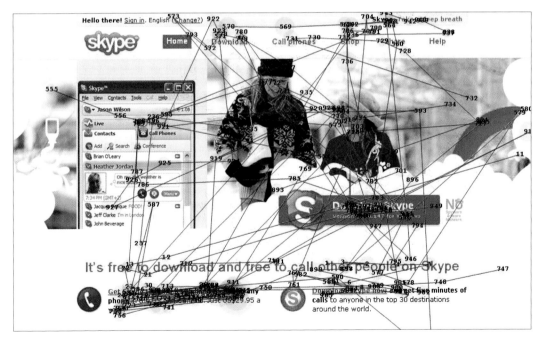

Figure 6.50 The user looked at the girls' faces several more times during her visit.

One reason images can't have too much detail on today's Web is the poor resolution on most computer monitors. It's simply not possible to get crisp photos at 100 dots per inch (dpi), which is a common screen quality. Research shows that 300 dpi is necessary for both images and text to have the highest clarity. Right now, displays with that quality are found primarily in IT labs and for highly specialized applications such as medical image analysis.

Unfortunately, among hardware technology, monitors are second only to laptop batteries in their slowness to improve. So, it's going to be a long time before you get a perfect screen for your PC.

But let's say that we get better screens by 2030. Will people look more at detailed images then? Probably, but clean and simple images will continue to have an advantage. People also prefer simple images because they are easier to scan. And scanning will be with us forever because of the browsing behaviors and incessant movement that characterize use of an infinitely big information space.

Gender Differences in How People Look at People

We wanted to see whether there is a difference in the way men and women look at faces on the Web, so we did some research. We found that there isn't a difference in how they look at mundane images. For example, men and women gave about the same fixations to the faces of the Gateway board of directors (**Figure 6.51**).

But when sexier images were introduced, men and women looked at them differently. For example, on the Neiman Marcus site, where people were looking for a shirt or top to buy for themselves, our female users focused on the task, analyzing the available tops and deciding which they liked most. They didn't look at the female models' faces (**Figure 6.52**). Men also looked at the shirts, but they gave as many fixations to the faces of the male models wearing them (**Figure 6.53**).

As we discuss in the next section, it may be that woman stay more focused on the task at hand and look only at related items, while men deviate slightly in their fixations during a task.

Figure 6.51 Men's and women's fixations on the Gateway board of directors' photos were about the same. Women's looks appear in the image on the left, men's on the right.

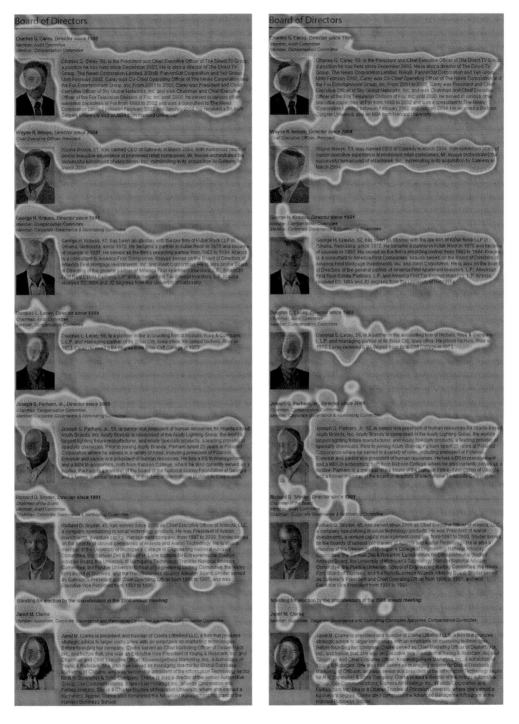

Figure 6.52 Looking at tops to buy on the Neiman Marcus Web site, women looked at the clothing, not the models' faces.

Figure 6.53 Men looked at the models' faces as much or more than at the clothing.

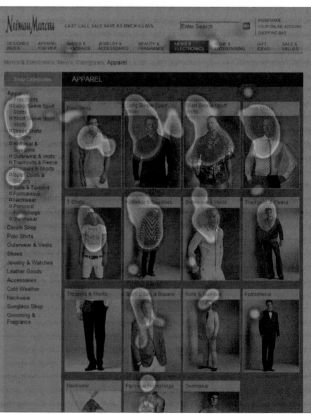

Who Gets More Looks—Men or Women?

Images of women and images of men each get looked at in about one-third of cases. But people spend 21 percent more time looking at images of women (1.15 seconds) than of men (.95 seconds). And they give women 4.51 fixations on average, compared to 3.95 for men.

Human Bodies and Sexual Body Parts

People like to look at human bodies and body parts on the Web—particularly faces and private anatomy. Why? After all, we can't talk to people in photos, make eye contact with them, flirt, or ask them on a date. We believe it is quite primal, something that is simply instinctive. An informal poll of colleagues, family, and friends yielded another reason: It's fun.

Even knowing how hardwired this is, we were still a bit surprised to find how much people look at these parts as they innocently browse the Web—and when they are focused on a task. They may not always be distracted or drawn in by a photo of good-looking, half-naked person, but often they are.

Take the photo of Lindsay Lohan on the Men.style.com site (**Figure 6.54**). Though our male users were reading about the latest electronics recommendations, they took time to look at the face and body of the young, beautiful actress in a small, hot, black leather bathing suit (**Figure 6.55**). Likewise, on the Neiman Marcus site, a male user who was very focused on finding the page for men's clothing still managed to steal a look at the female model's bare neck on the homepage (**Figure 6.56**).

Figure 6.54 The scantily clad actress Lindsay Lohan adorns the Web site for *Details* and *GQ* magazines.

Figure 6.55 A male user looked the image of Lohan up and down.

Figure 6.56 Looking for shirts on the Neiman Marcus site, a user looked at the menus and at a model's décolleté.

So, what happened when we compared how men and women looked at images of women? Again, on the Neiman Marcus site, many male shoppers looked at the cleavage of the woman in a red dress in the small image (**Figure 6.57**), but female shoppers did not (**Figure 6.58**).

Figure 6.57 Shoppers on this site mostly looked at the menus. But the male shoppers also looked at the cleavage of the woman in the red dress.

Figure 6.58 Women weren't drawn to the model's cleavage.

It may not come as a big surprise that women did not diverge from their task to look at a picture of another woman's breasts. But let's consider how men and women looked at some pictures of men.

Users researching George Brett on the Baseball Hall of Fame Web site thoroughly read the information at the top of the page and looked at the image of Brett at bat in old-style snug-fitting pants (**Figure 6.59**). In fact, they looked mostly at his face and crotch. But when we broke down the fixations by gender, we found that both men and women looked at Brett's face, but only men looked at his crotch (**Figure 6.60** and **Figure 6.61**).

Figure 6.59 Body heat: People looked quite a bit at the image of George Brett on this site, specifically at his face and groin.

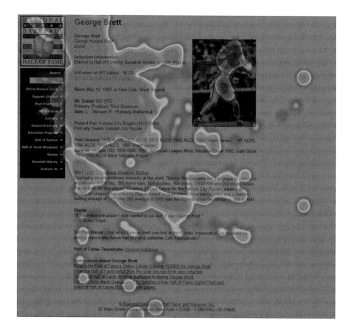

Figure 6.60 Women looked at George Brett's face but not his crotch when trying to learn what position and sport he played on this site.

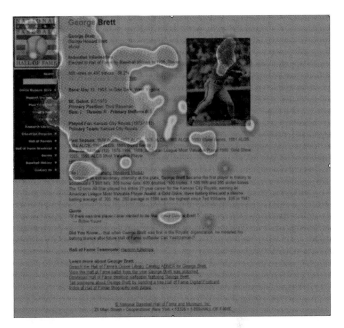

Figure 6.61 Men on the same task looked at Brett's face as well as his crotch.

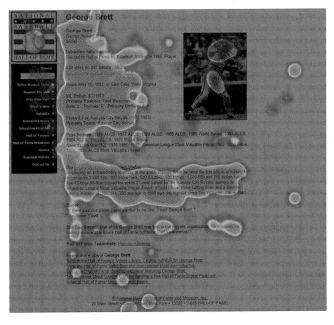

We wonder how people would respond to an image of Dodgers player Manny Ramirez, whose pants are so loose they'd surely fall off if he were not wearing a belt. But we didn't test this. We did, however, test some Web sites that cover another activity where men wear clothing that is tight in the crotch: ballet. Specifically, we asked people to learn about the great dancer Mikhail Baryshnikov.

As with Brett, women did not look at the male dancers' groins in images on the ballet sites (**Figure 6.62, left**). In fact, women didn't even look at the male ballet dancer in the photo on the left side of U.K. site Danceworks. But men did—at his face and even more so at his crotch (**Figure 6.62, right**).

Figure 6.62 Up close and personal: On the female users' heat map, there is no heat on the body of a male ballet dancer in an image on the U.K. Danceworks site (left), while the men's heat map shows heat on the dancer's face and crotch (right).

When images of Baryshnikov dancing were served up, things changed slightly for women. Users generally read the text extensively, because they were told they needed to discuss the dancer's background with a friend after they finished their task. Women focused on the dancer's face but looked a little at his crotch in one image (**Figure 6.63**). Men, as usual, looked at the dancer's crotch and face (**Figure 6.64**).

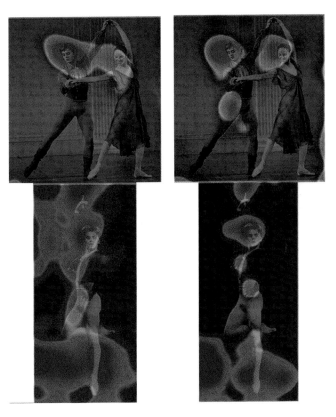

Figure 6.63 (left) Women looked a bit more at Baryshnikov's crotch in one image on the Danceworks site, but not much, and certainly not as much as men did. They looked more at the dancers' faces.

Figure 6.64 (right) Men looked the faces and private areas.

When focused on a task on the Web, men tend to look at sexual body parts more than women do. But it doesn't impact their task success rate or timing.

We don't mean to suggest that male users ogled these photos. Although they did look more at sexual parts of the body, they did not linger. The experience was over in just a moment, usually half a second or less, and their average task success rate was no lower than the women's.

A journalist once interviewed us about this phenomenon. She could not believe that women look less than men at images of men's clothed genital area. She was convinced that our research methods were flawed. After all, women have burned bras and run corporations. They've celebrated their sexual liberation in books like *Fear of Flying* and shows like *Sex and the City*. She said, "I looked at that heat map, and I looked at the crotches! Why wouldn't other women?" With all due respect, her strong feelings about this phenomenon may have colored the way she looked at the photos. And the fact that we are pointing out this gender difference would make most people look harder at the images.

The participants in our study, on the other hand, were not thinking about gender differences. They were asked to find information using the Web. They were "on task," and the tasks were certainly not designed to get them to look at particular body parts. In cases when they were not assigned a task, they were just looking at things that interested them and making up their own tasks. We did not direct them to the photos, nor did we ask them what they thought of the pages or images.

To be sure, women did look some at body parts, but far less than men did. Why is this? Analyzing people's psychological motives is beyond the scope of our study, but we have a couple of theories. One is that our female users were simply more focused on the task at hand and therefore less likely to be distracted by irrelevant images. Another theory relates to evolution and reproduction and the idea that men are programmed to "be fruitful and multiply." They are looking for people to mate with, and perhaps checking out their competition is part of the job.

Testing Porn Sites

With the Internet pornography industry making billions of dollars each year, we'd love to do a research study on porn sites. We figure this would need to be a field study in users' homes (or offices). And like all of our research studies, we'd have to watch users as they conduct their tasks on the Web. However, as you can probably imagine, none of our usability specialists have signed up to facilitate these studies.

An eyetracking research study conducted by Heather A. Rupp and Kim Wallen looked at how 15 male and 30 female heterosexual adults looked at sexually explicit photos on the Web. These photos were sexually unambiguous and not simply suggestive like an athlete in tight pants. The researchers found that men look at women's faces more than women do and more than they do at male faces; women look more at male faces than men do and more than they do at women's faces. They also found that men look at the female body more than they do at the male body and more than females look at the male body. Females look more at the male body than men do.

People looking at sexual parts of the body determine pretty rapidly that they can or cannot mate with the person in the photo. So, in the case of sexually explicit photos, they continue to look simply out of interest. But with photos that are not so sexually suggestive, such as those that users encountered in our study, it takes longer to determine mating possibilities.

Nonhuman Bodies

People don't just look at the sexual areas of humans in Web images. They also look at genital areas of animals, particularly dogs. Really. We discovered this when we gave tasks involving dogs, ducks, and sharks to large groups of users—more than 100 in each group. Obviously, the reproductive organs of ducks and sharks aren't all that visible, and participants did not glance at them. But dogs' genitals are much more evident, and they drew fixations. We did not expect this to happen when we assigned tasks.

One task we gave users was to adopt either a cairn terrier (like Toto in *The Wizard of Oz*) or a pharaoh hound, a rather regal-looking dog. We instructed them to learn about each dog on the Web before deciding which they would like to adopt.

People looked at and were even enamored with the faces of the hounds and terriers. They looked at the dogs' bodies to determine their size and look. They also viewed their reproductive organs regularly where they appeared, more than the dogs' other body parts. For example, on the Nefer-Temu Kennels' site, users looked at the pharaoh hounds' faces, teeth, and genitals (**Figure 6.65** and **Figure 6.66**). They also looked for the reproductive organs on the cairn terriers (**Figure 6.67**, **Figure 6.68**, and **Figure 6.69**).

Figure 6.65 Users looked at the faces of the pharaoh hounds on this page of the Nefer-Temu site.

Figure 6.66 On another page on the site, they looked at dogs' faces and body parts.

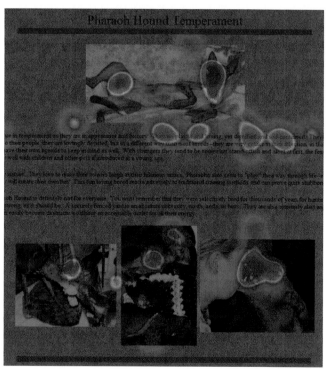

Figure 6.67 A user looked quite a lot at the cute cairn terrier pups on the Next-Day Pets site.

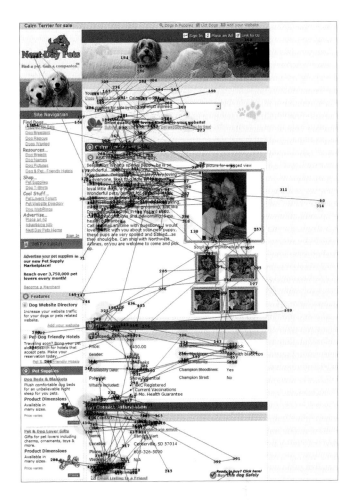

Figure 6.68 People looked at the cairn terrier's face and private parts on the American Kennel Club site.

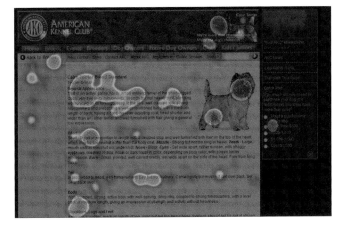

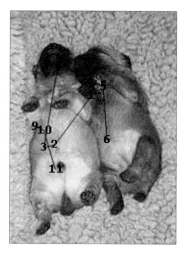

Figure 6.69 A user looked at the terrier puppies' faces, private parts, and chubby bellies on another site.

In one silhouette image where a pharaoh hound's sexual organs are hardly a prominent feature (unlike the belly shot on the Nefer-Temu site), people again looked at the dog's head, profile, and reproductive area (**Figure 6.70**). Even more interesting, they looked at—or looked *for*—the dog's genitalia in black-and-white line-art depictions (**Figure 6.71**).

Figure 6.70 On the Pharaoh Hound Club of America site, users looked at the silhouette of the dog's face and private area.

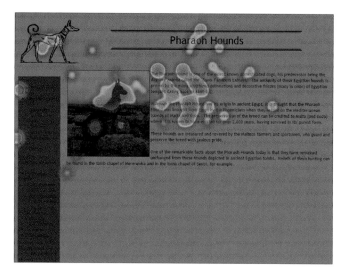

Figure 6.71 Even in black-and-white line-art drawings on this site, users looked at the dog's face and private area.

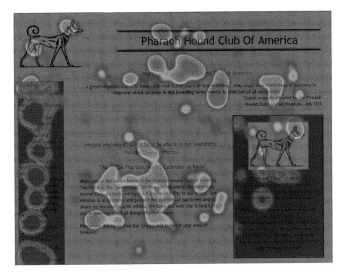

Although looking at the genitalia of other humans seems instinctive, we have to admit that we found this behavior a bit more confounding. But what drives it may be less a human instinct and more a mammal instinct. Bear with us for a minute. Way back in time, when we were dragging our slimy little selves out of the primordial sludge along with all different other types of beings, our brains weren't huge. One of our most important survival tasks was to determine which other beings we could mate with. Now really, we are not talking about bestiality here but an instinct that was critical to survival. And those who mastered it flourished. Fast-forward to today, and the first step to evaluating mating opportunities in a mammal (at least in a 2D environment where we cannot smell or usually hear them) is to look at their genitalia. So, perhaps that is what is going on. It's kind of fascinating, really, to think that here we are today, unconsciously playing out our primal instincts on the Web.

Keep in mind, of course, that we are just Darwin fans, and it would take some serious scientific expertise to determine the validity of this idea. But our research demonstrates indisputably that it's common for people checking out man's best friend on the Web to check out his private parts as well.

Nonsexual Body Parts

People are drawn to other interesting parts of humans and animals, including their skin and blood. The attraction to blood, though creepy, is not really surprising. Throughout history, people have chosen to see blood—at stonings, crucifixions, boxing matches, movies, and traffic accidents. And on the Web too, people want to see blood, skin, pointy things, and body parts.

When a lot of skin is showing, most people take a look at it. This happened with our users on the nytheatre.com Web site. All of them looked more than once at two shirtless actors in towels (**Figure 6.72**).

Figure 6.72 Users scanned the text and looked at the naked male torsos on this New York theater Web site.

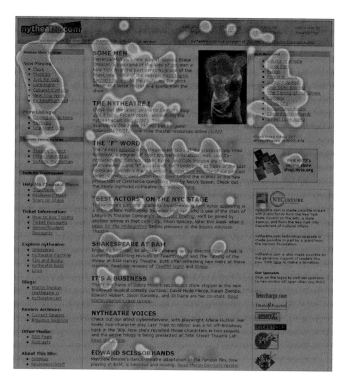

Even the skin on a human hand can draw the eye. Several users who were researching investment options were lured to the image of a hand on a computer mouse on the BNY Mortgage Web site (**Figure 6.73**).

Figure 6.73 People looked at the image of the human hand on the site of a Bank of New York mortgage company.

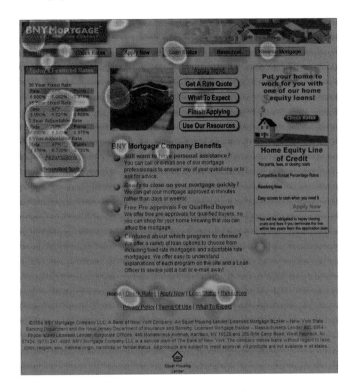

People in our study were also drawn to the skin of a chicken in an unusual food shot on the *New York Magazine* site (**Figure 6.74**). Because of its color, the skin might have looked human to them peripherally, but the peculiar way the chicken is contorted probably added some kind of disquieting interest.

Figure 6.74 A user was drawn to the chicken's skin and somewhat contorted body on this site.

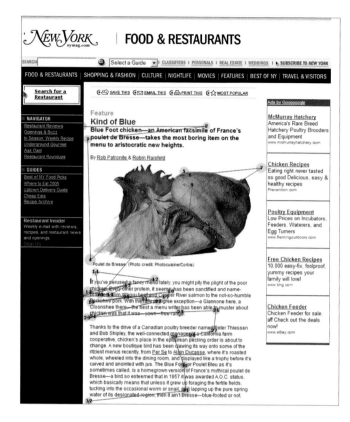

When some of our users were researching mako sharks, they read text and looked at several photos of sharks. They also ignored several photos of sharks, especially after they had seen a few. But their attention to images spiked on a page that showed sharks as they were caught on a fishing boat (**Figure 6.75**). People looked at photos of their bloody bodies slung on the boat's deck (**Figure 6.76**). They also looked at close-ups of a shark's teeth and jaw.

Figure 6.75 A user looked at the shark's body, teeth, and blood in an image on this page (shown cropped) on the Postmodern Web site.

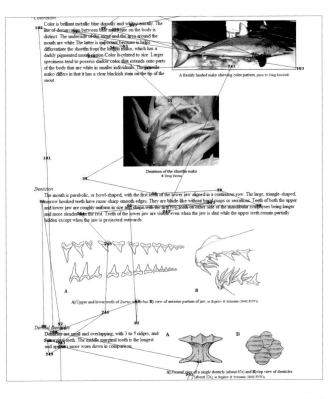

Figure 6.76 On a different part of the same page, a user looked at the shark's body, teeth, and blood.

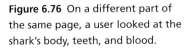

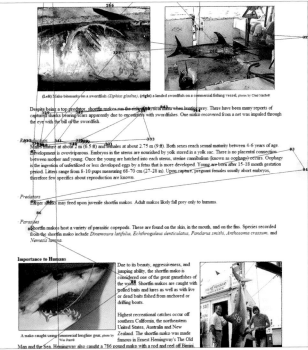

Objects of Attention

People are nosy. If a crowd is gathered on a street corner, other people will stop to see why. What is everyone looking at? Is a famous person nearby? We are curious, and we think if other people are spending time to look at something, maybe we should too. We see a somewhat similar behavior on the Web. When someone is looking at something in an image, users look at it too to see what all the fuss is about.

For example, when we asked users to perform a very specific task—to find the search function on the Sony Web site—they found it quickly (**Figure 6.77**). But a photo also caught their attention. Even while completing this very short task, they looked at the attractive man and woman and also at the camera the couple is looking at (**Figure 6.78**). Is the nice-looking couple in the photo looking at a photo they just took with the camera? Whatever they are doing, they appear to be enamored with this camera, so who wouldn't want to look at it too? Our users certainly did.

Figure 6.77 The Sony homepage shows two attractive people smiling at a camera that the woman is holding.

Eyetracking Web Usability

Figure 6.78 Users on a rapid-fire task to find the search engine on this page fixated mostly on that. But they also looked at the faces of the two people and the camera.

When looking at images on the Web, people are drawn to attractive people and the objects of their attention. To entice people to look at an object, use a photo of an appealing, smiling person facing the camera and looking at the object.

On the Comedy Central Web site, people looked at an advertisement of a man happily looking at a mobile device in his hand (**Figure 6.79**). He is not looking directly at the camera, but he is facing it, smiling, and seemingly enjoying the device quite a bit.

Figure 6.79 When entertaining himself on the Comedy Central Web site, a user looked at the smiling man as well as the object he was looking at in an advertisement.

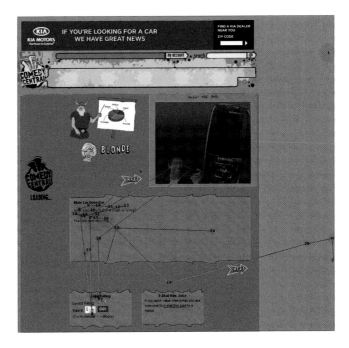

Apparently, our interest in what others are looking at extends beyond humans to other animals, including ducks. On the Berkeley Camera Club site, a user looking at an image of a mallard duck feeding just under the water's surface also looked where the duck was looking—at a shellfish in the sand that the bird appears about to feast on (**Figure 6.80**).

Figure 6.80 A user looked to see what the mallard duck was looking at below the water.

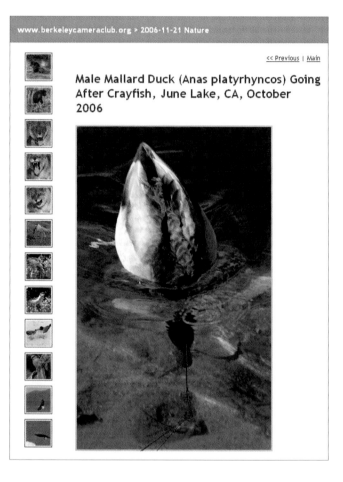

www.berkeleycameraclub.org > 2006-11-21 Nature

<< Previous | Main

Male Mallard Duck (Anas platyrhyncos) Going After Crayfish, June Lake, CA, October 2006

Delicious-Looking Food

Like the mallard duck looking at his shellfish snack, people cannot resist looking at photos of food that looks tasty. And greasy food seems to be one of the strongest sirens on the Web. Who could resist a fat Philly cheese steak or a blue-cheese cheeseburger nestled between two shiny buns (**Figure 6.81** and **Figure 6.82**)? Not our users.

Figure 6.81 Almost good enough to eat: A cheese steak got looks on the *New York Magazine* site.

Figure 6.82 A user looked at the mouth-watering cheeseburger also on this site.

Needless to say, desserts also summon users' fixations. Users who devoured a plate of pasta with their eyes still had room for the photo of a chocolate hexagon cake on the *New York Magazine* site (**Figure 6.83**). And the chocolates on pastry chef Jacques Torres' online store were eye candy for users shopping for a gift there (**Figure 6.84**).

Figure 6.83 A user's eyes greedily consumed the appetizing chocolate cake and plate of lasagna on this site.

Eyetracking Web Usability

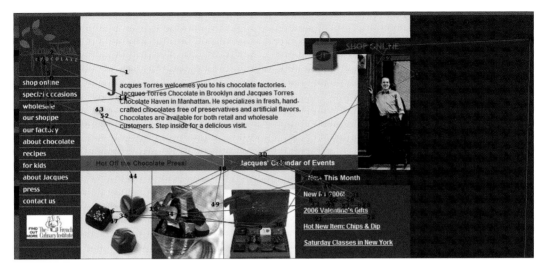

Figure 6.84 Chocolates get looked at on Jacques Torres' site.

The FreshDirect "little man" resurfaces on the upper-right bakery page of the site to draw attention to a seasonal item, Easter cupcakes. But users ignored him to zero in on photos of cookies, just as they did on other pages where he or one of his "colleagues" appears (**Figure 6.85**). (See more on him in the "Originality" section of this chapter.)

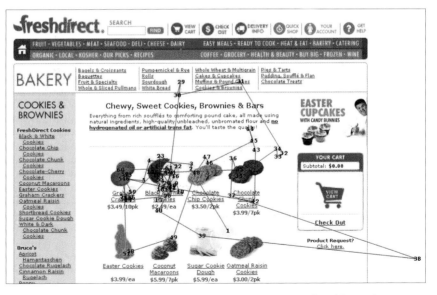

Figure 6.85 A user looked at the images of cookies as she shopped for confections on this site.

Fortunately, people cannot get fat by devouring food images on the Web. And we're happy to report that when they are presented with photos of healthy food—such as a piece of fish on a bed of vegetables —people also look at it (**Figure 6.86**).

People look at images that convey information or processes.

Informational Images

Images that convey information or instructions are the converse of superfluous or generic images. People often give them a good number of fixations, and they are especially helpful for those who are visually oriented. Informational images can stand alone or be used to reinforce or further illustrate text.

With these images, the simpler the presentation, the better. When assigned the task of learning how windmills gener-ate power, many of our users found themselves on kids' Web sites with informational illustrations (**Figure 6.87**). They usually didn't leave, at least right away, because the descriptions and images were especially helpful at breaking down a complex subject (**Figure 6.88**). In fact, in the course of our study, people who came upon children's sites used them for various tasks.

Figure 6.87 On a kids' page of the Energy Information Administration Web site, an adult user found both the text and illustrations about wind energy and windmills very useful.

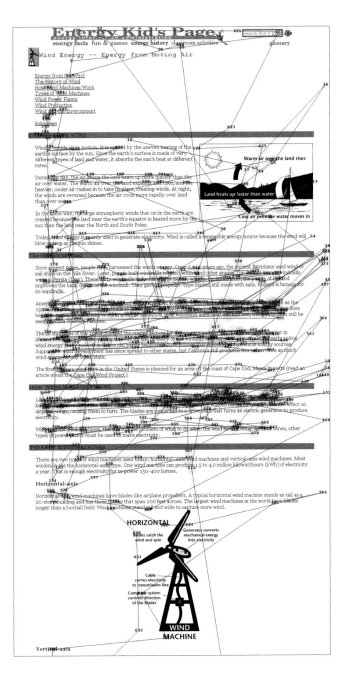

Figure 6.88 These explanatory images make sense of warm and cold air movement.

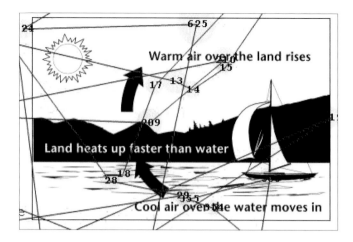

An image certainly does not need to be on a kids' page to be clear and understandable to adults. On another site, a user looked several times at a close-up image of a turbine with the text *How does a wind turbine work?* (**Figure 6.89**). This cue probably coaxes users more than the image without text would. Short explanatory text at the top of the image, callouts, and red arrows work together to attract the user's eye.

Likewise, when researching a telephone headset to buy, users found an instructional image of one headset very helpful (**Figure 6.90**). The image shows how to convert the headset from over-the-head to over-the-ear functioning. People also looked at the short text around the image.

Why Adults Use Kids' Web Sites

Several times during our study, users landed on kids' Web pages, usually via a search engine. Even when they knew or assumed the site was designed for children, they often stayed and used it because the text and images on these sites make difficult information easy to understand. Adult sites can learn from this. Lowering the reading level of your site and offering simple images that convey an idea clearly may help you reach a wider audience.

Eyetracking Web Usability

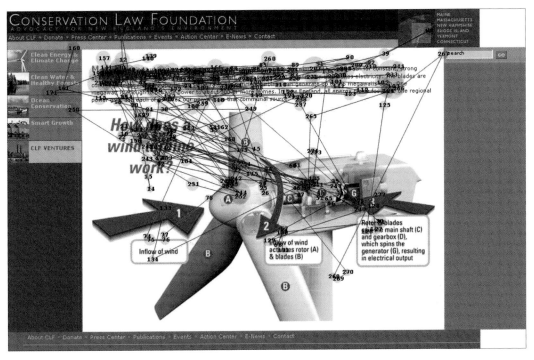

Figure 6.89 A user dissects an image showing how a windmill works on the Conservation Law Foundation Web site.

Figure 6.90 Users found this illustration useful in showing how this headset converts.

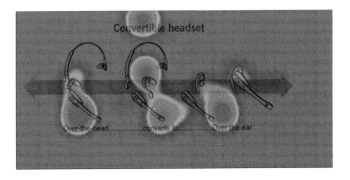

Sometimes people are more interested in an image than text—especially when the technology is the subject. When researching Skype, for example, users were very interested in images of the product's interface (**Figure 6.91**). Even an image on the download page was useful.

Figure 6.91 An image of the Skype interface conveyed a lot of information about the product to this user.

A user researching Skype on another site, Wikipedia, looked thoroughly at a paragraph of text before looking at the image (**Figure 6.92** and **Figure 6.93**). She used the image to supplement what she read about the product in the text. In this case, the image and text worked well together to explain the product.

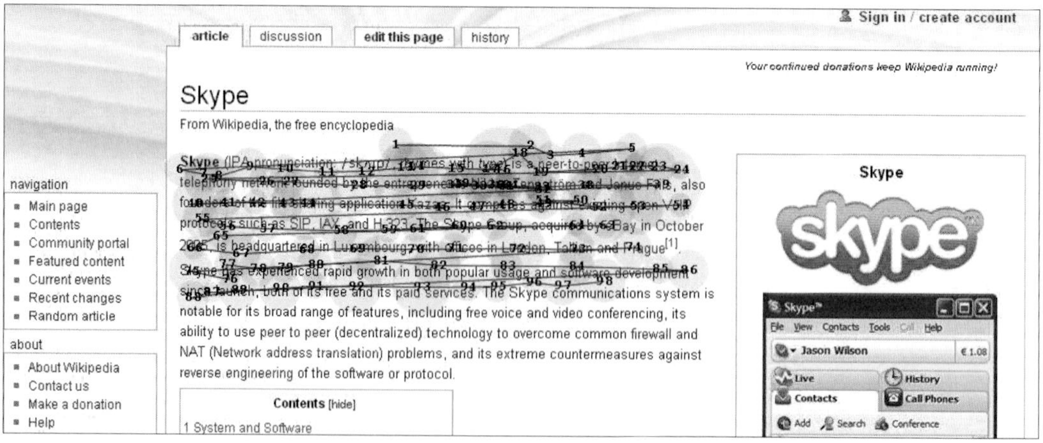

Figure 6.92 A user first looked at the text about Skype on this Wikipedia page.

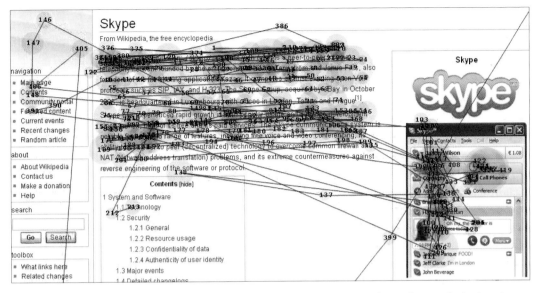
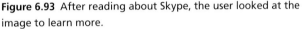

Figure 6.93 After reading about Skype, the user looked at the image to learn more.

Show Screenshots

We know from our separate report on business-to-business (B2B) Web sites that users treasure screenshots on sites that sell software ranging from PC utilities to complicated enterprise solutions.

Why do people look so much at screenshots on software sites? It's because they can often illustrate better than text what software does—and certainly better than the florid and vapid text that B2B sites often employ. Screenshots can also convey an impression of what it feels like to use the product. (And no, it's not enough to offer free downloads of a trial version. Busy systems administrators don't have time to try new software unless it's highly promising. This promise can be demonstrated through screenshots.) Our tip for software screenshots: Whenever possible, offer them in full size.

A page on the Web site for Siemens graphically illustrates how people respond to informational and noninformational images. One user trying to learn about the electronics and electrical engineering organization was drawn by the image of a circle with photos (**Figure 6.94**), which displays the five challenges on which Siemens is working. But he did not look at the generic—and useless—images of a city skyline. Even a human hand could not save this boring grassy field. The lighting takes away any human aspect of the body part.

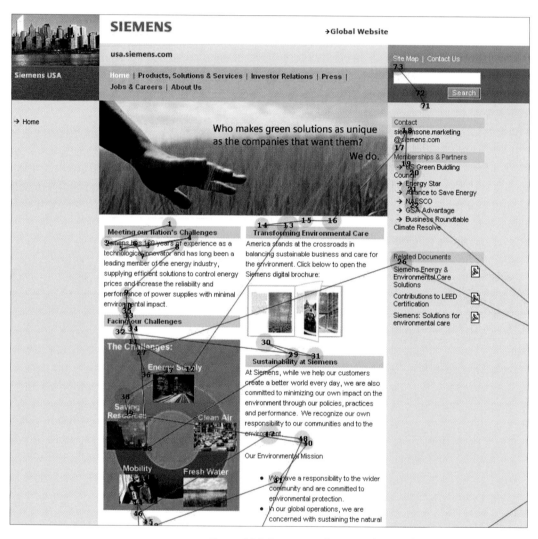

Figure 6.94 A user was drawn to the circular graphic about Siemens' challenges.

In some cases it is easier to explain and understand something via an image than a written explanation. For example, most people know by now that they need to enter the number and expiration date of their credit card to make an online purchase, but they sometimes forget what the verification code is. When buying a gift on the JCPenney site, users looked at the image of a Visa card that shows what the code is and where it's located (**Figure 6.95**).

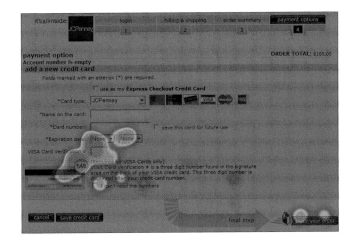

Figure 6.95 Users looked at the Visa card verification image for help when placing an order on this site.

Instructional Images Shouldn't Leave Users Tied in Knots

To see how well instructions are presented on the Web, we gave users a piece of rope and asked them to go wherever they wanted on the Web to learn how to tie a bowline knot. Most did a Google search and ended up on one of the top-selected pages, such as the U.S. Coast Guard Auxiliary site.

The site displays seemingly simple, numbered steps along with illustrations on how to tie the knot, but users had difficulty following them (**Figure 6.96**). First, the text called for action with "the bitter end" of the rope, and most users had no idea which end of the rope was "bitter." Second, the illustrations were almost too detailed. The texture of the rope made it difficult for people to decipher which end was to loop over or under the rope to make the knot (**Figure 6.97**).

Figure 6.96 Users were confused by instructions and illustrations about how to tie a bowline knot on the Coast Guard site.

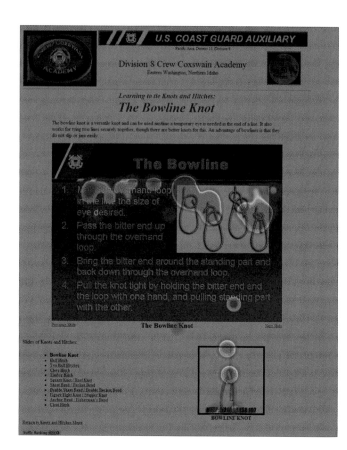

Complex illustrations may look impressive, but simple is better for instructional images. Make them consistent, from using simple illustrations to providing easy-to-follow text.

Figure 6.97 Users looked intently at illustrations of the knot they were trying to tie, as this close-up shows.

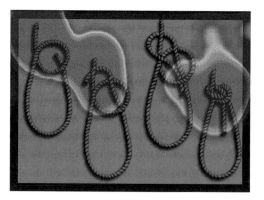

On the other hand, the less-sophisticated illustrations on the Roper's Knot page of Realknots.com tricked users into thinking that tying the knot would be a breeze. Because the rope drawings were simpler—without the rope texture—they were better at depicting when to loop over and under. But by the second illustration, users were still confused. They ended up backtracking to the first step and exhaustively reviewing the images and accompanying text (**Figure 6.98**, **Figure 6.99**, and **Figure 6.100**).

Figure 6.98 The simpler rope drawings on this site should have been easier to follow, but they weren't.

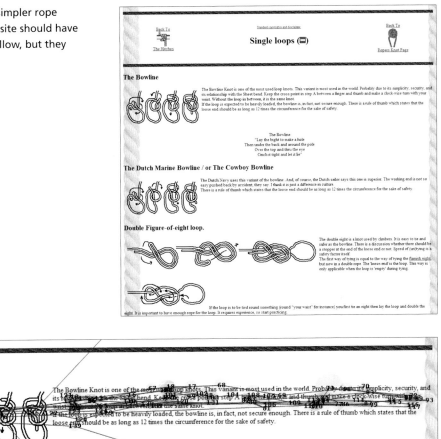

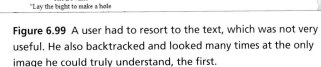

Figure 6.99 A user had to resort to the text, which was not very useful. He also backtracked and looked many times at the only image he could truly understand, the first.

Figure 6.100 Most people who perused images of how to tie a bow-line knot on this site got lost at the second step.

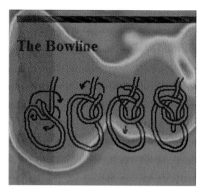

When designing instructional images, tease out each step. It's generally better for users to have clearer images that thoroughly explain a process than fewer images that try to convey too much information.

Maps

People look at maps on the Web, but only those that are easy to read and understand.

On the Sony site, users assigned to find a store location came to a page that featured a map with numbers corresponding to various outlet store locations. But they barely looked at the map because it was difficult to make out the numbers on it (**Figure 6.101** and **Figure 6.102**).

Figure 6.101 Users did not find the Sony Web site's map with hard-to-read numbers very helpful.

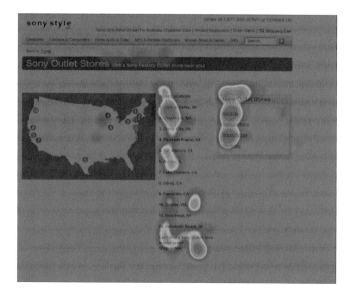

Eyetracking Web Usability

Figure 6.102 A closer look at the map shows that it was hardly looked at.

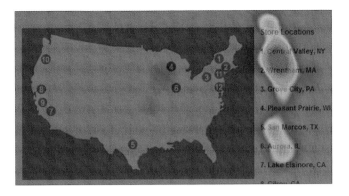

In contrast, users gave many looks to a map of the best stores for men on the *GQ/Details* Web site. The map is well labeled, is legible, and shows good contrast.

Skype uses colors to display its rates for calling areas around the world (**Figure 6.103**). For purposes like this, a map can convey information to users quicker and easier than a list would. But map interfaces should still offer a text alternative for accessibility.

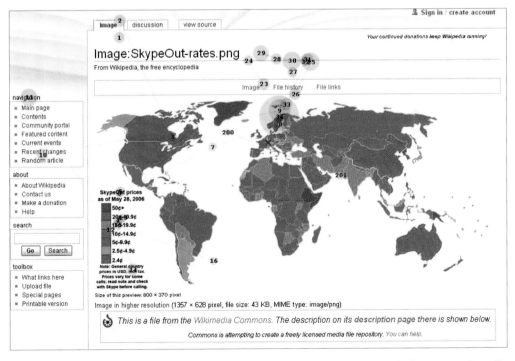

Figure 6.103 A user could see at a glance the least-expensive calling areas of the world on this site.

For people who need directions, maps can help visualize the route to a location and its general whereabouts. For example, users could see the location of various restaurants in a gourmet ghetto on the *New York Magazine* site (**Figure 6.104**).

Ensure that maps have good contrast and labels. Legible maps that convey information get looked at, but confusing elements are ignored.

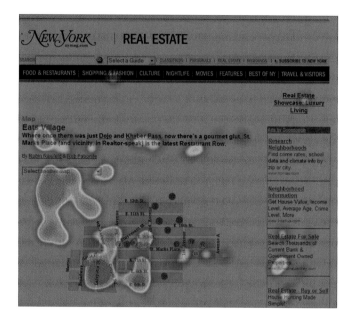

Similarly, good seating charts for theaters, stadiums, and airplanes can also be helpful. On the nytheatre.com site, a chart helped one user choose mezzanine seats over the more expensive orchestra seats for a performance at the Gerald Schoenfeld Theatre (**Figure 6.105**).

Figure 6.105 A seating chart helped this user choose seats for a show.

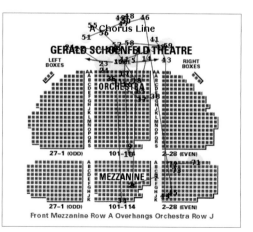

Images That Resemble Advertisements

We often talk about the great role peripheral vision plays in Web navigation. Using this evolved skill, people tune out in advance the images they think will be useless or might hinder their experience, like advertisements. People look at advertisements on the Web sometimes, but if they are not interested in ads at the time, they ignore them. And sometimes people disregard images that only appear to be ads. We refer to this as *erroneous image ignoring.*

Designers may not even realize that an image they are creating looks like an ad. In fact, they may intentionally implement ad-like traits such as bright colors to catch users' eyes on a page of muted tones. But this has the inverse effect.

Users may mistakenly conclude that an image is an ad in the following cases:

- It deviates greatly from the rest of the site in color and style.

- It is placed and shaped like an ad, such as a top, horizontal banner or a long rectangle on the right side.

- It has a single-color background.

- It shows highly formatted text or text and images in the same box.

- It is animated.

For example, users shopping for stereos on the Pioneer Web site consistently ignored the callout navigation in the right-side column of pages. The location, shape, text, and images make this area resemble advertisements (**Figure 6.106**).

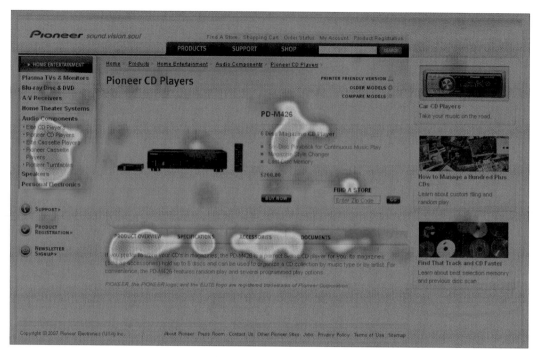

Figure 6.106 Users on this site may never learn how to find tracks and CDs faster because they ignored the ad-like links to the information on the right.

The folks at SpringerLink, a database for journals and references, wanted to advertise to their site's users that the company had won an International Information Industry Award. Too bad they made it look like an ad. Users ignored the blue, white, and red box because of its heavy formatting (**Figure 6.107**).

We discuss traits of advertisements further in Chapter 7. But the message from these few examples is this: If you want people to look at an image, don't make it look like an advertisement.

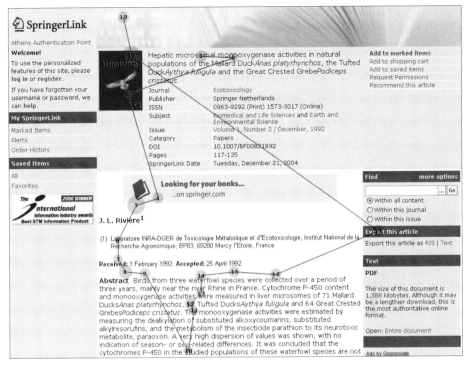

Figure 6.107 Users missed the award badge just below the menu on the left because it was formatted like an ad.

Cartoons and Illustrations

People in our study came across a good mix of photographs, illustrations, and drawings on the Web. We decided to measure whether users look at photos and illustrations equally or at one more than the other. We found that they look at 23 percent of photographs and 14 percent of illustrations and drawings.

In general, people are more attracted to real-life images than to hand-drawn ones on the Web.

Once people look at Web illustrations, however, they look longer and harder at them than at photos. On average, people look at illustrations for 6.59 seconds and about 20.64 fixations and at photos for only 1.18 seconds and 4.4 fixations.

Why such a big discrepancy? The main reason is that illustrations are used more often than photos to demonstrate a process and give instructions. So, users may need to look for several seconds at an illustration that is conveying intricate information but just for a fixation or two at a photo of a person. And many photos simply confirm something users already know, such as what tortellini looks like. An illustration may show them how to fold squares of pasta into perfect little cheese purses and would elicit more fixations.

To be sure, photos can also demonstrate processes and steps. But in general, technical illustrations are more common on the Web than technical photos.

On the opposite end of the spectrum are the cartoon-like illustrations that don't get any looks. When using a kid's Web site to research mako sharks, our adult users typically ignored all the cartoon images (**Figure 6.108**). (If we had kids test on this site, we probably would have seen a different result. We know from our research with children that they love many kinds of pictures on the Web.)

Figure 6.108 An adult user looked at the text but ignored most of the cartoon images of sharks on a kids' educational site.

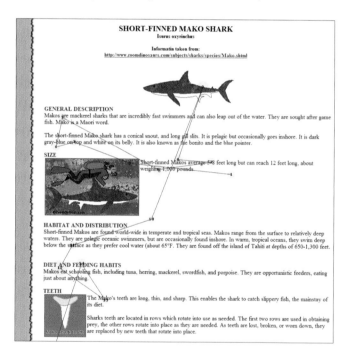

They also ignored them on adult sites. Through a search, a user looking for information on mallard ducks came to a page titled *Canadian Waters* on the Web site for the Fisheries and Oceans of Canada. She was greeted by a cartoon drawing of a flirty fish—which incidentally took up a large chunk of real estate in the upper right of the content area.

Some people might find the fish a friendly addition to the site, but those on a serious search are more likely to ignore it. She looked at the text and other icons but skunked the fish.

However, lured down the page by its clear headings and chunking of text, she did look at other illustrations—those of ducks (**Figure 6.109** and **Figure 6.110**). They are good, clear images with no background, so they are also quite iconic. And they related to both the content of the page and her task.

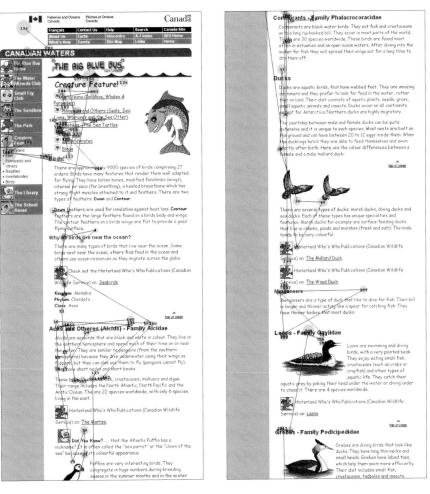

Figure 6.109 A user ignored the cartoon of the silly fish on this site, despite its size and color.

Figure 6.110 She looked at the illustration of ducks farther down the page, however, probably because they were more real looking and relevant.

Earlier in this chapter, we discussed how people often disregard icons on a page. Similarly, users very skillfully avoided almost all the images of a dog in a man's suit that pepper pages on the Dog Owner's Guide site (**Figure 6.111**). Still, they managed to look at much of the text.

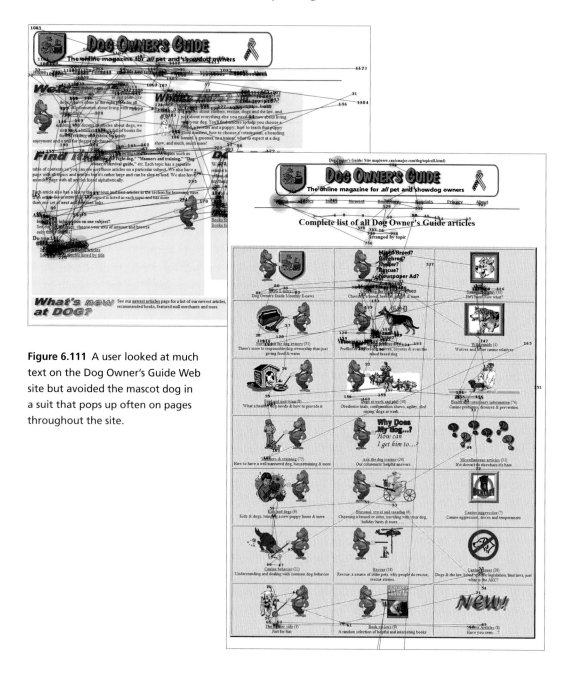

Figure 6.111 A user looked at much text on the Dog Owner's Guide Web site but avoided the mascot dog in a suit that pops up often on pages throughout the site.

> *Don't waste your money or pixels on clip art illustrations. Instead, commission a professional illustrator to draw custom images that can serve as value-added content for your products or services.*

If we exclude instructional illustrations, the time and fixations that users spend on illustrations drop significantly—far below those that they allot to photos. This is not to say that noninformative cartoons or illustrations can't be intricate and highly related to content. But the illustrations we see on the Web are usually more generic—and often ignored.

The lesson? If you can get people to look at your illustrations, they will probably stay for a while. So, make them relevant and worthy of users' attention, with accurate, easy-to-understand details. With photographs, however, ensure that people can get the message you are sending in a very short time and a few fixations because that's all most photographs are ever going to get.

Images in E-commerce

Web designers and marketers have long known the importance of displaying clear images of the products they are selling. For example, when asked to buy a coffee pot on the Mr. Coffee Web site to replace one that a fictitious friend broke, users looked at the model number and description to make sure they found the correct model (**Figure 6.112**). They were also interested in what the pot looked like, so they looked at the image. (This is one case where *we* didn't look at the image carefully enough ourselves. The first user looked at it and said, "I'd really make fun of my friend for this one. How do you break a metal pot?")

Figure 6.112 Users looked at what the replacement coffee pot looked like on the Mr. Coffee Web site.

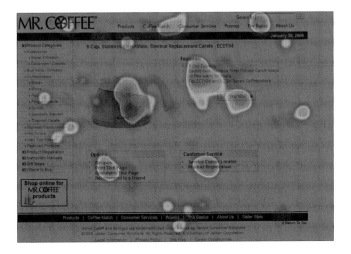

Navigational Images in E-commerce

Even small product images that are often used as navigation should be clear. For example, when looking for items to buy on the Flight 001 Web site, our users looked at the smaller images of travel bags, selected the one they were interested in, and then examined it in the larger image that appears in the upper right of the page (**Figure 6.113**).

Figure 6.113 People looked at the small images of travel bags and especially at the larger image and text on this site.

When category-related navigation images are not different enough from one another or detailed enough to be helpful, people may spend more fixations on the accompanying text and headings. For example, when shopping for a flat-screen TV on the Panasonic site, users looked more at category titles such as *plasma TVs, framed,* and *LCD TVs* than at the images of each type of television (**Figure 6.114**). The titles were simply more helpful than small photos of very similar-looking rectangular boxes. But once users chose a type of TV, they looked at the images on that page (**Figure 6.115**). For example, people who chose to go to the LCD TV page looked at the price, title, details, and small images of various LCD models.

Figure 6.114 People didn't look very much at the tiny, nearly identical TV images on the Panasonic site.

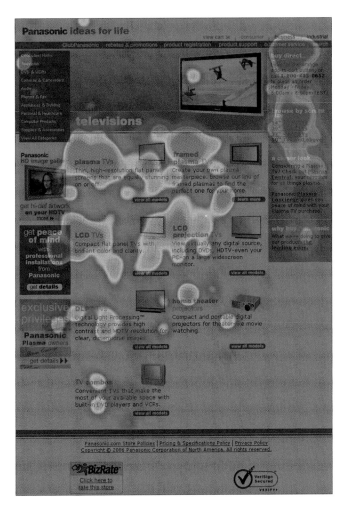

Figure 6.115 But once users chose a category of TVs, they looked at the images in that category.

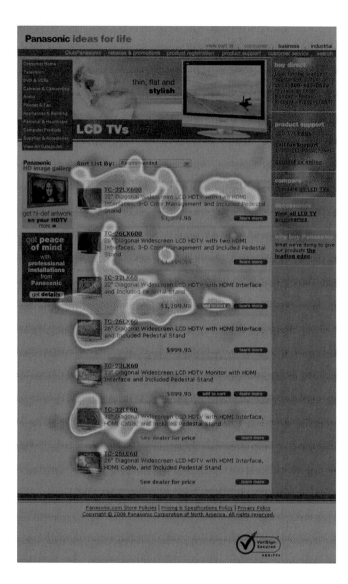

Eyetracking Web Usability

On the FreshDirect site, however, users shopping for apples looked at small images of the fruit even at the category level. Unlike the category-level television photos on the Panasonic site, these images are easy to distinguish from one another because apple varieties look different (**Figure 6.116**). The apples are clear, iconic, and set against a stark white background, which is not boring here because the fruit provides enough mouthwatering color.

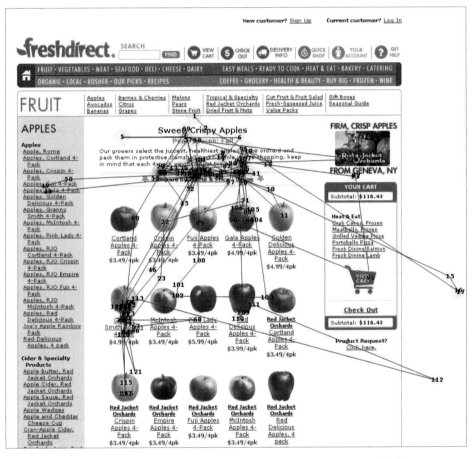

Figure 6.116 Users looked at the small images of different types of apples on this grocery site.

The users also looked extensively at images of the specific apples they were interested in on the product pages on the site (**Figure 6.117**). And they perused images of cheese, wine, meals, and even cuts of meat, even though they were not purchasing the exact item in the photo.

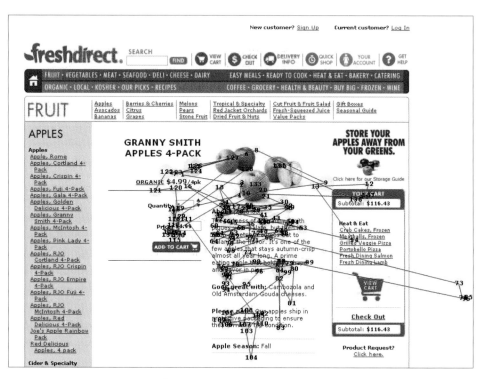

Figure 6.117 A user who selected Granny Smiths looked at the close-up images on the product page. It was a nice touch to display one apple sliced and open.

Display Value-Ad with Product Images

If displaying a product image in various ways will drive home the value to users, then by all means add images, zoom in, or rotate features. Even showing a simple image with a few variations of the product works. For example, when picking a headset to buy on the HeadsetZone site, several users looked at a close-up of the M220C model, along with the descriptive text (**Figure 6.118**).

An image can also help people sort through or remember different products. On the Sears site, we asked users to buy a humidifier for a specific size room and in a specific cost range. A compare table on the site helped them check which of the available models met their criteria (**Figure 6.119**). Even though people paid the most attention to the model descriptions, they still looked at the images of the humidifiers. Some said the images helped them keep the different models straight in their minds.

Figure 6.118 Users found the close-up image of a headset useful on the HeadsetZone site.

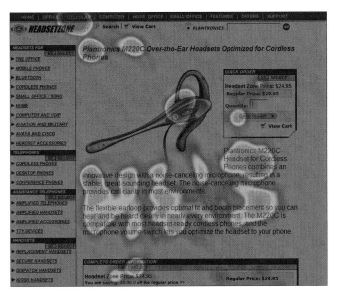

Figure 6.119 For some shoppers, images of different humidifiers on the Sears site kept the information about them from becoming a blur.

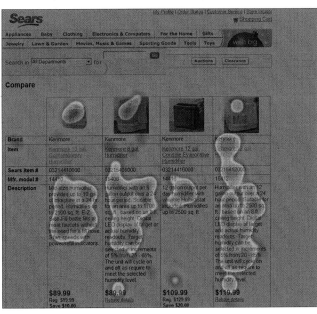

People should be able to zoom in on products that include details they want to see before making a purchase. Typical thumbnail-size images are too small for most people to make out writing in them.

On the Neiman Marcus site, some users were looking at T-shirts with writing on them. Even though the name of each T-shirt is based on the words on the shirt, people don't necessarily look at clothing names. Users always opened the detailed product page, and several people even chose the *Views: Larger* link. Disappointingly, however, this opened a new window with the same size image (**Figure 6.120**). One user remarked, "That's silly. Why would I buy a T-shirt if I can't tell what it says on it?" He's certainly right. The site could have included the text that appears on the T-shirt in the product description or run a close-up image of the writing.

Figure 6.120 Users looked at the writing on the large image of a T-shirt, as well as at the up-sell image on the bottom of this page. It helped that the small image was of high quality.

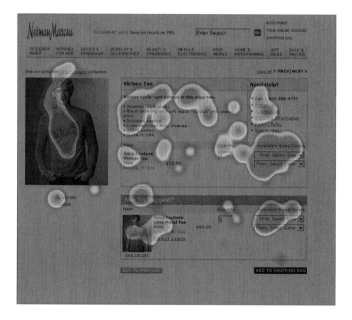

On the Panic Goods Web site, the T-shirt photos were also quite small, and people could not see as much detail as they would have liked. But users who double-clicked the photos could see a close-up of the image on the shirt (**Figure 6.121**).

Eyetracking Web Usability

Figure 6.121 People looked at the T-shirts on the Panic Goods Web site.

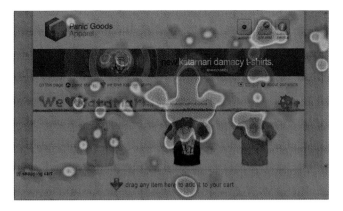

A user who was shopping for a television on the Panasonic Web site chose one by size and price to examine in more detail. A larger image of the TV appears on the page with the detailed description (**Figure 6.122**). The user looked at it extensively and then said, "This looks nice (**Figure 6.123**). I like that it showed the base and they didn't show it mounted on a wall because it would be standing on a base on a piece of furniture in my bedroom."

Figure 6.122 The large images of televisions on the Panasonic Web site are clear.

Figure 6.123 A user inspected the base and screen of a television he was interested in.

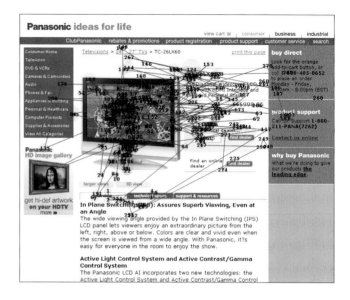

Users try to make out detail in products they are interested in, even in small photos. They are willing to open up larger images too.

In some cases, the name of items in an image can be as important as the image itself. When shopping for paint on the Benjamin Moore Web site, people looked at the color samples, of course. But they also looked quite a lot at the names of the paints (**Figure 6.124**). One user said, "I like the Nantucket Fog and White Dove. I like the names too."

Figure 6.124 A user looked at many evocatively named paint samples before selecting a color.

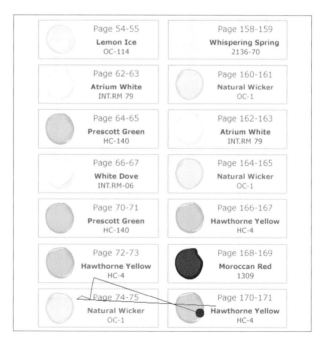

Users looking for a gift of music for a fictitious teenage nephew searched for popular CDs and groups on the Amazon site. They looked at album cover art for clues to a good choice (**Figure 6.125**).

Figure 6.125 Users look at CD cover art, even in small images.

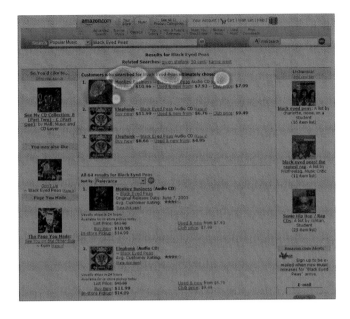

Album Cover Art

We assume that we hardly need to issue a guideline to include album cover art when selling music. Music sites seem to have already figured this out. But why is it that album covers are so useful on music sites?

Ultimately, of course, it's most useful to be able to hear the music—or at least a sample of it—before purchasing a CD, music download, ringtone, or opera ticket. But you can't scan audio clips; you have to listen to them sequentially. In contrast, text and images are scannable.

An album cover is usually a highly designed piece of art that is instantly recognizable. Even the Beatles' *White Album*, which is entirely white, can be recognized by its cover. The style of cover art also evokes the style of the music in a way that a title often can't. A cover with silhouettes of men in powdered wigs playing violins in candelabra light evokes something very different from one of a skinny punk smashing a Fender guitar.

Even though album cover art may seem like the type of frivolous illustration we usually warn against, it is very useful for identifying a specific album, artist, or style of music.

Even when buying products that are not that important to see, people still look at associated images. For example, users looking to buy an antifogging product for their car windshield found Rain-X on the Aum Auto Web site (**Figure 6.126**). Even after thoroughly reading the product description, most users still looked at the Rain-X bottle (**Figure 6.127** and **Figure 6.128**).

Figure 6.126 The Aum Auto Web site offers clear pictures of products.

Eyetracking Web Usability

Figure 6.127 When first learning about Rain-X, a user read the text but did not look at the product image.

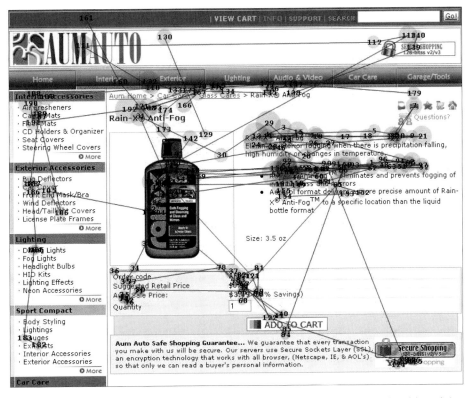

Figure 6.128 After reading the text, he looked at the image of the Rain-X bottle, although it didn't yield new information about the product.

As we have seen elsewhere, when people are really motivated to see certain items, they will put up with subpar images. This is what happened with users buying a baby gift on the *Unique Gifts* page of the JCPenney site. It didn't matter that the images were not incredibly clear because the shoppers had selected to go to this page so they could see images of gifts, and they were willing to look harder at them (**Figure 6.129**).

We are not encouraging you to put bad images on your site, just pointing out that motivated users sometimes cut designers a little slack on detail clarity and size of images.

Figure 6.129 People were willing to look at the somewhat fuzzy images on the JCPenney site because they had selected to go to this page to see baby gifts.

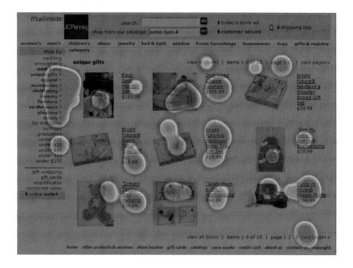

Moving Images

Web sites use animation for five main purposes:

- To get attention
- To show a process
- To show different images and messages on one piece of screen real estate
- To entertain or make a topic more fun or interesting
- To communicate

To users, however, some animation is helpful, and some is distracting and annoying. Keep these general facts in mind when considering whether to put animation on your site:

- People watch instructional animations closely.

- Animations are helpful if they are slow, clear, and controllable.

- It is difficult to read text while watching a demonstration.

- People watch animations when they have time to kill.

- People can be distracted by animations that are not related to content.

And here are two things to keep in mind about Web videos:

- People easily become bored with "talking head" videos. They look away from the video quickly and often, although they still listen to the audio if they are interested in the topic.

- If people choose video content to watch, such as a TV show or well-produced movie trailer, they watch it closely until the end.

At the time of this writing, it is not possible to capture animations and videos in gaze-plot images or heat maps. The researcher must watch the interaction live and in gaze replays. Obviously, we cannot portray moving images in book format, but we can discuss our findings about them.

Animated Progress Indicators

Progress indicators are a must-have for sites with applications, travel sites, and many e-commerce sites, which often need to convey to users that the site is working (not down) or searching for something. They must keep people informed, and maybe even interested enough to wait. If people leave, the organization loses sales. Progress indicators are an excellent use of animation on the Web.

Progress indicators are an excellent use of animation on the Web, communicating to users that the system is working for them. It is helpful to include short explanatory text with progress indicators.

Simple progress indicators help people understand that they must wait a few moments while something loads onto the page. Users often look at text that accompanies animated progress indicators, so in general, it is helpful to include short explanatory text with them.

For example, when people select an MP3 player on the Sony Web site, a progress bar appears (**Figure 6.130**). One of our users read the text that accompanied it and said, "It's loading a 3D product tour." Then he waited for that to happen.

Figure 6.130 The progress indicator animation on the Sony site caught the user's attention.

At checkout on the Kiehl's site, a row of squares animates across the page to indicate to users that they should wait while their order processes. People in our study looked at the words *Processing Order* and the image of people buying items in a Kiehl's store while they waited (**Figure 6.131**).

Figure 6.131 Users looked at the progress indicator animation on the Kiehl's site that told them when their order was processing.

Progress indicators are essential on travel Web sites because people must wait while a plane ticket, hotel, or tour that meets their requirements is searched out and returned. On airline sites, people may wait once to see whether the product they want—such as a ticket from St. Louis to Edinburgh on May 10—is available and then again to find out the price.

The Yahoo Travel site explicitly tells people not to close the window while their search is processing. The ellipsis at the end of the line *We are searching for your hotel...* animates from a period to two dots, then three, back to none, then to one again, and so on. Similarly, Expedia asks users to *please wait* while dots at the bottom of the page animate from left to right.

Some sites use animated progress indicators and their explanatory text as an opportunity for a mild plug—to remind the waiting audience what is special about the site. For example, text on the Cheap Tickets travel site signals to users to wait while the site is *searching for the best deals* for them. Our users read the text because they were waiting (**Figure 6.132**). What else was there to do?

Figure 6.132 The text and progress indicator animation, arrows moving in a circle, drew a user's attention on the Cheap Tickets travel site.

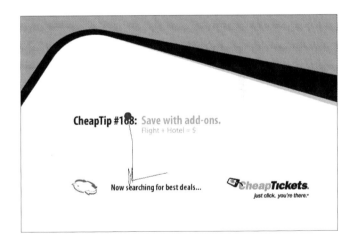

Some sites communicate to users how long they may have to wait for something to process. Liberty Travel tells users that their search may take *up to one minute*. People read this and the text below it—which, incidentally, informed users that the site was checking two databases and *over 1 billion*

fare combinations to better serve them (**Figure 6.133**). And they glanced periodically at the five squares that grew and shrunk to indicate progress.

Figure 6.133 Users looked at the animation and text in the progress indicator on the Liberty Travel site.

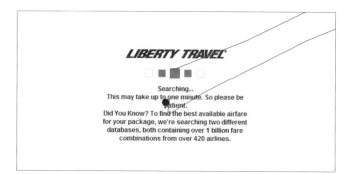

Giving people a processing time can backfire, however. The Priceline progress indicator indicated to users that their ticket search *will just take a few more seconds more!* Unfortunately, this message cycled through three or four times while the search was working (**Figure 6.134** and **Figure 6.135**). Reading a message like this can be reassuring the first time but vexing several times. People start to distrust messages that seem disingenuous. Priceline also runs a few other messages while the search is processing. People read them too, at least the first time they showed up.

Figure 6.134 The *This will take a few more seconds!* message did not fulfill its promise on the Priceline Web site.

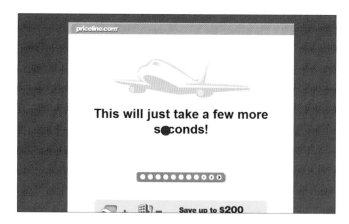

Eyetracking Web Usability

Figure 6.135 Priceline rotated different messages while the yellow progress bar animated. Unfortunately, the same message promising that the search would only take a few more seconds, cycled through a few times during this user's search.

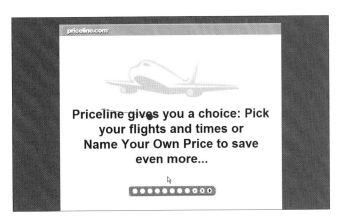

It's a good idea to give people a sense of how long the wait will be but even better to be specific because users appreciate feeling as though they are in control and not at the mercy of a site. But process time is often unpredictable. Our rule of thumb in this area is to under-promise and over-deliver.

Some sites give people links that take them away from their tasks (usually to an ad) while they are waiting for the information they need to complete it. We discourage this. Do you really want to risk losing a captive audience? Users who are waiting for airplane ticket options to appear are full tilt on a purchase, and leading them somewhere else is e-suicide. But giving them information—a little information—without links elsewhere is a good idea.

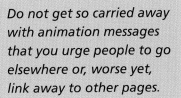

Do not get so carried away with animation messages that you urge people to go elsewhere or, worse yet, link away to other pages.

Whimsical Progress Indicators

Some progress indicator animations add an element of delight to the waiting process. If they are too elaborate, however, users sometimes think they are slowing down the actual process they are waiting on. But a clever, simple element can be appealing to users. For example, a plane flies from left to right on the United Airlines site while a user's flight search processes (**Figure 6.136**). People watched it as it flew, and some smiled. On the Benjamin Moore site, a small can fills with paint as a site search progresses (**Figure 6.137**).

Figure 6.136 The flying airplane progress indicator is a nice touch on an airline site.

Figure 6.137 A user looked at a paint bucket filling up on the Benjamin Moore site. The increasing percentage under the can indicates how much of the search process is completed—and how full the bucket is.

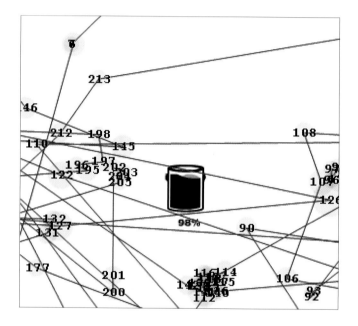

When the subject lends itself to it, an animated progress indicator can be positively dazzling. While the trailer to the Harry Potter movie *The Goblet of Fire* loads on the Warner Bros. site, users are treated to the image of an animated blue flame intensifying and expiring repeatedly in a goblet. Users were mesmerized by it, and it established a magical ambiance even before the trailer began (**Figure 6.138**).

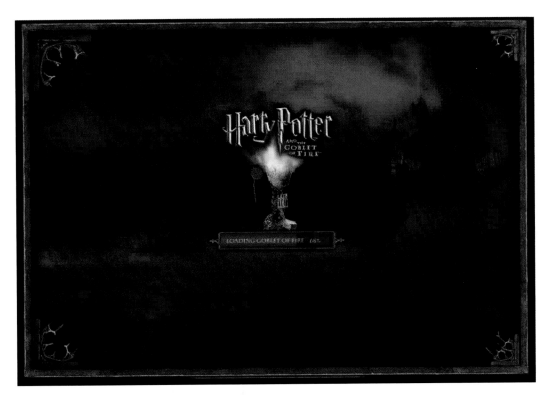

Figure 6.138 People were riveted to the flame progress indicator for a Harry Potter movie trailer.

Give the captive audience some tasty tidbits while they are watching progress animations. Rewarding information or something fun for the eye can make the wait more palatable.

Some progress indicator animation bombs with users even when it is professional and imaginative, however. On the Panasonic site, a flower unfolds as a page loads (**Figure 6.139** and **Figure 6.140**). One of our users said it was pretty, but the rest preferred to look at the pink bar showing the percentage of the page that had loaded. Why didn't people appreciate some lovely animation while they were waiting? First, the animation appeared at the start of users' visit to the site, when they just wanted to load the TV page. They didn't expect to have to wait for pages to load. Second, the blossoming flower was elaborate and unrelated to electronics, which users came to the site to see.

Figure 6.139 Useless beauty: Unlike most users on the Panasonic site, this one looked at the flowering image.

Figure 6.140 She also looked at the percent bar animation to see how soon the page she was waiting for would load.

Designers take a risk when they add unrelated, lengthy, and unexpected multimedia on pages. Some people will find it fun and cool, but some will really dislike it. It's best to do some usability research to see which camp most of your target users fall into before implementing an interface like this on your live site.

Distracting Animation

There are many cases of Web animation that is useless or, worse, distracting. Remember the spinning globes on so many Web pages in the mid–1990s? They became a joke. Sure, they were there to indicate to users that they were on the World Wide Web. But as new as that was, people hitting a site already knew they were on the Web. After all, they had typed in the URL. It was like putting a picture of a bus on a bus so passengers would know they are on a bus. We admit that there was some delight initially in knowing that things could spin on the Web and that we could make it happen. But the novelty wore off, and fast.

On the Panasonic Web site, a large animation of various HD TVs above the heading *Living in High Definition* appears at the top of the homepage. At first, users waited for the animation to finish. But when it continued for more than 20 seconds, they decided to go ahead and make a selection elsewhere on the page. This was not a good way to greet users to the site.

Eyetracking Web Usability

The distracting animation proved to be a bigger issue for a couple of users. They selected the *Live in HD* link in the animation but did not like where it took them, which was to an animated menu with images of products speedily flying everywhere (**Figure 6.141**). They selected *Back* and, when they returned to the homepage, mistakenly selected the link again. It seems that the animation hindered their concentration.

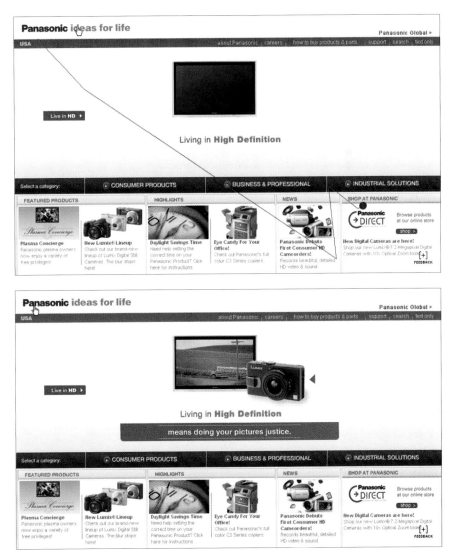

Figure 6.141 Watch out for flying objects: On the Panasonic Web site, products fly across the top of the page. This distracted users.

A cute jumping bunny on the How2 Web site turned out to be a rascally rabbit for some users. The site shows illustrations of a bowline knot in various stages of being tied (**Figure 6.142**). The accompanying text is actually the words of a little ditty that has helped many a Girl Scout or Boy Scout remember how to tie this kind of knot: "The rabbit comes up the hole, goes around the tree, and back down the hole." The jumping bunny, sitting in the middle of the text, is meant to add a cute touch.

Figure 6.142 The hopping bunny in the upper right was meant to be whimsical on this site.

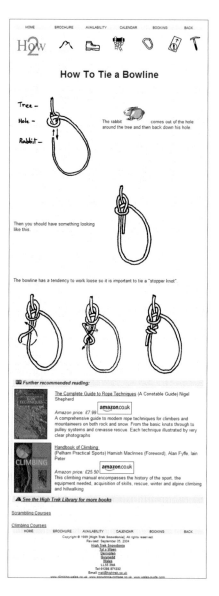

Eyetracking Web Usability

Users couldn't take their eyes off the bunny—even though they wanted to (**Figure 6.143**, **Figure 6.144**, and **Figure 6.145**). They found its hopping, which continues for the duration a page visit, very distracting. One user ended up looking at the bunny as much or more than he looked at the images of the knot or the text about it. He was ultimately very distracted by the energetic hopping, and it hindered his success in tying the knot.

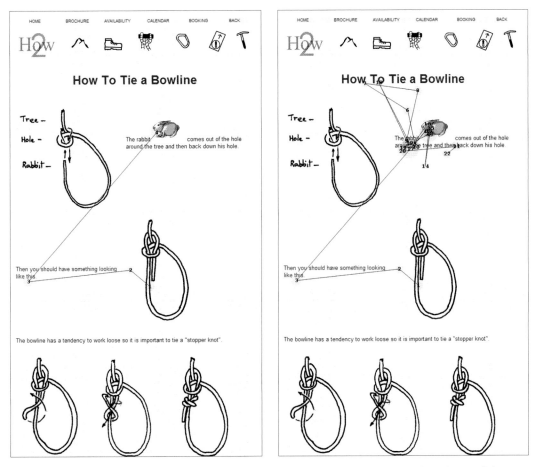

Figure 6.143 A user was instantly drawn to the hopping bunny.

Figure 6.144 The bunny kept hopping, and the user kept looking at it.

Figure 6.145 It keeps going, going, and going: As a user consulted the page while trying to tie a bowline knot, his eye kept getting drawn back to the bouncing bunny.

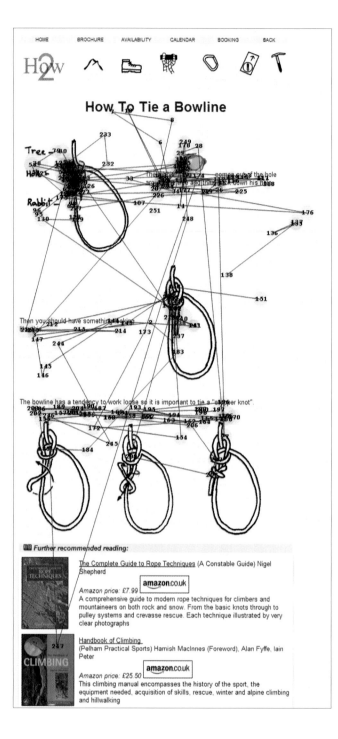

Eyetracking Web Usability

Text that accompanies instructional animation is helpful because it backs up the moving image and can add more information. People consult both. This is also good for accessibility.

A welcoming hop when users first hit the page could be cute, but incessant motion is distracting to people who are trying to concentrate. This was really not a successful animation. In fact, most users who tried to tie the knot using this site failed miserably.

Users had a much better experience and more success with the animation on the Tollesbury Sailing Club Web site (**Figure 6.146**). The animation shows the bowline knot being tied again and again. People looked at the animation and the text that accompanies it (**Figure 6.147**).

Figure 6.146 A rope is formed into a bowline knot repeatedly in this sailing site's animation.

Figure 6.147 By the end of her visit, a user was able to tie the knot correctly after following the animation and reading the text several times.

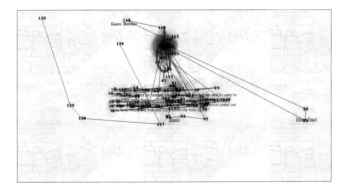

Animation Controls

People are control freaks when they use the Web. And dealing with animation brings out their biggest freak. They want and expect to be able to start, pause, and exit the animation as they see fit. As the ability to do this becomes more and more commonplace on the Web, people become less and less tolerant when they don't have these options.

There were no controls for users to pause, rewind, or fast-forward the knot animation on the Tollesbury site. But this was OK for three reasons:

- The animation is only a few seconds long.

- The animation replays itself automatically, so people can consult a section again, when necessary.

- Users were using their hands to try to a tie knot, so working the PC controls would have been cumbersome.

But in most cases if an animation doesn't have these traits or is missing some of them, it loses it efficacy. The Sony Web site is missing controls for its product tours. A user interested in an MP3 player selected its item details, and a product tour loaded and played automatically (**Figure 6.148**). It is essentially a view of the item as it rotated a full 360 degrees. He watched it closely (**Figure 6.149**).

Figure 6.148 The product tour of the Sony MP3 player shows the product from every angle.

Figure 6.149 A user's eye followed the MP3 player make a full circle on the Sony site.

After it was finished, in about four seconds, he said, "Interesting, but I'd like to see that animation again because I think it just told me how thick it was." He looked all around the item, especially below it, for controls. He continued, "I'd like to see that animation again, but I'm not really sure how." He finally reloaded the page and that worked. But this is a fairly advanced action, and some users did not think to do this, nor should they have to.

On the John F. Kennedy Presidential Library and Museum Web site, the controls for animation are used inconsistently and are not standard, which is confusing. A user taking a virtual tour of the museum watched with interest as a slide show automatically showed many family photos and images of JFK in his youth (**Figure 6.150** and **Figure 6.151**). There was no way to control the tempo, but she didn't notice because she was following along happily.

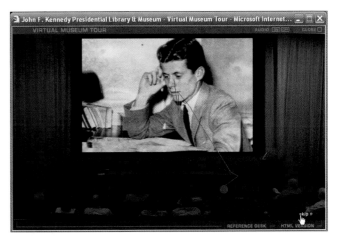

Figure 6.150 A virtual tour of the JFK Library and Museum begins with a narrated slide show of the 35th president's life.

Figure 6.151 A user watched the slide show.

After the two-minute intro, the museum tour began. The user lost interest but did not know how to hide or control it. The rewind, stop, and forward buttons that appeared underneath the image did nothing when she clicked them (**Figure 6.152**). She ignored the photo and started reading the text on the right that accompanies it. Then she looked at the smaller slides at the bottom of the animation window and found that she could use the controls to move through them at the pace she wanted. She continued to look at these for the duration of the tour because they were of more interest to her than the main "show."

Figure 6.152 The user lost interest when the show moved on to a virtual tour of the museum, but she looked below at the images in the film strip, which she could control, as the video continued.

TV and Movies

If people won't even waste one fixation on an image that doesn't interest them, imagine how parsimonious they are with animated content. Especially if they have invested time waiting for it to load, it had better be worthwhile.

Some content that was created for another medium, such as television or the movie screen, does not translate well to the Web. For example, people are quickly bored with "talking head" newsreels because visuals of a single person staring at the camera and talking get old quickly to users. One person on the CNN site looked at a doctor talking about the Hurricane Katrina rescue efforts, but his eye also wandered to the sign behind the man, the video controls, and elsewhere on the page as he listened to him speak (**Figure 6.153**).

Figure 6.153 A user looked at the VCR-like controls and links to other stories when he grew tired of looking at the "talking head" on the CNN site.

Note: Gaze plots do not work for video, so this is a rare heat map of a single user's visit to a page.

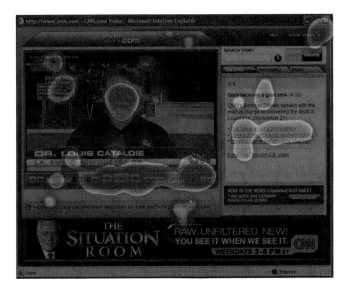

On the other hand, the trailer for the Harry Potter movie *The Goblet of Fire* translates well to the Web. Although it is small, the quality is high, the subjects appear mostly in the middle, and the content is fast-moving and exciting. Those users who found it were riveted to it (**Figure 6.154**). The only negative to watching the trailer on the Web is trying to read the tiny *coming soon* text that appears at the end. It was obviously designed for a large movie screen.

Figure 6.154 From Professor Dumbledore and the goblet of fire to a row of students from Beauxbatons Academy of Magic to the faces of Harry and his friend Ron, users were riveted to the *Harry Potter* movie trailer at the Warner Bros. site.

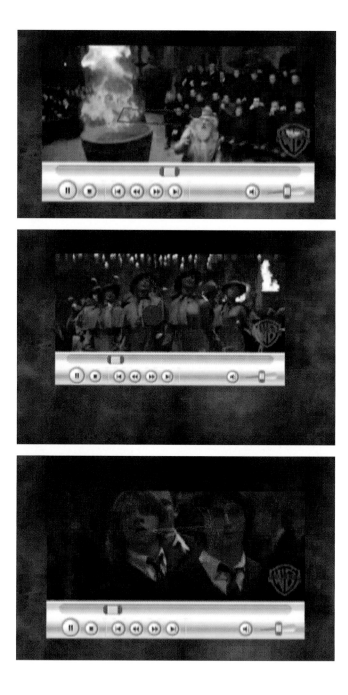

People can easily switch gears from actively navigating to passively watching TV shows on the Web. As long as they have selected to watch a show, they enjoy and pay attention to it, even if it is very small.

On the Comedy Central site, users looked at videos of the *South Park* television show. Although the videos were not created for the Web, they were clear and simple enough that people had no trouble seeing and focusing on the characters (**Figure 6.155** and **Figure 6.156**). And while waiting for the videos to load, people could look at a list of other featured videos to see what else they might want to watch.

Figure 6.155 A user looked at the face of the *South Park* character Butters as he spoke in a video on the Comedy Central site.

Figure 6.156 The user found the face and backside of a mooning Jesse Jackson easily decipherable in another *South Park* video.

The Evolving Web User

Remember, as the presentation of photography, illustrations, animation, and video gets better and better on the Web, users will come to expect more of them. Years ago people did not want to watch video in usability sessions. They were conditioned to it being too long, poorly produced, or crashing. But today, in our test sessions, several people chose to watch TV shows they had missed, such as a recent episode of *American Idol*. Others wanted to go to YouTube to see something a friend had recommended. For example, one had been told about a video of two otters floating and holding hands. People watched these videos intently, as if they were watching television.

It is impressive to see how smoothly users can switch gears from *pull media* such as the Web, where they are in control and clicking furiously, to *push media*, where they sit back and watch content streaming to them once they have chosen what video to watch. It's also intriguing to see people ignore bad images and fixate on helpful, interesting ones. These are signs of how people are evolving and flourishing on the Web. We can't wait to see what happens next.

7 Advertisements

Eyetracking usability research helps us determine when and how much people look at advertisements on the Web and what attributes of ads attract their attention. This interaction occurs before those that business stakeholders and ad executives use to measure an ad's effectiveness, such as clicks, site visits, and revenue generated. Eyetracking tells us that people look at ads that seem helpful at the moment they encounter them—whether they are rushing to find specific information or just shopping around. The look of an ad is important, but so is its placement on the page. In this chapter, we discuss what makes an ad attract or not attract people's eyes.

As people traverse the Web, they look at a little more than one-third—36 percent—of the ads on the pages they visit, except on search engine results pages (SERPs). This is not a bad rate of looks. However, the time and fixations they give to ads is quite low—an average of about one-third of a second and only 1.5 fixations. One-third of one second is not long; it was over before you read the entire word *one* at the beginning of this sentence. That's certainly not much time to convey a complex marketing idea.

This leads to the most ironic finding in all of our eyetracking research: The ads that are usually the most expensive to produce—graphical ads and graphical animated ads—are usually much less attractive to people than simple text ones. And by *attractive*, we mean what users naturally gravitate to and look at *in practice*, not what people *say* is attractive when asked to look at a particular ad. We get different answers in in interviews, focus groups, and surveys than we do when we analyze actual behavior. And we'd probably get different answers if we studied ads on billboards or the side of a bus.

Advertising on the Web is said to generate billions of dollars. One look can be the difference between a sale or no sale. And getting no looks definitely means no sale. Yet we commonly see users ignoring many ads while they look all around them. Read on to see how to make sure your ad is look-worthy.

It's a Jungle Out There

Unlike our ancient ancestors, modern Web users don't need to defend themselves against all manner of physical danger—from starvation to saber-toothed tigers to scarlet fever. But sitting in front of a glowing computer, sometimes for eight hours a day, has its own dangers. It has made people vigilant about protecting themselves from the barrage of ads and useless material multiplying on the Web. Users have developed instinctive and nearly instant ways to weed them out, almost without even looking at them. Ignoring unhelpful ads is simply a survival technique.

This evolution of the Web user is a rapid and unforgiving process. As fast as ads and user interface (UI) elements transform, so do users. Even new users quickly learn about

> People only look at
> 36 percent of ads.

Eyetracking Web Usability

user interfaces and the UI elements that will help or hinder them. It's not clear if people even realize that they are purposefully "defending themselves" by avoiding poorly laid-out text or unrelated animations on the Web, but they certainly do it when they think information or ads might waste their time or, worse, open a myriad of pop-up windows they did not mean to conjure.

Since even Web early-adopters have been using the Web for less than 20 years, we could call this defense mechanism a rapid evolutionary response. Scientists used to believe it took thousands of years for a species to change and defend itself against a new predator, but now we see examples of a faster form of evolution. In 2006, researchers discovered that the blue mussels of Maine were being easily crushed and gobbled up by a new marauder, Asian shore crabs, which had somehow made their way to the northeastern American coast in the late 1980s. Yet within about 15 years, the unprotected mollusks noticeably thickened their shells as a defense against crustaceans.

So it is goes with the Web. Like the blue mussels of New England waters, thin-shelled users—those who have no defense against ads and other elements—are easy prey, while those who thicken their shells against attack survive and thrive.

When People Look at Ads

Users may tune out items that simply appear unneeded, at least peripherally, even if a closer look could have revealed some usefulness.

Before we discuss the attributes of ads that draw or repel Web users, let's look at how a user's state of mind and what the user is doing on the Web affects fixations.

Doing Tasks vs. Browsing

First, let's consider people's behavior off the Web—at a supermarket. Say a woman needs gorgonzola-stuffed Spanish olives, and she is a brand loyalist. She is not very likely to notice sales or new products as she beelines to the olive section to do this specific, directed task. But other times she may stroll the grocery store aisles in search of sales and ideas. At these times, she's open to checking out the two-for-one granola special and tasting a guacamole sample.

Not surprisingly, users with a specific task look at only about one-third of the ads they encounter. Surprisingly, users browsing freely on the Web look at only 5 percent more ads than those on task.

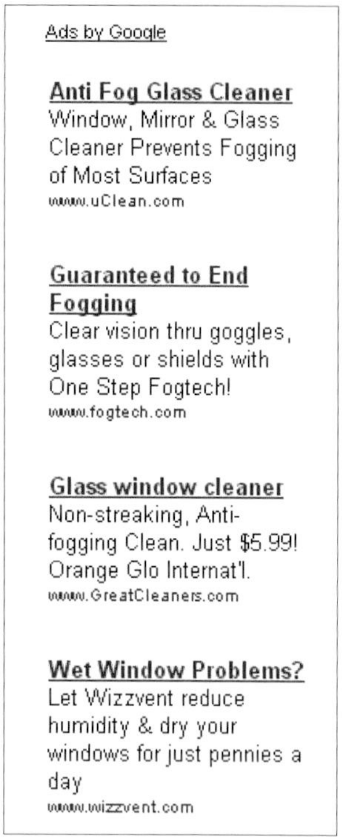

Ads by Google
Anti Fog Glass Cleaner
Window, Mirror & Glass Cleaner Prevents Fogging of Most Surfaces
www.uClean.com
Guaranteed to End Fogging
Clear vision thru goggles, glasses or shields with One Step Fogtech!
www.fogtech.com
Glass window cleaner
Non-streaking, Anti-fogging Clean. Just $5.99! Orange Glo Internat'l.
www.GreatCleaners.com
Wet Window Problems?
Let Wizzvent reduce humidity & dry your windows for just pennies a day
www.wizzvent.com

Figure 7.1 A close-up of the sponsored links, which advertise many defogging products.

Similarly, on the Web, users who want to check their bank statement or find the best way to prune a weigela shrub are less interested in ads than in getting that specific information. As designers, we might then expect that when they're not on task, they'd be far more likely to look at ads, like the woman browsing at the grocery store. However, this is not the case. People who are browsing look at only 5 percent more ads.

When focused on specific tasks, people look 34 percent of the time, for an average of 1.44 fixations, at text and graphical advertisements (not including sponsored links on SERPs). When browsing openly, people look at 39 percent of ads, for 1.56 fixations on average—an increase of about one-tenth of a fixation.

People Doing E-commerce Tasks

The exception to this rule is when people are doing e-commerce tasks: They tend to look at ads more than when doing other types of tasks or browsing. This is partly because today's Web shopper is painfully aware of discounting. We frequently see Web shoppers searching for coupons.

People also look at sponsored links because they help them answer a variety of shopping questions, such as the following:

- Does a product even exist that meets my need or desire?
- What are some related products that I might also want to buy?
- I know what I want to buy, but where can I buy it and get the best deal?

For example, when we asked users to find out how to keep car windshields from fogging, several people ended up on the eHow Web site. They read the site's instructions for keeping windshields clean but also got an idea of products they could buy for that purpose in the sponsored text links on the right (**Figure 7.1** and **Figure 7.2**).

Figure 7.2 A user on a mission to find a windshield defogger was as interested in the related sponsored links as the instructional text on the eHow site.

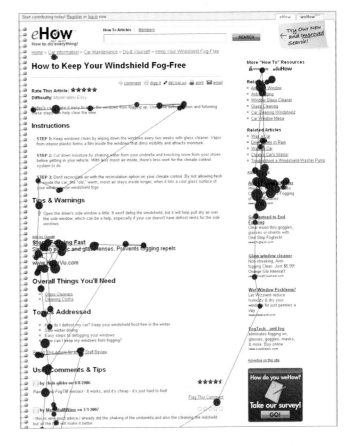

Even when open to viewing advertisements while shopping, users are more attracted to text ads than to glossy ones. One user trying to find a CD gift for a teenager looked for suggestions on the right-side sponsored links on the Google SERP (**Figure 7.3**).

One might think that only people who are decidedly shopping would read sponsored links. Not true. People who aren't looking for suggestions for products to buy also look at text ads. A user interested in investing for retirement did a Google search for his bank, UBS. He looked at the organic results on the SERP but also looked thoroughly at the sponsored results on the right (**Figure 7.4**).

Figure 7.3 A user looking for a music gift seached for "music Web sites for teenagers." On the results page, he looked thoroughly at the sponsored links on the right for some helpful suggestions.

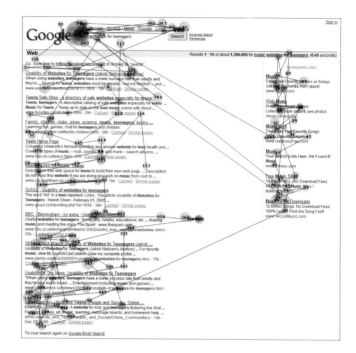

Figure 7.4 A user searched for the UBS bank specifically but also looked at the sponsored links on the right.

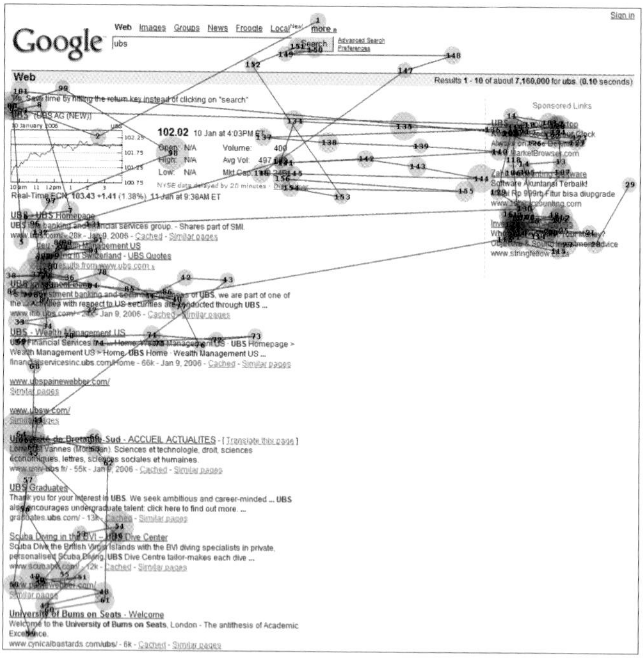

Sometimes people look at ads and sponsored links that they have no use for. For example, a user researching how fast a mako shark swims didn't want to buy a shark no matter how good a deal was offered. Yet he looked at the two sponsored links at the top of a Yahoo search page (**Figure 7.5**). Or what of the user trying to learn how to tie a bowline knot? He just wanted instructions, not a new necktie, but he looked at the sponsored links for neckties on the right (**Figure 7.6**).

Figure 7.5 A user researching mako sharks was not shopping for a shark, but he still looked at the top sponsored links on a Yahoo SERP.

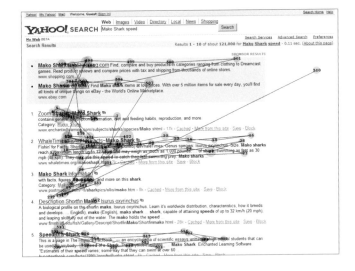

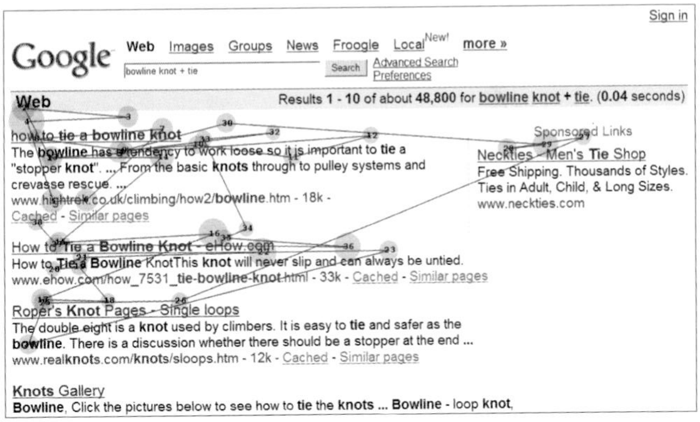

Figure 7.6 A user gave three fixations to a sponsored link for men's neckties on a Google SERP, although his task was to learn to tie a bowline knot.

Tasks usually have very little effect on how much people look at ads specifically. But tasks affect how people look at Web pages in general. The simplest examples of this in our study occurred during "rapid-fire" tasks, when we asked people to locate various elements of Web pages and then launched the sites to see where they looked for them. Depending on what we asked people to do, their eyes would shoot to various places on the page, even on the same Web site. For example, users automatically looked to the upper right for the site's search or shopping cart, but they looked to the top left for the logo and the top and left rail for the menu—all different places, depending on the task at hand. And when we asked them to read the news on a news site, people often looked first at the headlines and then at the content for only the headlines in which they were interested. They didn't look first at the actual stories or the menus for other choices. But when specifically looking for sports news, for example, users looked to the tabs or menus for the *Sports* section.

How Different Types of Ads Fare with Users

People look most at ads that they can get something from in less than a second and a couple of fixations. Here's how that breaks down by type of ad (**Figure 7.7** and **Figure 7.8**):

- **People look at 88 percent of ads that match the style of the site.** This may be because they think that these ads are internal promotions, which users have learned are more credible and usually more helpful for their tasks. They may also mistake these ads for navigation because they look so much like other features on the site.

- **People look at 52 percent of text ads.** Text, text, and more text may not be exciting, but it gives people the feeling that they will get information soon and without having to look very hard. Also, in recent years, many users have come to feel that Google = Good. For this and other reasons, text ads sponsored by Google, which are often on the right side of a page, have positive connotations and get looked at.

Figure 7.7 People most often look at ads that match a site's style.

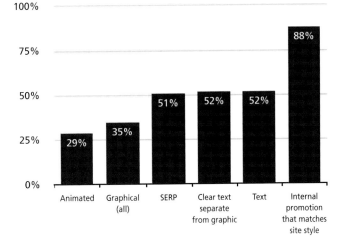

Types of Ads: Percent Fixated On

Figure 7.8 People look the least at animated ads.

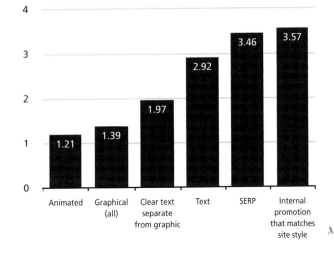

Types of Ads: Average Fixations

- **People look at 52 percent of graphical ads with separate images and text.** People like ads in which the text is separated from the graphic and is legible. Images give some excitement to these ads and draw the eye, but a few accompanying words of big block text on a plain colored background is a draw as well.

- **People look at 51 percent of sponsored links on SERPs.** This includes sponsored links on the top and right of pages, but not on the bottom. Users have evolved to expect that sponsored links on SERPs are related to their queries and can be helpful. Some less-experienced Web users may also look at them because they mistake them for organic links.

- **People look at 35 percent of graphical ads with text on an image.** Users look at 35 percent of ads where text appears on top of a textured background. Text on any kind of pattern or embellished backdrop is more difficult to read and thus less attractive to users than text on a plain background.

- **People look at 29 percent of animated ads.** Users look at animated ads less than at any other type of ad. Animations may sometimes catch the eye, but most users have been annoyed by animated ads in the past and have sworn them off.

Not surprisingly, people give more fixations to the types of ads they look at most often, with one exception. They give more fixations to SERP-sponsored links than one might expect. It seems that once people decide to look at one of these links, they are somewhat hooked, because the topic often relates to their query.

The Impact of Ad Placement

An ad's position on the page helps determine whether users look at it. No matter what the shape, content, or design of an ad, a poor location can keep it from getting even a look from users.

When it comes to graphical ads without text, people look at more ads on the right of pages, 37 percent, than at those at the top, 27 percent. They also give more fixations to ads on the right (provided they are "above the fold"), 1.51 on average, compared to 1.05 for those on top.

There are a few likely reasons for this, none having to do with content. The first is **banner blindness**, the phenomenon of users tuning out banners. Ignoring right ad banners is slightly less ingrained than top banner blindness. (As Web users continue to advance, this may change.) Second, the right rail area of the page often includes related links, menus, and other information that's part of the UI. So, people are more likely to look there because they expect UI elements to be there. Third, once you tune out a top banner, there is really no reason to be hanging out way up at the top of a page. But people are often near the right rail area when using a page, particularly when using the scroll bar, so they have more chances to see ads there.

The opposite is true with text ads on SERPs, where people look more than twice as much at sponsored links at the top of a page, 78 percent, than at those on the right, 33 percent. They also give right-side links just 1.93 fixations and about .7 seconds, compared with 5.35 fixations and 2.1 seconds on top sponsored results.

People have come to trust search engines to return information they want, even in sponsored links. So, they are unlikely to ignore sponsored links that appear first on the page, before and above the search results. People also tend to think that the content on the right side of a SERP is less important, and they're not likely to stop scanning the center of the page, where the organic results are, to zigzag way over to the paid ads on the right. (For more information about user behavior on SERPs, see our report about eyetracking search, available for download at *www.nngroup.com/reports/reading.*)

Ad Relativity and Competition in User Interfaces

More important than where an ad is placed on a page is its placement in relation to other content. For advertisers and internal marketing teams, choosing which pages to put an ad or promotion on is a challenge because everything on a page is vying for users' attention. On the one hand, you want your ad or promotions to be on a page that gets many hits because it increases the probability of your ad getting looks. On the other hand, pages are usually hit-getters because they have good, desired content. And if the content is very riveting, users may never even look at the ads.

Advertisers, marketing professionals, and site designers should consider how an ad will work with the rest of the items on a page. They should assess what other elements will compete with the ad and whether interface elements that meet the needs of most users' top tasks appear before the ad. (See more on top tasks in Chapter 3, "Page Layout.")

In an example from our study, many users who were asked to set up a ski vacation to Colorado went to the Expedia site, where they were greeted with an application to book

> On most Web pages, people look at graphical advertisements on the right more than at the top. The opposite is true on SERPs, where people look at sponsored ads at the top more than those on the right.

air and hotel—probably the site's most important feature—right on the homepage. This is appropriately placed, and users appreciate not having to hunt around for it, click menus, or search. Instead, the input fields for their destination and dates of travel are very handy.

There is also a major promotion for travel deals on the right side of the homepage, next to the input area. It is a professional graphic design, has images and text, animates, and takes up at least 20 percent of the page "above the fold." And almost every user ignored it (**Figure 7.9**).

Figure 7.9 Users scheduling a trip to Colorado ignored an ad for Las Vegas on this site, even though it is large, is colorful, and animates.

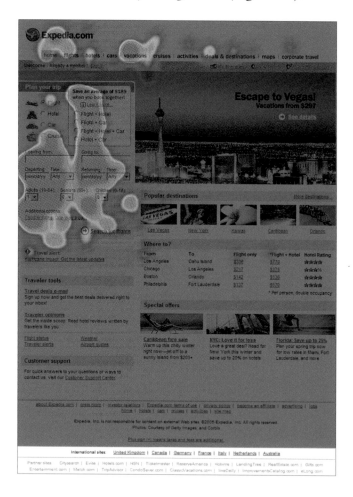

Eyetracking Web Usability

The ad designers probably thought this promotion would attract people because it is large, is colorful, is at the top of the page, is pretty to look at, and animates periodically. But these are not traits that attract people to ads on the Web. Instead, our users checked the logo and site name to confirm where they were, saw the fields to book a trip, started doing the task, and did not look further around the page or at the ad, even when it animated.

Users responded similarly on the MapQuest Web site. When they hit the page, they saw an input field and a search field in the upper left. Most did not look around the page for more features, and they didn't look at the large, colored Dell computer ad in the prominent top-right position. It didn't stand a chance against the core site features (**Figure 7.10**). And if users had looked, the ad's irrelevance to their reason for being there would have deterred them from lingering for another fixation. Another problem is the ad's presentation: Graphics with tiny text squished toward the top of the box on an embossed background add up to an ad that people ignore.

Figure 7.10 Users zoomed in on the two features that could aid them in their tasks on this page—an input field and a search box—and never looked at the large ad for Dell computers.

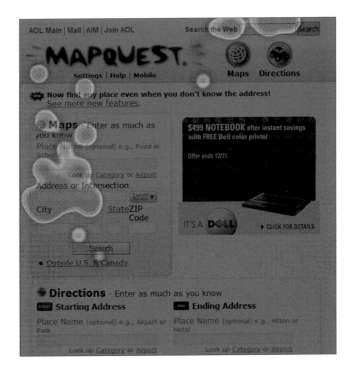

Some ads are victims of momentum behavior (discussed further in Chapter 8, "User Viewing Behaviors on the Web"). As you know, many users doing a Web task block out what they don't think they need. And if they see something that works well enough for them, they don't bother looking further for something even better.

In one very extreme example, a user who was determined to do a search on Yahoo looked at nothing but the search box, ignoring all the other information on the page, including the text ads on the right, when they could have helped her (**Figure 7.11**).

Advertisers should try to place their ads on a page with content that interests users or helps them get a task done but doesn't monopolize their attention. Advertisers may choose to place their ad on a page that includes the application that users come to the site for, but that application will be tough competition for their ad.

Figure 7.11 Too much information: A user went to the search box and stayed there, avoiding the rest of this busy page.

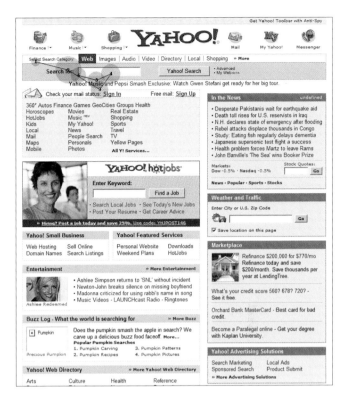

Banner Blindness

Although banner ads at the very top of pages are the first thing presented to users, people still manage to tune them out because of banner blindness.

As we have mentioned, ads at the top of a page are often doomed by users' banner blindness. In one task, we took users to the *New York Post* Web site and asked them to see whether anything there interested them. Several people went to the daily horoscope page, where they could choose their astrological sign from a drop-down list. Most users read the short horoscope very thoroughly but did not look at the animated Verizon advertisement below the main horizontal navigation and above the page content (**Figure 7.12**). (They also did not look at the graphical ad to the right about a "terrifying new thriller.")

Figure 7.12 A user with well-developed banner blindness read every inch of her horoscope but snubbed the prominent Verizon ad above it.

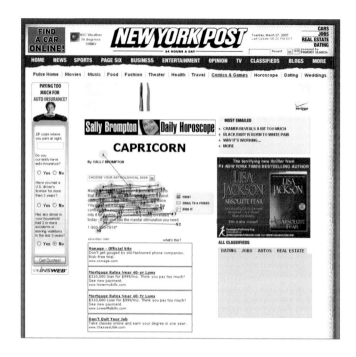

Similarly, on the LiveScience Web site, a user reading about how windmills generate power scanned text ads on the right but was blind to the Neiman Marcus banner ad at the top (**Figure 7.13**).

There are also cases of **reverse banner blindness**, when users look at an ad that appears in an area where they are expecting to see something else. On the Learnthings site, for example, a user looked at the banner ad that appears where a logo would normally be and then to the right to find the organization's logo (**Figure 7.14**).

Figure 7.13 A user ignored the top banner and instead read about the workings of windmills on this site. Two saccades pass across the vertical SkyQuest ad, but the user didn't see either one. Remember that the human eye is blind during its fast and blurring movement from one fixation to the next.

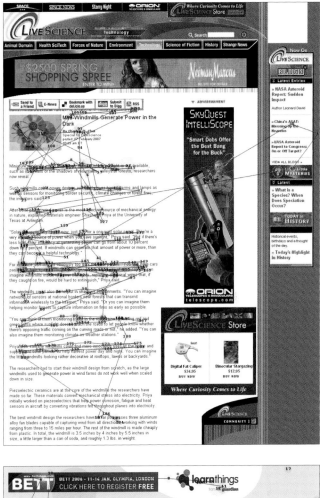

Figure 7.14 A user accidentally looked at the ad on the left when she was actually looking for the organization's logo, which appears, unexpectedly on the right.

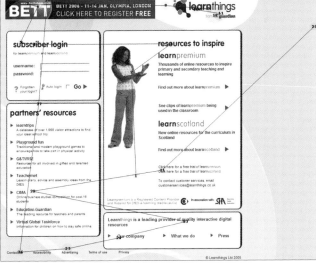

Text (Sponsored Link) Ads

The most unexciting ads visually, sponsored links, are magnetic for a few reasons. First, they are now a standard feature, and many people know what they are. Second, their content is related to the topic users are interested in. Finally, their design—simple black or blue text on a white background—is easy to scan and read. It doesn't compete with the message. In fact, sponsored links may be more of a challenge for advertisers than graphical ads because they must convey everything with only a small number of words.

Why People Look at Sponsored Links on SERPs

Text advertisements on SERPs are a completely different animal from ads on other pages. Various traits of sponsored links on SERPs make them especially intriguing to Web users:

- Sponsored links are almost always exclusively text, and text ads are generally easier to register than graphical ads.

- Sponsored links typically are related to the user's search query and therefore more likely than random ads to lead to something of interest to them. And as Web users have evolved, they have learned that the best deals are often found in the smallest ads.

- SERP ads are easy to pick out because they are in two standard locations: across the top and down the right side of the page. Some also appear at the bottom, but they are very rarely looked at.

- Sponsored links are almost always labeled *Sponsored Links.* Although most people don't necessarily see that label, those who do read it know what these items are.

- It's less of an imposition to look at a sponsored link on a SERP than to look at an ad on other pages. Users on a SERP are scanning results. The only competition in the UI are other results, all formatted similarly, so users need not break their focus to look at them (**Figure 7.15**).

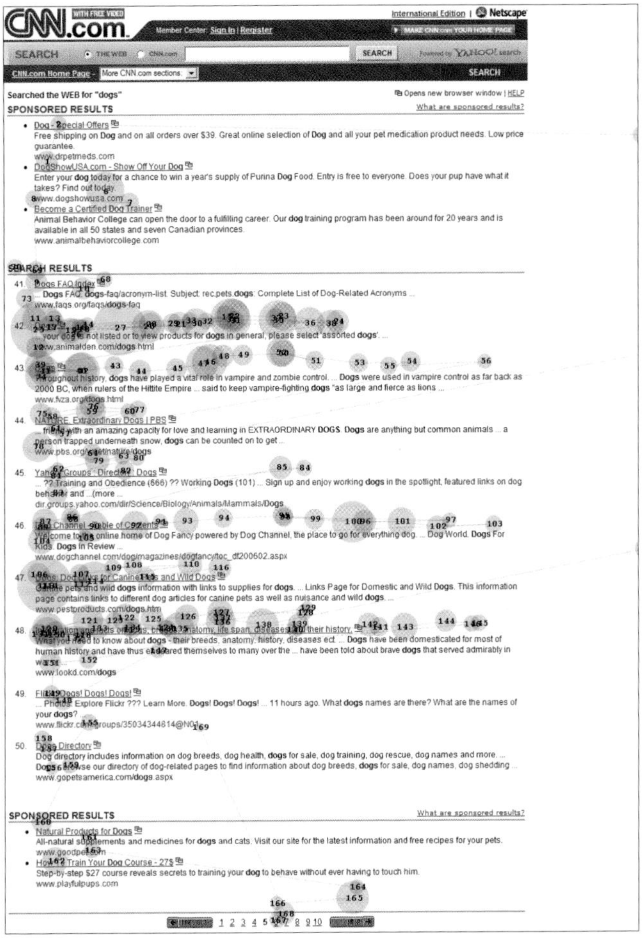

Figure 7.15 A user looked at sponsored links at the top and even the bottom of the CNN site. She came across the bottom ads naturally as she scrolled down the results on the page.

Sponsored Links on Other Pages

Users look at sponsored ads on non-SERPs because they know from experience that they are generally relevant and related to page content. When given a task to perform, participants in our study often looked at the Google text ads on the right of non-SERP pages.

In one session, for example, several users planning a Colorado ski vacation found themselves on the EzineArticles site after doing a Web search. They actually paid more attention to the text ads there than to the page content. This was for a combination of reasons. Also, they were deterred by the wall of text on the page. The content is hardly competition for the ads—it's unattractive and, worse, off-putting. This left users with a few choices: to select the *Back* button, type in a new URL, look elsewhere on the page, or type a new query into the Google toolbar. (Note: The last option was not available in our sessions, so users would have had to type the Google URL in the address field. The Google toolbar field might have been a more attractive option had it been available.) Most users made the choice that required the least effort—to look at something else on the page (**Figure 7.16**). And the simple, readable text ads, enhanced by Google's reputation, helped make this the obvious choice (**Figure 7.17**). In fact, because the first ads in the list were very related to the topic they were interested in, users were encouraged to look at more ads.

Figure 7.16 Users found the text ads on the right easier on their eyes than the thick block of content in the middle of the page on the EzineArticles site.

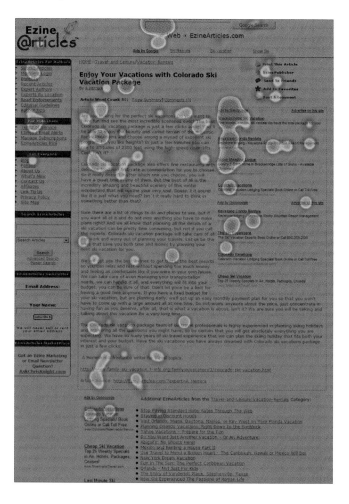

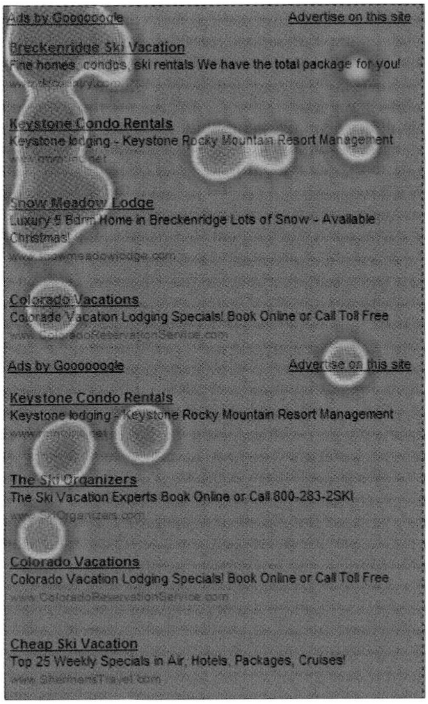

Figure 7.17 Users read words and phrases such as *Breckenridge ski, fine homes, Keystone, Snow Meadow,* and *Colorado,* which let them know the ads were relevant to their task, planning a Colorado ski trip.

Sponsored Links and Hot Potato Behavior

Hot potato behavior occurs often with sponsored links. When users look at an ad that they expect to be helpful but quickly determine that it is not because its title doesn't seem to relate to the current topic, they feel burned and "drop" it to move on to something else.

People are quick to scorn an ad that is not related to the content they want, especially when they were expecting the ad to be helpful. We see this **hot potato** behavior often when users feel burned by sponsored links. People do not like being tricked, and they are especially unforgiving of ads that defy their expectations. They will look at the ad for just a fixation or two, and then they don't look at the area again ever—or at least not for a long time.

For example, when looking for information about Fiorello La Guardia, people were presented with two small paragraphs of text in a column. They read about half of them, but reading in the typical F-pattern for this type of design, they missed information on the right side of the paragraphs.

The second text paragraph reads as follows:

> *Extra Credit: A 1959 Broadway musical about the mayor,* Fiorello!, *won four Tony Awards and the Pulitzer Prize for drama. The mayor was played by Tom Bosley, later famous as Mr. Cunningham on the TV series* Happy Days.

But the only words people read in the paragraph were these:

Extra Credit: A 1959, mayor, Fiorello!, *won, Awards, Pulitzer Prize for drama, The, Tom Bosley, later,* and *series.*

Reading this way, users missed the fact that there was a 1959 Broadway production about La Guardia. So when they turned their attention to the Google text ads on the right and the first word they read was *Broadway,* they very quickly looked away, uninterested in reading on (**Figure 7.18**).

Figure 7.18 Users felt duped by the sponsored ads related to Broadway shows because they did not read that there was a Broadway play about La Guardia.

It's difficult to say what an advertiser should do in this kind of case. The ad relates to information on the page, but not much, nor is it in a priority spot. One solution would be to offer contextual ads that relate only to the highest-priority and most likely read information on the page—such as information in headings, bullets, the first paragraph on the page, and other priority spots.

In another example, a user was trying to get instructions for tying a bowline knot. He gave only one look to the right sponsored link because it's about bowling, not bowline knots (**Figure 7.19**). Although providing suggestions based on similar spelling may sometimes pay off, this shows that it can also bomb.

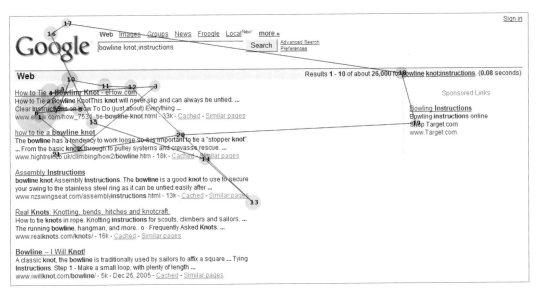

Figure 7.19 A user felt misled by the sponsored link for bowling instructions. It may have been spelled similarly to bowline, a word in his search term, but it was on a very unrelated topic.

Despite possible setbacks such as these, sponsored links are still very valuable and looked at on both SERPs and non-SERPs, our studies show. In fact, we feel so strongly about their effectiveness that we have used them ourselves.

Do Graphics Belong in Web Advertising?

Some ads—and, probably to a lesser degree, internal promotions—are created for the sole purpose of getting clicks. Others are meant to convey a message. Still others are simple reminders that a company or product exists, and advertisers deem them successful if they just do that. But all ads are a call to action—to buy something, remember something, or learn something new. Yet 65 percent of graphical ads are completely ignored. They don't get people to act. They don't get clicked. They don't get read. They don't even get one glance.

We are not saying that people don't *ever* look graphical ads. Advertising on the Web is a multibillion-dollar business. And with so many ads plastered with color and all-around mayhem, some are bound to get looked at and clicked.

Graphical ads are certainly not a lost cause, and graphics do belong in Web advertising. They simply need to be tailored to the Web user. So, don't go firing your design department—you'll need it to design the kinds of graphical ads that people *will* look at. The following are some characteristics of ads that win looks.

People ignore 65 percent of graphical ads.

Internal Promotions: Match the Site's Style

Users look more at promotions and advertisements that match the layout, color scheme, and style of the Web site they're on than at any other type of ad. Many of these are not paid-for ads but internal promotions—ads presented by the organization the Web site represents. Our number-one guideline for designing internal promotions is this: Match the style of the Web site.

Design an internal promotion to match the Web site's color scheme, typeface, and overall style. Do not introduce different branding. And place the promotion within the page borders, not as an offset banner at the very top or far right of the page.

Some organizations do not do this. In fact, they seem to go out of their way to make their own promotions look like external, paid-for ads. This is very misguided. Matching their site's style is probably easier and will almost certainly attract more users. Coming up with a different promotion style is like walking a mile out of your way to step on a hornet's nest. Take the short route home, and you won't get stung.

We have some theories about why people look more at ads and promotions that match a site's style and color scheme:

- If people are scanning and reading on a site, they already have some trust in it. They reason that an area or item that looks like part of the site probably comes from the same source as the site itself, so they trust it too—at least for a look.

- In appearance, these items usually look somewhere between an ad and the site itself, so people assume they have useful information or offers.

- Because they look like the rest of the site, some people think they are not ads or promotions. Instead, they assume they are interface elements to help them progress through their tasks.

The Adelphia television cable company presents its internal promotions in the same typeface, color scheme, and overall branding as the rest of its site. In other words, the promotion looks like it is designed and presented by the site. And although it is in an outlined box, it appears within the page borders, not as a banner offset at the top or on the right. The price of the ad's *Exclusive Web Offer* is presented in numeral form, which also attracts the eye. It makes the content feel more specific (and thus useful) than that in many ads.

Our study participants who hit this page gave the promotion much attention, despite that they were on a mission to learn about digital video recording. Since this promotion that had nothing to do with their task drew their eyes, it exemplifies a particularly winning format (**Figure 7.20**).

Figure 7.20 Winning formula: For users, it was a smooth segue to the *Exclusive Web Offer* promo on the Adelphia site because it looked and felt like part of the site.

Several users researching what Skype costs hit the *Skype Shop* page on the company's Web site. The page has four internal promotions: a top banner, two left-side boxes, and a bottom banner. They all match the overall site style, and users looked at them all (**Figure 7.21**).

Figure 7.21 People looked at the promotions peppered around this *Skype Shop* page because they match the site's style.

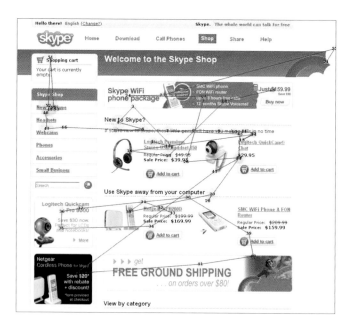

On the Citi Web site, users were looking for information about investing in retirement. One user looked at the expected text toward the left of the page, focusing on a few links, and then looked at the similarly styled promotion on the right (**Figure 7.22**).

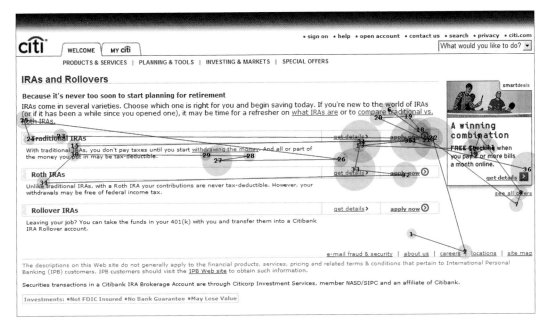

Figure 7.22 In addition to reading text and links on the Citi Web site, a user read the promotions, which were created in the style of the rest of the page.

A page on the Encyclopedia Britannica site provides a case study in how users respond to different types of ads (**Figure 7.23**).

Figure 7.23 There are five different types of ads on one page on the Encyclopedia Britannica site: 1) an animated external advertising banner at the top; 2) three graphical internal promotions on the right; 3) three text and graphical internal promotions on the left; 4) three Google text ads in the middle; 5) a graphical external advertisement on the bottom.

Eyetracking Web Usability

When researching windmills and wind power, some users found themselves on a particularly long page, where there are several internal promotions and external advertisements:

- An animated external advertising banner at the top of the page, which does not match the site's style at the top of the page

- Three graphical internal promotions on the right of the page, all matching the site's style

- Three text and graphical internal promotions on the left side, some "below the fold"

- Three Google text ads in the middle of the page, "below the fold"

- A graphical external advertisement at the very bottom of the page that does not match the site's style

A user's interaction with the different sales elements is telling. Ultimately, he looked most at the internal promotions that appear "above the fold." He also looked at the Google text ads in the middle of the page, at least those that are "above the fold." But he ignored the animated external ads at the top and bottom of the page (**Figure 7.24**).

Figure 7.24 A microcosm of ad look behavior: This user's experience encapsulated that of many others—he looked most at the internal promotions that appear to come from the people who sponsor the site and looked at sponsored Google text ads, but not at animated ads.

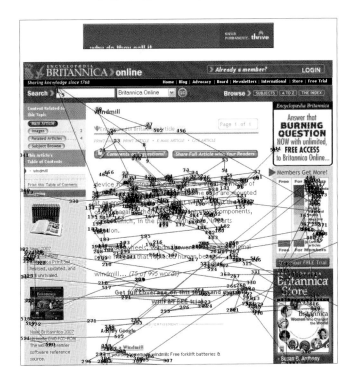

We'd say that the internal Encyclopedia Britannica promotions that appear "above the fold" are successful because they beckon the user to look at them several times. But now let's look at *when* he looked at different elements on the page. In his first 45 seconds, he read the text about how windmills work and the links and buttons on the page, but he did not look at the promotions or ads. So, the ads are not usually the first priority; people are going for good content.

Moving on, the first promotion he looked at is on the right side, looks like the site, and is eye level with where he was reading at that point. This could mean he was ready to look at promotions or that he was still studying the content and thought this promotion was part of it. Since he gave the promo only two fixations, the second hypothesis is more likely. But then he turned to the Google text ads in the middle of the page and fixated several times. Finally—probably thinking by this time that he had exhausted the content and was moving on to the ads— he looked at the promotion on the left for the Encyclopedia Britannica Print Set, which is a combination of text and graphics (an open book and set of books).

All of these promotions (and ads) are successful because the user fixated on them multiple times. However, as this example shows, to Web users, even successful ads are usually the less desirable—even ugly—step-cousin to good page content.

Assess Your Promotion for Lookability

Try this exercise. Give your promotion one point for each of these three criteria that it meets:

- It is static.
- It matches the site style or uses very plain text on a plain background.
- It is "above the fold."

The higher the score, the more likely the promotion will get looked at (at least the first time users encounter it).

The following table shows the results when we scored the ads and internal promotions on the Brittanica site. We then checked them against the findings from our eyetracking study. The higher-scored ads and promotions got looked at; the lower ones did not.

Promotion	Static (Not Moving)	Matches Site Style (or Is Plain Text)	Above the Fold	Score	User Looked
	0	0	1	1	No
	1	1	1	3	Yes
	1	1	1	3	Yes
	1	1	0	2	No
	1	1	1	3	Yes
	0	0	0	0	No

External Ads: What Works

It makes sense that internal promotions should match a site's style. A more nagging question is whether advertisements for unrelated organizations, products, or services should match the style and color palette of the Web site on which they appear. We believe they should not, and we'll explain why.

Imagine that a user who is searching for tires on a car parts site sees an ad in the same typeface and colors of the site. He looks at it, hoping it will be about a tire deal, but it is about home mortgages. How will he react? He will probably look away instantly, and he may be annoyed. And if he is burned like this a few times, he may even stop looking at advertisements and promotions that look like the site they're on. Considering the rapid evolution of the Web user, he will probably find a way to peripherally filter out these types of ads in the future, maybe even on this same visit. And he may grow to mistrust both the advertiser and the organization whose site houses the ad.

In cases where people are actually looking for external ads, they usually look for elements that do not look like the site they are on. That's another reason for external ads to match their own brand identity and style, not that of the site.

Large, Readable Graphical Text Alone or Separate from Images

On the Web, people are attracted to large, readable text that contrasts well against a background color (ideally a solid). If they can tell in a glance that they will not have to work to see text as they would on a watermark or image in an ad, they are more likely to look at it. Remember that people look at graphical ads with distinct text 17 percent more than at those with text over an image.

> *Give designers in your organization guidelines for how to create promotions to match the Web site's style. Communicate to them that promo areas are not the place to stretch their creative wings.*

For example, users researching a music gift on the *USA Today* site were attracted to unrelated ads that had these traits (**Figure 7.25**). In a top banner ad, the bright white text *Visit Florida* stands out against the lush green foliage. Although we do not recommend using images as backgrounds to text, this text is bright and the background is monochromatic, so there's no chance it will get lost. People also looked at a Careerbuilder.com ad in an orange rectangle on the right of the page. The ad's white circle with clear text inside—not to mention the separate image of monkeys in suits—attracted attention.

Figure 7.25 No monkeying around: The designers of two ads on this *USA Today* page knew what they were doing. The bright white lettering on the top green banner and the orange banner with monkeys and a white circle of text drew users' eyes.

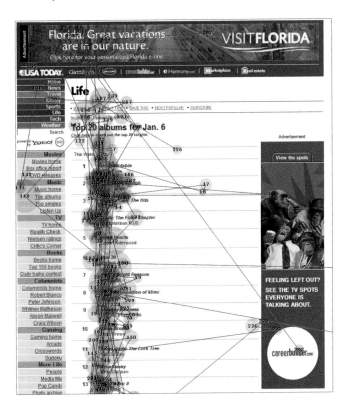

A promotion on the Fidelity Web site features a few words of text in a colored box. It also got several fixations (**Figure 7.26**).

Figure 7.26 A simple, subtle, and relevant ad drew a user's eyes on the Fidelity site.

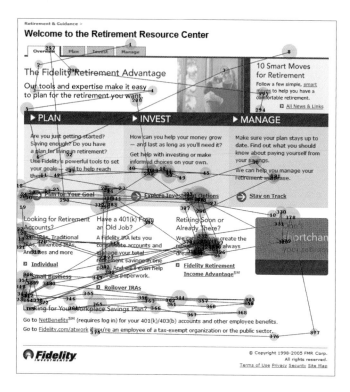

Portal pages, pages that appear portal-like (because they have delineated sections, each with varied information), and news site pages are often so bloated and busy that it can be difficult for users to decide which sections to look at, ads or no ads. It's more of a guessing game for them. Still, people can often tune out busy ads.

A page on the CNN Web site has two graphical ads with text not separated enough from the graphics. Both the small green and gray Dell ad on the left side and the large Blockbuster ad on the right are a mix of hard-to-read text and graphics. They got no looks at all from users who were browsing the page for something of interest to them (**Figure 7.27**). Users repeatedly skipped these graphical advertisements, but they read headings, links, and articles.

Figure 7.27 Not interested: When browsing this page for something of interest to them, users looked at the headings and text, but not the busy graphical ads.

Magnetic or Thrilling Graphical Properties

As we discussed in Chapter 6, "Images," people look at body parts, smiling faces, and UI elements. These magnetic elements can also attract people to ads. But they have to be a little more brazen in a small image. For example, an image of a person in a small ad needs to show more face and less body. And an image of a body needs to show skin to draw users to it.

Smiling Faces

Users look at ads with healthy, smiling, close-up faces looking straight at the camera. Sometimes these magnetic faces are exactly what draws users' eyes to the ad. For example, users looking for restaurant reviews on the *New York Magazine* site stole a look at the attractive stylist in the Maybelline Beauty Studio ad on the right (**Figure 7.28**).

Figure 7.28 Woman cannot live by bread alone: Even when looking for restaurant reviews, a user looked at the image of the good-looking makeup artist.

On the Web site of the *Monterey County Herald,* a user looking for financial advice still scanned over to look at a smiling mother's face and hair in an ad for life insurance (**Figure 7.29**).

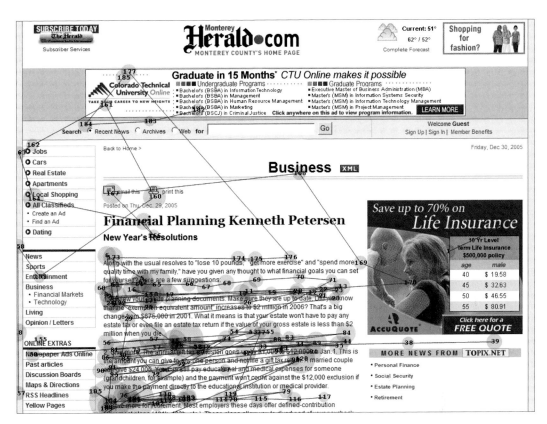

Figure 7.29 For love or money: Even when looking for financial advice, a user looked at the "hot mama" in the image.

Skin

People often give a glance to ads that have images of exposed human skin. For example, when reading about mallard ducks, a user glanced at the ad showing a person swimming in a pool on the UnderwaterTimes Web site (**Figure 7.30**).

Figure 7.30 The user is coaxed away from the textual information to the swimmer's skin in the ad on the right.

Needless to say, some ads appeal more shamelessly to prurient interests. For example, when reading his Web-based email, a user looked at an ad featuring a woman in a bikini positioned for, uh, true love in an ad for True, an online dating service. Interestingly, however, he fixated on the woman's face and chest once but on the text five times (**Figure 7.31**). The image drew him in, but the text kept his interest longer, showing just how powerful text in ads can be.

Figure 7.31 That "come hither" stare: A man looked at the sexy model in an ad for True. He looked even more at the text, demonstrating the power of clear text in Web ads.

Note: Normally we would not make a heat map with only one user's experience, but the technology did not allow a gaze plot in this case. Each rounded red blob represents one fixation.

Figure 7.32 News wins: Even a half-naked model cannot compete with news that people are interested in.

When designing graphical ads for the Web, give attractive images equal or a little less space than text. Images should also be adjacent to text, not background for it.

Still, sex doesn't always sell, and it still must play by the rules of competition in user interfaces. For example, people reading the news on the CNN site read the news but ignored a Victoria's Secret ad with a hot model in yellow underwear (**Figure 7.32**).

User Interface Elements

UI elements such as open fields and drop-down lists attract the eye, even when they are part of an advertisement. People are so conditioned to look for and use these controls that they will look at them anywhere on a page.

For example, on MyrtleBeachOnline.com, users reading about retirement plans still fixated on the scrolling list interface elements in the ads on the top and right of the page (**Figure 7.33**).

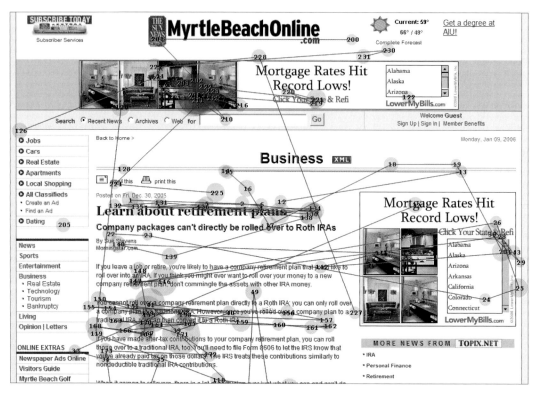

Figure 7.33 A user read headings and text and fixated several times on the UI controls in the two graphical ads on this page.

Animated Ads

People look at animated advertisements less than static graphical ads, text ads, and ads on SERPs. This is probably because, in the past, the dodgy, in-your-face, and downright obnoxious ads were also animated. Web users have learned to stay away from them.

But today's animated ads have chilled out quite a lot. The ones that get looked at are usually subtle and do not flash frequently. They also display the attributes of eye-catching static graphical ads, such as clear text separate from interesting images. For example, a Hyundai ad on the right side of the Comedy Central Web site features a car and clear text on a white background. Even while engrossed in a joke, a user looked at this ad for a few fixations (**Figure 7.34**).

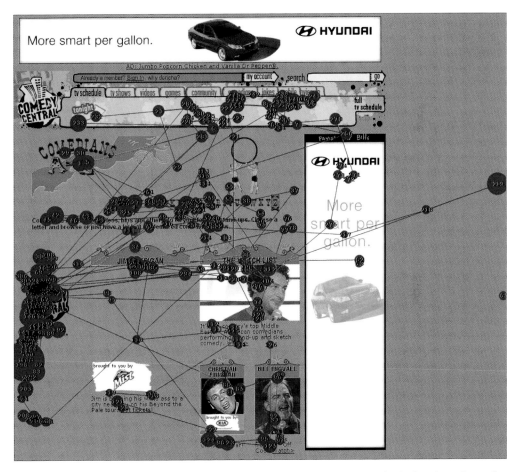

Figure 7.34 No laughing matter: A user looked at the animated Hyundai ad on the Comedy Central site because it was subtle and had simple text.

Similarly, on the Web site of the *Chicago Sun-Times*, a user looked at the clear text in the animated ads on the top and right (**Figure 7.35**). The animation elegantly changed from a text ad that was light blue and white to another without a lot of gimmick.

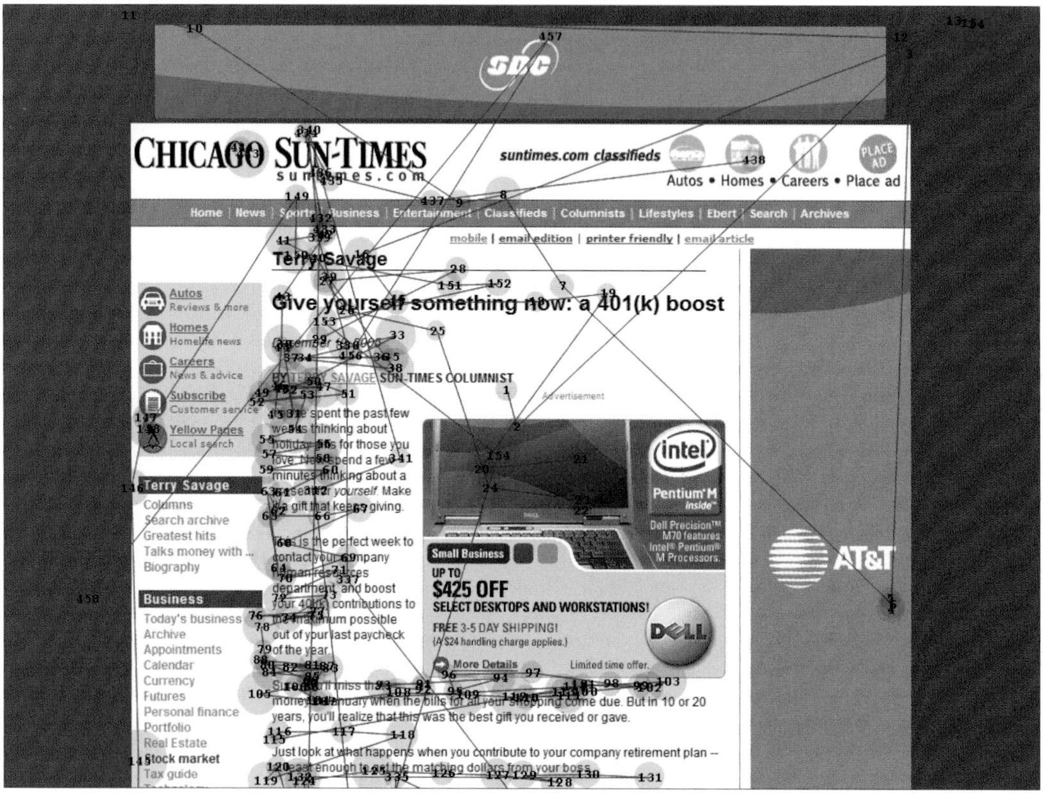

Figure 7.35 The understated AT&T ad animation did not deter people from looking at the block of text in the ad.

Users often look at animations as a page loads because only the first part of the ad has appeared and has not yet animated; the rest of the page has not yet loaded and there is nothing else to look at; or, as the page loads, everything is "animating" in a way.

Regardless of why, animations seem to bother users less during the behavior we call **impatient viewing**, when people look at whatever is available at the time—be it a banner that displayed first, a progress indicator, or whatever other lonely element is visible. For example, in a banner on the VH1 Web site, the user Sylvia looked at an Oil of Olay ad that is faintly animated. The text is clear, and the images appear on the right and left of the text. The images are easy to make out; one is the Olay brand logo, and the other the product itself. The ad has attractive traits and is competing with nothing, so Sylvia gave it several fixations.

What looks like a small spotlight moved horizontally across the ad. As it started to move across the word *will,* Sylvia's eye followed it (**Figure 7.36**).

Figure 7.36 The user looks at the animated word *will* as a spotlight effect moved to it as she waits for the rest of the page to appear.

Her eye remained there as the light moved across the next word, *a* (**Figure 7.37**). And when the shimmer was gone, her eye went to the image of the product (**Figure 7.38**) as she continued to wait for the rest of the page to load.

Figure 7.37 She followed the spotlight to the word *a*.

Figure 7.38 When the animation ceased and she had looked at the text, she looked at one of the images in the ad.

Eyetracking Web Usability

In another example, a user first looked at the ad in the upper right as the *New York Times* homepage loaded. He then looked at the animated promotion on the left, which has clear text and a separate image of a scrumptious-looking croissant (**Figure 7.39**). There was very little else on the page at this point.

Figure 7.39 This part of a gaze replay shows a user looking at the pastry ad in the upper left (after he looked at the clear text ad in the upper right), while there was little else on the page.

The user then looked to the animated internal promotion in the right rail—plain, large text on a black background (**Figure 7.40**). As he looked this way, the rest of the page loaded. The user either was interested in the ad or was practicing momentum behavior: He still fixated on the promotion even when other content became available.

Figure 7.40 Still waiting for the rest of the page to load, the user snuck a look at the ad on the right. As he did so, the content loaded to the left.

At least initially as the page was loading, there was no other content to see, so these ads are in the coveted position of having the user's full attention for a few seconds. And the *Times* took full advantage of this by also giving people a clean, simple promotion that they could scan and get information from.

We believe that ads, promotions, and content can coexist amicably on Web sites as long as designers carefully plan how the ads and promotions look and where they are placed. To motivate people to look at internal promotions, ensure that they are designed in the same style as the rest of the site. To get people to look at your ads on external sites, buy a sponsored link. Or use clear text, use interesting images, and by all means keep the text and the images distinct from each other. Web users can function happily in the presence of both ads and content as long as the ads look like ads and do not get in their way.

8 User Viewing Behaviors on the Web

In Web design, we aim to influence the way people look at our pages. With images, we illustrate. With words, we cajole. And with layout, we lead. The way we present page design, menus, and text affects much of what people look at first, keep looking at, and ultimately select. And although a designer's reward is usually a user's click, we should also honor the power of the look. A fixation is a necessary first step to getting a person to read about something, learn about something, understand it, or select it. In watching hundreds of people using the Web with eyetracking technology, we never saw people select something they did not look at first.

> *People click only the things they have looked at. So, getting clicks begins with attracting the eye.*

Eyetracking exposes user behaviors at a detailed level that is not possible with more traditional usability studies. We have mentioned some of these behaviors in specific examples throughout this book and these behaviors are summarized in the glossary. In this chapter, we examine them in more detail. Consider each of them in relation to your own Web site design. The more you can predict how a person will deal with the sites they encounter, the better your designs will be.

Exhaustive Review vs. Necessary or Desired Review

When users cannot find what they are looking for, they can either leave the page or site or look harder. If a site is unusable, the person will often choose to leave. The *Back* button is always at the ready, and often they turn to Google, where competitors beckon. If they choose to look harder on a cluttered site, they may try to use the on-site search.

For example, one of our users, Dori, knew the Circuit City store and chose to go to its Web site to buy an MP3 player (**Figure 8.1**). But when the site loaded, the homepage was chaotic. Since she knew the store's brand well, she stayed on the packed page. But she scanned it only minimally and saw the open search field. She opted to use this rather than attempting to find and then pilot the navigation.

Why People Stay on Bad Pages

Users may be motivated to stay on sites that have very poor layout for a variety of reasons, such as past experiences with the brand or referrals from Google or a friend. These are some of the most common motivators for staying on a poorly laid-out site:

- A referral from a friend, a newsletter, or another site the user trusts
- A Google referral—for example, a clear link name from a Google SERP, which "promises" the user the answer
- A site/brand with a good reputation
- A credible-sounding site
- A need to be on the specific site—for example, to return a product or get information from a certified agency

---

Figure 8.1 The user Dori minimally scanned the exceedingly cluttered Circuit City homepage and went right to the site's search function in the upper right. This is the opposite of exhaustive review.

As Dori's experience shows, sometimes outside influences charm users into staying on a subpar site or a page. These can include referrals, credibility, or brand. Probably the strongest reason people stay is the idea that the site may be the only place for the information they are seeking—a belief that can come from a high Google referral. Or an organization may have a hold on particular information, especially official data. Or the user has dealt with a particular organization and needs to continue the relationship. For example, perhaps a user bought a product from a particular company and needs to find the product manual on the company's site. Or perhaps an intranet is the only place people can reliably find information about their employer's vacation policy. In these cases, users must spend time and fixations to examine the options on a page, sometimes many times, in the hope of finding the right information.

This scouring—looking and relooking at links, areas of a page, and menus—is one of the least-constructive and most wasteful behaviors we see in eyetracking research. We call it **exhaustive review**, and it usually occurs when a page or site is disorganized and often has too much on it or when the link to the page pledged something other than the page's content.

Watching and listening to people as they use your site may help you determine whether exhaustive review is common on it. But without eyetracking, it can be difficult to pinpoint whether this behavior is actually happening.

In conducting our studies, we have noticed many instances of users repeatedly looking at elements on a page not because they are engaged with its content but because they are frustrated. Their looks seem to be saying, "Where the heck is that menu?" or "I swear I saw that article here before!"

One example of exhaustive review occurred on the U.S. Census Bureau's homepage, where users were looking for the populations of the United States and Texas. People knew that this information should definitely be on this site, so they looked hard before abandoning it.

The heat map shows exhaustive review—several people looked fruitlessly around the page, on the left and middle (**Figure 8.2**). Many of the fixations on the right rail, however, are good fixations, signifying that people used this helpful section and found answers. But several people did not look at the area at all. If this page had been very well designed, there would be much more heat on the right and a great deal less heat elsewhere on the page.

When people repeatedly look at an area of a page, it can be an indication that the page is not well organized or is too crowded. We call this unconstructive combing of pages and menus exhaustive review.

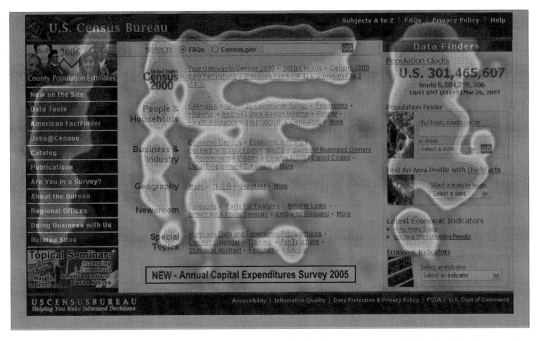

Figure 8.2 Users looked extensively and often fruitlessly around the page on the Census Bureau site, exemplifying exhaustive review.

There are, of course, many examples of extended looking that people choose to do and take pleasure in, which we call **desired exploration**. If a person likes the content and spends time reading, watching, or shopping, they are enjoying themselves on the site. Even when there are many fixations, this is a positive and expected experience for the user.

In some cases, a user may not be enjoying exploration, but it is still productive. We call these obligatory or acceptable looks **necessary review**. For example, the heat on the population features on the Census Bureau site means people were accomplishing something with the feature they needed. Dedicating many looks to find something is rarely, if ever, positive and would not be considered necessary review. But for people to use and engage with a feature, they simply must look at it more. This is predictable and tolerable.

When you are doing your own research, keep in mind that there are even times when one user doing very similar tasks on the same site can experience both exhaustive review and desired exploration. For example, let's say a woman has a gift certificate for her daughter to a kids' online clothing store. She takes her time to really look at the offerings. It's fun. There will be a lot of red, indicating desired exploration, on a heat map for the product pages in this scenario.

Now let's change the tasks minimally and say that her daughter came home from school saying that she has won the role of "tree number seven" in the school play, and she needs brown pants and a dark green top for her costume. The mom's experience shopping for these items could be quite different. What if she can find only yellowish green shirts? And the only brown pants in her daughter's size are plaid? Some sick-looking tree her kid will be. So, she continues looking, this time racking up much exhaustive review heat on our imaginary heat map.

Same general task (shopping) and same site (children's clothing), but very different experiences. This is why it is critical to know the user's motivation and goals to correctly interpret usage data—whether eyetracking, server logs, or anything else—and to watch people as they are working.

Another example of necessary review occurs often on e-commerce sites. When shopping for multiple items, people may refer to the list of items in their shopping cart several times. This has nothing to do with poor presentation or misunderstanding; it's just a case of users confirming what they are planning to buy and the site helping them to do so. For example, users shopping on the FreshDirect site often consulted the shopping cart on the right, which also enabled them to see the dollar amount of their purchases as it added up (**Figure 8.3**).

Figure 8.3 This user referred to the shopping cart many times on the FreshDirect Web site, simply confirming what groceries he was buying.

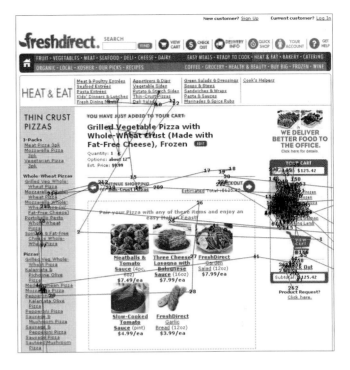

Retail Product Presentation: Stick to the Basics

Eyetracking research reinforces some of the standard, long-standing design rules for presenting retail products. For typical consumer products, we know that people want to easily see the following:

- A clear image of the item
- The product name
- The price
- A short description
- A link to a longer description (for people who are more invested in the product)

Of course, for some more complex products—service items, major equipment, B2B transactions—it can be difficult to include all these. Then it's a good idea to offer clear contact information. But with common items such as a flower arrangement, an overnight bag, a pair of jeans, or a TV, people need this information, and they need it right up front.

Exhaustive Review Can Be Downright Exhausting

On the Mr. Coffee site, we asked users to buy anything they wanted. Susan looked at the left-side menu on the homepage. *Coffeemakers* caught her eye, and she selected it, saying, "I am going to look at coffeemakers because my son would like to have one in his dorm."

She looked at a few images and then clicked the *View All* link in the lower right. Then she began to consider and comment on the features she was looking for. She said, "I have to make sure I get one with an automatic shut-off because they are not allowed to have a model that doesn't have that [in the college dormitory]."

She looked at several images of coffeemakers, but at this stage there was no information about an automatic shut-off. Still, the images and information presented helped Susan recall another important feature. First, the number of cups each model brews is under its image and model number. Second, some of the images featured a coffee cup alongside the coffeemaker, giving potential buyers a sense of the scale and size of the product (**Figure 8.4**).

Images that are clear and give a sense of the size of a product can be helpful in making a sale. Summary text about popular features also helps users choose what to buy. Not including summary information makes users look harder than they should ever need to look.

Figure 8.4 The Mr. Coffee Web site displays images of products and a very short description of each on its products list page.

She looked at both the brew size and the coffee cups and said, "I am also looking for one that is kind of small because space is very limited" (**Figure 8.5**). She scrolled up and down and added, "I would assume that one that makes four cups would be good since there will be two of them living there." Her gazes were productive and helped her evaluate the pots. This is an example of necessary review.

Figure 8.5 Based on the images, Susan started to zero in on coffeemakers, particularly those with four-cup size carafes. The coffee cup and saucer in some of the images gave her a sense of the size of the coffeemakers.

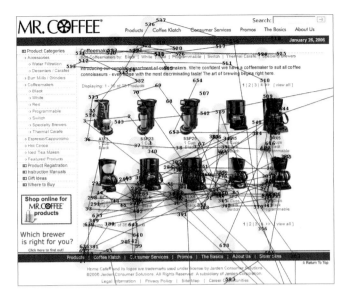

Susan focused on one pot and said, "I am going to look at this one, NLX5. Four cups, and it's programmable." When she got to the product details page, she scanned around and started to read the bulleted items about that model (**Figure 8.6**). The bulleted information helped her, but soon she realized something was missing. She started to quickly fixate all around the page, exhibiting exhaustive review. She said, "It is not telling me how much it costs"(**Figure 8.7**). She fixated around the periphery, the upper right, the lower right, and near the *Buy Now* button, looking for a price.

Figure 8.6 There is no price on the product details page on the Mr. Coffee Web site. Since listing prices is relatively standard practice on e-commerce sites, people looked for the price all over this page and expressed a desire to have the information here.

Figure 8.7 The user Susan looked everywhere for a price on the product details page, exhibiting exhaustive review.

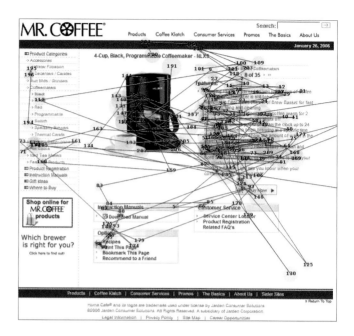

It's beyond us why any site would make users click past not only the initial product list page but also a details page to find a price. And, of course, most users will not click an action button such as *Buy Now* until they know the price. But Susan, committed and with nowhere else to look, did click *Buy Now* to see whether the price would be revealed that way. As she hoped, it was disclosed as a new window opened. She looked at the price, *$29.99*, in the upper left of the page. She also saw a note there that the item was out of stock. Now they tell her? To add insult to injury, there was another note that the item usually ships within ten business days.

Susan decided to add the coffeepot to her shopping cart "to see if it'll give me any information about when it will be available." (This is a highly superstitious act but one that was somewhat justified by her recent experience of getting a price by clicking the "buy" button.) She looked around the page and got no help. She said, "Hmmm," and clicked the *Back* button. This just took her back a page, so she closed the secondary window to get back to the page with all the coffeepots. She said, "I am going to choose a different model then. Maybe a different color."

Eyetracking Web Usability

"Here's another four-cup that's programmable," she said, pausing to ponder exactly what *programmable* means. (This would be a very good place for a hyperlink to a detailed explanation.) But then she added, "Maybe I don't need programmable. I am just trying to make sure it has the automatic shutoff."

She opened an item that was not identified as programmable, read the bullets, and said, "No, it doesn't have it." She looked at another nonprogrammable model and said, "It doesn't have it either." (This would be a great place for a coffeepot "compare" feature.)

She finally found another pot that suited her needs, but there was no button to add it to her cart. She scrolled up and down and looked all around the page. At this point, she needed a cup of strong java just to get through this convoluted site. Instead, she said, with a mother's patience, "That's odd. I don't see something that lets you purchase."

Needless to say, this was a taxing and drawn-out process. Why did the site withhold so much information along the way? Maybe we should call the user's behavior in this case *exhausting* review, rather than *exhaustive* review.

Bad Record for Some Baseball Sites

Exhaustive review was also prevalent on some of the baseball Web sites that many people used in our study. You may recall that one of our assigned tasks was to find which sport and position George Brett played. Many users searched with Google to find their way to three baseball Web sites: one very helpful, two not so helpful.

On the Baseball-Reference site, users landed on a page that is very long but visually delineates sections with colored boxes and tables (**Figure 8.8** and **Figure 8.9**). It's often easier for people to scan this kind of layout than one that is straight prose because they can check a section title to see whether it has what they are looking for and ignore the rest.

But this page was not very helpful. The problem wasn't the excessive page length. In fact, some people had little or no idea how long the page was because they didn't try scrolling very much, for reasons we'll explain shortly.

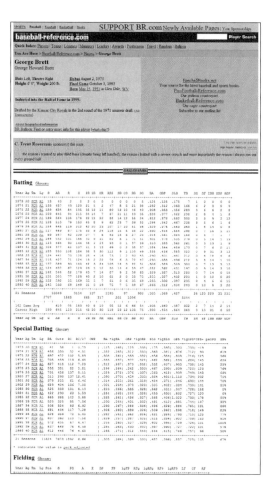

Figure 8.8 George Brett's page on the Baseball-Reference Web site is very long, with designated sections that are visually distinct.

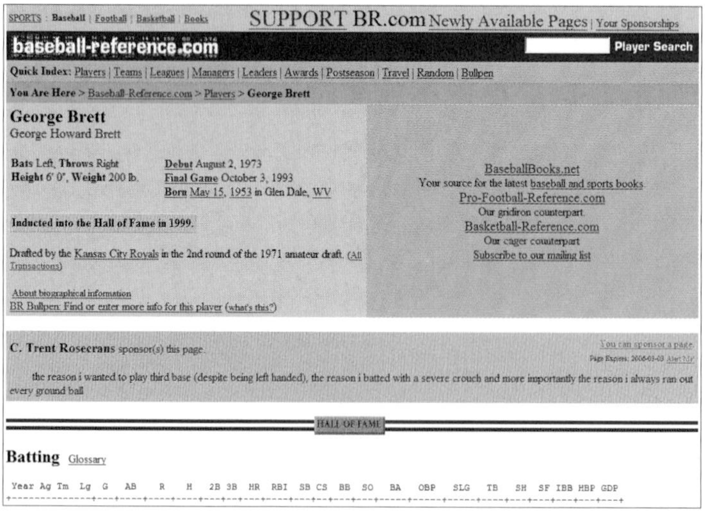

Figure 8.9 A cropped view of Brett's page on the Baseball-Reference site shows the area "above the fold."

The main issue was that important information about the baseball player was not available in places where people expected it to be: in the gray or blue section at the top. The gray box on the left houses all sorts of interesting facts about Brett—he bats left, throws right; his debut game date, final game date; and so on. But not his field position. Now Brett was certainly a slugger, but he was also a very good third (and sometimes first) baseman. Unfortunately, this is not listed in the gray box.

What enticed people to think Brett's position would be listed here? It was its relationship to other content: Important information about Brett is housed in this priority spot.

Only raw endurance allowed some users to find the answer in the yellow band below the gray box, where it is buried in what seems to be a fragment of a quote from Brett: "the reason i wanted to play third base (despite being left–handed), the reason i batted with a severe crouch and more importantly the reason i always ran out every ground ball." This is a prime example of exhaustive review, showing how many fixations users can spend examining an area where they expect information to be (**Figure 8.10**).

Figure 8.10 People looked repeatedly, extensively, and unsuccessfully for George Brett's field position in the gray, upper-left section of the page.

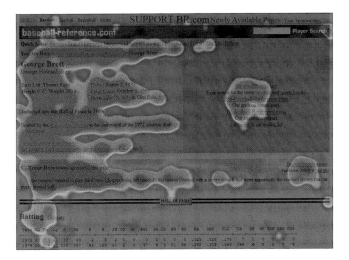

This should have been a very easy task—we'd classify it as level 1, easiest, on a scale of 1 to 3. We hope that most people would be able to complete it successfully on the Web. And overall, the completion rate for this task on all sites was 87 percent—not bad. But it was lower, 83 percent, for people who found their answer after using only this site. Four percentage points may not seem like much, but users also spent an average of 2 minutes on this site, 15 seconds longer than the average overall. So, people who used only the Baseball-Reference site spent more time and had less success.

Additionally, users who found Brett's playing position on this site were not very confident in their answer. They rated their overall confidence as 6.29 on a scale of 1 to 7. Users' average overall confidence using all sites (including Baseball-Reference) was 6.55. Their satisfaction rating was 5.57 on this site vs. 6.18 on all sites.

It might seem unfair to make these comparisons between one site and multiple sites because users will be more knowledgeable and confident if they consult a few sites. But for many simple tasks, they should really only need to use one authoritative and well-laid-out site.

For this task, users visited an average of 1.13 sites from the search engine results page (SERP), with 64 percent visiting only one site (in addition to the Web search page and SERP). In fact, people did better when they visited only one site than when they visited multiple sites or just the Baseball-Reference site. The average success rate for those who used only one site was 92 percent; the time spent was 1 minute 26 seconds, the confidence rating was 6.71, and the satisfaction rating was 6.48 (**Table 8.1**).

Table 8.1 User Experience on Baseball-Reference vs. All Sites

	Success Rate	Time Spent	Confidence Level	Satisfaction Level
Using one site only	92%	1:26	6.71	6.48
Using multiple sites	87%	1:45	6.55	6.18
Using Baseball-Reference site only	83%	2:00	6.29	5.57

The lesson: One site is enough for a user to have high success and feel confident with information if it's a reliable-looking site with easy-to-understand information. But one bad site can make users waste their time and leave them feeling discontented.

Now, we are not trying to pick on the Baseball-Reference site, which has many good traits, including very comprehensive details about players. All sites have some bad usability elements, and we present these numbers simply to show the impact that exhaustive review can have on a user's experience on any site. Other sites had issues as well. But the Baseball-Reference site was attractive in the Google results page, mainly because it was the second organic link and the first three words in the link title, *George Brett Statistics*, were clear. So, many users visited it, and we were able to learn from their experience.

Users also experienced exhaustive review on the Baseball Library site. Important information is hard to find on the site, which is ironic because it seems that the designers tried hard to make it visible (**Figure 8.11**).

Figure 8.11 A page on the Baseball Library site chunks information into various boxes and bulleted lists, making it difficult for people to determine where the most basic information is.

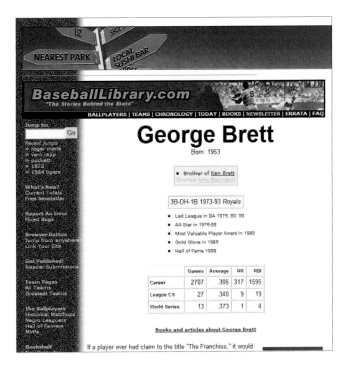

For example, Brett's position is the third piece of content on his page. But three aspects of its presentation are a problem:

- The information is presented in a box. Depending on the look and placement of boxes, some people tune them out, as they do banners.

- The information is abbreviated: *3B* instead of *third base*. Abbreviations can be fine, and for a user experienced with baseball and this site, *3B* might be obvious. But for people who may be scanning for a fast answer and are not familiar with this site, abbreviations are easy to overlook.

- There are no labels. Depending on the spacing and surrounding words, labels are not always necessary. But if there were a bolded *position* label near *3B,* more users would have probably found the answer faster.

The user Karla first looked almost exactly at the answer to the question on this site (**Figure 8.12**). But then she quickly looked below it to the bulleted list. The abbreviation probably did not catch her eye, but bulleted lists are also a magnetic element. In this particular case, however, the list could arguably be considered a miscue: It seemed as if it would have the most basic information about the player, but instead it lists his awards.

When she did not find the answer there, Karla looked to the text on the page, especially scanning the links and the beginning of paragraphs (**Figure 8.13**). Still not finding the answer, she went back to sections she had looked at already. She then looked to the box near the top of the page, where the abbreviated answer *3B* is located. Her eye fixated on this, but she did not register it as the answer and instead again looked to the bullets. Like the users on the Baseball-Reference site, she probably couldn't believe that something as basic as Brett's position would not appear in the bulleted list about him. In the final segment of Karla's visit to this page, she looked further at the box with the answer, at the bullets, and at the text.

Abbreviations, especially uncommon ones, are more difficult to scan and understand than the complete words.

Figure 8.12 In Karla's first fixation on this Baseball Library page, her eye almost went over the answer she was looking for, but instead she was drawn to the "magnetic" bulleted list and then to the table and the text.

Note: This gaze plot shows the user's first 40 fixations on this page. Figure 8.13 shows her entire fixations on the page.

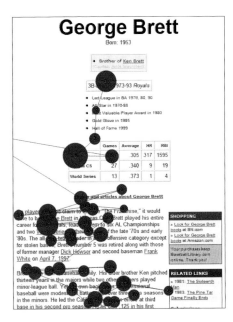

Figure 8.13 By the end of Karla's full visit to this page, she had viewed the answer she was looking for in the yellow-shaded box a few times—and suffered exhaustive review.

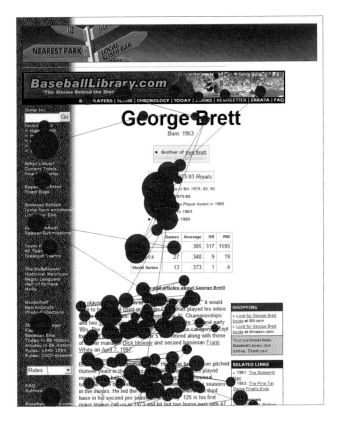

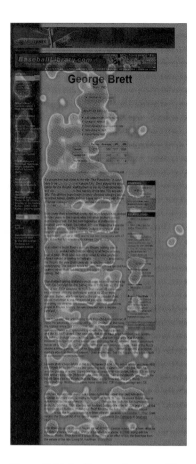

Figure 8.14 Red hot and wrong: The large blobs of heat on this heat map indicate exhaustive review—users searching all over for an answer— not necessary review or desired exploration.

If we had done this study without using eyetracking technology, we might think that she completely missed the box with the answer. But because of eyetracking, we know that she looked at the box a few times, but the content wasn't understandable to her.

In this example of miscues and exhaustive review, the user spent about 200 fixations. And when she finally offered her desperate and fatigued answer to which sport and position Brett played, it was: "Baseball, batter." She had no idea that he played third base.

Other users had the same problem, and a few were thrown off by the mention (in the first box, under the year Brett was born) of Brett's older brother, Ken, who also played in the major leagues but as a pitcher (**Figure 8.14**). Some mistakenly answered that George Brett was a pitcher.

Not all users were hobbled by exhaustive review on this task, however. Many hit a third site, the National Baseball Hall of Fame, where it was easier to find the answer (**Figure 8.15**). The words *Primary Position: Third Baseman* appear in the fifth content chunk on the page, with other important information about Brett. Users were more successful here than on the other two baseball Web sites because:

- The page layout is consistent, and the basic content type is either regular text or bolded text, so there are not a lot of mixed treatments for users to sift through.

- There are labels, and they are in bold.

- The player's field position is listed in an expected and high-priority area.

- The position is spelled out, not abbreviated.

Figure 8.15 George Brett's primary field position, third base, is labeled and appears near the top of the page on the Baseball Hall of Fame site.

Special callout treatments can be distracting and miscues for users. Consistent, simple layout often works better

There are still issues with this layout, the worst being that the word *primary* appears before the word *position*. People scanned the first word and not the second. Of course, the label was quite accurate because Brett's primary position was third base. But putting the most relevant word, *position*, first is easier for users to scan. For example, it could be presented: *Position (primary)* or *Position: Third Base (also played first base on occasion)*.

Users had to do a little looking to find the answer to the assigned question on the Baseball Hall of Fame site, but not as much as on the other two baseball sites. On average, the success rate was much higher—100 percent, actually—and the task time lower for people who used only this site. People who used only the Baseball Library were 91 percent successful, and those who used only Baseball-Reference were 83 percent successful.

People who used only the Baseball Hall of Fame site spent just one minute and five seconds on average to complete the task. People who used only the Baseball-Reference site spent almost twice that, two minutes, on average. And people who used only the Baseball Library site spent more than three times as much time, three minutes and twenty-one seconds.

Finally, after using only the Hall of Fame site, 96 percent of users felt finished, believed they knew the correct answer, and did not look at any other Web sites. But after using just Baseball-Reference, only 45 percent of users felt they had enough information. **Table 8.2** compares the user experience on the three baseball sites.

Table 8.2 Comparison of User Experience on Three Baseball Sites

	Baseball Hall of Fame	Baseball Library	Baseball-Reference
Success rate (this site only)	100%	91%	83%
Minutes spent (this site only)	1:05	3:21	2:00
Visited this site first and then no others	96%	89%	45%
Visited this site first and then one or more other sites	4%	11%	55%

What Happens When Information Is Too Complicated

We saw a different kind of exhaustive review on a page of the Skype Web site. Overall, this site is pretty well organized, and pages are often uncluttered. But layout and content have to be just about perfect when the goal of a page is to educate people about a new concept. In fact, the page where our users went to learn about Skype is meant to teach people about both Internet telephony, an idea that is new to many people, and what Skype offers. A Web page with dual goals like these really has its work cut out for it.

Many of the product features are attractive but not laid out in a simple, comparable way. So, users could miss the fact that with Skype you can use your computer to make calls and use any of the following choices:

- Call someone else who has Skype from your Skype, all for free

- Call any phone from your Skype for very cheap (you buy chunks of minutes at a time and use them until they are gone or you buy more)

- Buy a subscription where you get a phone number that any phone can call and that you can call from

A few of our users did not actually grasp the idea that there are products such as Skype that enable people to use computers to call one another. Some read the words *use your computer to call any phone* number, but this—combined with explanations that relate to more traditional phone plans—confused matters. Without this central understanding, they did not have the foundation to recognize the specifics and benefits of Skype. Most people did not pick up on a very important attraction: Calls made from your PC with Skype to another PC with Skype, even using video, are free. The *Skype to Skype* references, while looked at, were meaningless to users.

So much different information on pages also can prevent people from understanding that the rates to call any telephone with Skype are less expensive than regular calling rates. While people looked at these offerings numerous times, they conjured their own interpretations of them. One participant, Ed, said, "My understanding is that domestic calls are free but not international calls."

Other elements added to the confusion. For example, on one page, a yellow sticker calls out *$29.95 per year* (for a subscription calling plan)—a bargain if you are looking to have a set phone number. In fact, people who had started to grasp the other big concepts—free Skype to Skype and less expensive calls even without the plan—were so enchanted with this cheap rate and sunburst sticker that it muddied the other concepts.

One user had just begun to understand the ideas of free Skype to Skype and cheap calls (with no permanent number). Then he hit a page about calling plans and was drawn several times to the bright *$29.95 per year* yellow sticker (**Figure 8.16**). He looked all over the page and then back to the sticker. Looking at this same sticker so many times indicates that he was confused, or at least questioning the offers that he had read. We call this behavior **Repeated Review**. This is when the user looks at the same specific element multiple times. This is different from exhaustive review, where the user looks at many different things (too many of them, in fact). There will usually be a large amount of repeated review during an exhaustive review, but there can also be repeated review as a stand-alone behavior as

Repeated Review occurs when users looks at the same specific element multiple times. This is different from exhaustive review, where the user looks at many different things many times.

seen in this Skype example. In this case, the problem is not that the layout is confusing or that users don't know where to locate the items of interest. The problem is that the items themselves are difficult or somehow confuse the main message.

Figure 8.16 A user looked at the price stickers on the Skype site several times, indicating that he was confused.

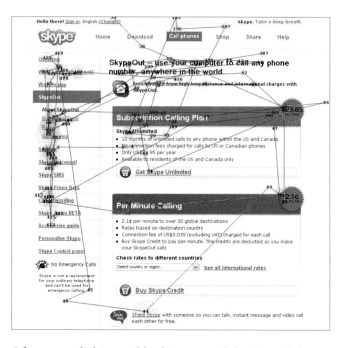

After some clicking and looking around the site and three visits back to the homepage when he was trying to understand the offerings and the costs associated with them, he headed for home yet again. This time he saw a line of text on the bottom-left side that read this: *Just $29.95 a year.* He looked at this and said, "Here, $30 a year." Let's face it, it's easier to grasp a set price than the concepts of free Skype-to-Skype calls or buying cheap minutes.

The layout of the homepage compounds the complexities of the information. Consider the elements a user must choose from: the menu, a screenshot of the product, a picture of happy girls, an option to download, and a note in large blue type. The user did not want any of these things. He skipped the blue note that *It's free to download and free to call other people on Skype*—possibly because he thought it was part of the images above it (**Figure 8.17**). Or perhaps he had read it earlier and didn't register the somewhat complex concept. So, where would he look next? The two small chunks of text look more informative than the rest of the items on the page, and they house more information than anything else on the page, so he looked there. But this text describes the $29.95 calling plan and an offer for five free minutes of calls to any destination.

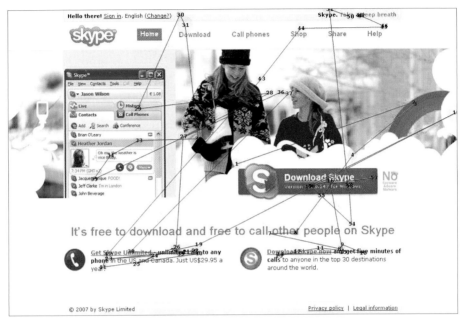

Figure 8.17 The user regressed to this homepage—his fourth visit there—and got an answer about the cost for the product. But he missed the fact that Skype can be free or very inexpensive.

When pages and concepts are complicated, users often retreat to the elements they understand. This can cause them to miss important ideas and draw erroneous conclusions.

These layout issues beguiled the user to believe something that was simply untrue—that using Skype always costs money. What's worse, they did not encourage him to want to download the product.

People form incorrect perceptions on Web sites for two reasons: when the correct information is the least attractive, least believable, or least understandable element on the page, and when a very attractive element is simply stated or much more attention-grabbing. Users' concentration is then focused on that instead of on finding what they need.

When people reread letters, parts of words, or words, it exemplifies **regression**, a well-known eye behavior, and it often means the word or writing is confusing.

Momentum Behavior

Momentum behavior occurs when people look at but do not choose an option that could help them because they have already selected a course and are sticking to it. Even within moments, users can become loyal to the route they have chosen and oblivious to other interface elements.

Momentum behavior happens when parts of the interface are not strong enough to call to users when they need them. In other words, a name, style, or placement is not enough to draw people to the path they should take. Another cause of momentum behavior is the fact that people don't always look for the most direct route—they'll follow what we call an **inferior path** just to get their task done, even if it ends up being the scenic route. If it does occur to them that there may be a better route, they feel that either they won't find it or it will take too long to try.

People want to find a successful path for getting tasks done. Even a less efficient path that works will suffice, and people will continue to use this inferior path every time they use a Web site. Instead, make the best path blatantly obvious even on the user's first try.

Since we often see this in usability studies in a lab, we could conclude that people in a lab setting may not have a relationship with the Web sites we are testing. Or perhaps they just want to finish a given task. But we also see this behavior when they choose their own sites and tasks and in field studies where people are in their own home or office and are used to working with the Web sites. In fact, people sometimes adhere to their inefficient methods for doing tasks throughout their entire session at a site and possibly every time they use a particular site.

We saw cases of momentum behavior on the Census Bureau site, when users were not called away from their current path even by the right answer in front of them because of poor placement, terminology, and overall page clutter on the site.

Kara witnessed a rather extreme example of momentum behavior in the 1990s, when working for a software organization that produced powerful applications for writing and managing hefty publications such as books, manufacturing documents, and clinical trials at pharmaceutical organizations. The design team did many site visits to watch people using the product over the life cycle of dealing with the published pieces. One user worked at a pharmaceutical organization, primarily keeping the clinical trials in order for their seven-year life. Her small cubicle was jammed full of blue loose-leaf binders housing a plethora of papers on different versions of drug trials, which she also had in digital format filed similarly on her computer.

Also surrounding her were a number of squeeze balls, keyboard and wrist lifters, gimmicky hand massagers, and the Queen Mother of carpel-tunnel syndrome alleviators: wrist guards. She had several wrist guards in different colors (perhaps matching different outfits and moods), some longer and more padded than others.

Seeing these artifacts did not worry the design team much because at that time many of us did not know that there is a correct way to sit at a desk and hold our wrists. And most of us using PCs for extended periods came down with sore wrists or needed therapy or surgery, or some combination of these. Still, this woman had a serious stash of wrist-relief devices. And after a few visits with her, the team realized, to its chagrin, that it was their fault.

Years prior, she had found a path to doing a task with the software. It involved using the third button on the mouse (a torture device on her Sun SPARCstation). It would have been a fine path had she not had to press it about a zillion times a day and had there not been a much better, faster, safer way to do it. But her path worked, so why would she think there was a better way to get her task done and search that way out? Like many users, she stuck with what she knew—through pain, surgery, and a small fortune invested in wrist paraphernalia. She was caught in momentum behavior on a grand and global level.

Note that after seeing many other customers outfitted with wrist guards, the team did its best to fix this feature in later releases. The goal was to make the better path much more visible and attractive than the dangerous one.

When designing Web sites and other consumer software, we often consider ourselves to be 2D designers and thus free from considering ergonomics and physical safety in product use. "That's for manufacturing people and industrial designers," we say. Not true. Many Web interface elements can put undue physical pressure on a user's body. These include the following:

- Cascading menus that users must hold open as they search for the right link with the mouse
- Miniature links and links that are so close together it feels like a dexterity test to click them
- Tiny, unclear, or poorly contrasted text that users must squint at or lean into the monitor to read

We see some people, especially those older than 65, shake while they hold the mouse or squeeze the mouse hard, as if they are trying to get mouse juice from it. They often need to make several tries at clicking the item they want. And poor contrast between the text and the background, text on background images, tiny text, and flowery typefaces also make people work too hard just to read the content on a page. We have seen users leaning far into the screen and squinting for long periods of time. This can thoroughly strain the eyes—and how's your back?

For those who plan to do eyetracking testing on their site, this can also be a problem. The eyetracker loses the eye when users lean way into the screen. So, if you have hard-to-read text, be sure to pilot-test first to ensure that you can keep a lock on the users' eyes as they work.

Link names and placement, as well as competition between the features on a page, can have strong effect on momentum behavior. For example, we asked people to watch a trailer for the Harry Potter movie *The Goblet of Fire* and decide whether they wanted to see the film. We navigated with the eyetracker directly to the movie's site, where users were presented with a page with a large photo of a few of the main characters. A note appeared center stage in this large photo: *Click to begin the adventure* (**Figure 8.18** and **Figure 8.19**). Our users were supposed to click the *View trailer* link at the top of the left-side navigation, but this other feature derailed them. It grabbed their attention for a few reasons:

- Its commanding tone: *click here*

- Its placement in the center of the page

- Its engaging content (who wouldn't want to *begin the adventure*?)

Figure 8.18 People thought an animated pan around the Harry Potter characters on the Warner Brothers site was the trailer for *The Goblet of Fire*. They missed the link in the left-side menu to the far more exciting real trailer.

Figure 8.19 A cropped view shows the links for *View Trailer* and *Click to begin the adventure.*

Several people looked at the relatively pathetic *View trailer* link on the left after seeing the link in the center of the page. Most did not click it, though. They had already selected what they thought was a good path and would not be distracted by the right path. And when they ultimately selected the *Click to begin the adventure* link, ominous music started to play and the animation panned 360 degrees around the images of the main characters, who were standing still (**Figure 8.20**). People assumed this slow panning was the movie trailer. In fact, the real movie trailer, which they didn't look at, *was* exciting: faces, bodies, fire, action, blood, booming music...it had it all. But the anemic *View trailer* link simply didn't stand a chance against the sirens of excitement that the adventure link promised.

Figure 8.20 The *View trailer* command, which people needed to see the trailer, disappeared once the animation began.

Once the user selected to begin the adventure, the *View trailer* link collapsed away into a tiny vertical *Menu* button. So, the option to view the trailer wasn't even visible while the panorama was animating.

People who attempted to watch the trailer were only 71 percent successful, compared to an average success rate of 78 percent overall for the tasks we assigned in this round of testing. This included some complicated tasks that required several steps of research, such as buying a humidifier for a specific-sized room and finding out what a person needs to legally cross the United States/Canada border in a car. The Harry Potter task was far easier than all the others: People just had to select a link at the top of the list of links. So, although the success rate for it may not seem much lower than the average success rate in the round, given the task, it was a serious disappointment.

Even worse than the low success score is the fact that people who looked at the panoramic animation (instead of the trailer) were not excited about the movie. People were positively bored with it. After watching the clip, one user said, "No, I don't really want to see that movie."

Here again is a case where users felt they had found a good enough path and went down it, never really being successful. This was not likely a conscious decision on their part. Everything happens so fast on the Web—who has time to reason and talk to themselves before making a selection? It's more likely that people can really only focus on one thing at a time.

Low Vision and Momentum Behavior

A variation of momentum behavior is people stopping a task when they have found information that is "good enough." One of the places we have observed this in our studies is with people who have low vision and use screen magnification technology.

A sighted person can scan a page for visual cues about content, but a person with low vision often cannot make out images. Even with a magnifier, which enables people to zoom in far on pages (and thus see only very small parts of them at a time), users with low-vision sometimes need the additional help of a screen reader, which reads words on pages aloud via a synthesized voice. So, simple words as link names can be a good cue for users who have very low vision.

In one scenario, our users with low vision went to the New York City Department of Sanitation Web site to find out whether it is OK to put a plastic bottle, pizza box, and wire coat hanger into recycling bins. At that time, the department's Web site had many sections and links, and the users worked for several minutes without success. But most of them eventually found a link to a poster (meant to be printed and put on a wall) that had columns displaying cartoon images of what could and could not be recycled. This was a useful interface for sighted users, who could print the poster and keep it by their recycling bin. With some effort, they could also scroll around the poster online, make out the images of items, and, most importantly, see which column they were in. But a person with low vision could not make out an image of a coat hanger any better than that of a Styrofoam cup. And scrolling up to the column header while keeping the item's context was impossible.

Since most of the users found the poster, however, they assumed it was the only place on the site with information about what is recyclable in New York City. So, they said they could not complete the task. What they did not know was there was an alternate, harder-to-find feature that presented the same information in text. This text feature would have made it possible for people with low vision to do the task and easier for sighted users to do it online. But a very small percentage of the users found the text feature at all because they had already found what they thought was the only answer.

Although it might be necessary to hide interface elements to make room for other items, this usually incurs a big usability penalty because, for users, out of sight is out of mind. In general, menus and other important features should collapse only for an incredibly good reason. It's not always easy, but if you can streamline pages, choosing the main points and eliminating the rest, it will help people make the best choices the first time.

Logging

The goal of design should be to make pathways simple and straightforward enough that users do not get caught up in momentum behavior. But if they do get caught up, it's still possible to change their direction if an element in the interface exudes a strong enough signal to convince them it is worth investigating.

When people see something but don't act on it immediately —instead noting it for future reference—we call it **logging**. They are intentionally doing something else but still depositing the command in their brains, knowing that it is another possible way to complete their task. And if the path they are following does not prove fruitful quickly, they return to the option they logged away.

Selective Disregard

When analyzing eyetracking results, people frequently ask us how often users look at a specific element. This is a fair question and certainly an important one if the answer is "never." Sometimes users are just not drawn to a particular element or area of the page, but usually it is not that simple. When users choose to ignore something—be it a menu, an image, a logo, or breadcrumbs—we must consider why.

There are many occasions when it is perfectly appropriate for users to ignore elements of Web pages. If they know something is available to them but they don't need it at that moment, they may confidently choose to ignore it. For example, after people use the menu to get to a page with the content they need, they don't bother looking through the menu again on that page. Instead, they employ **selective disregard**.

This behavior is highly related to the well-documented "selective attention" phenomenon, in which people (and monkeys and fruit flies and surely other beings) pay attention only to the things that are currently important to them. It is simply impossible to pay attention to all sensorial stimuli. There's not enough time in the day. Or, more to the point, we don't have enough brain cells to process everything our senses pick up. Any being with more senses than a slug must ignore most of the stimuli around it, or it won't survive.

In eyetracking, we see this behavior further enhanced. People not only don't waste their thoughts; they don't even waste a *look* at things they don't think they need at the time. These are common reasons why people use selective disregard:

- They have already used an element on a site, know it is there, and don't need to look at or use it again at that time.

- They are confident in a Web site's layout from using other sites with similar controls and choose to ignore elements they do not need right then.

- Barring the specific design of the current site, they subconsciously expect the element to appear in a certain place based on general Web usage, so they ignore it at times when they don't need it.

- They don't think an item seems useful based on its rough appearance, as perceived through peripheral vision, so they don't fixate on it and never find out what it actually contains. Banner blindness is the most well-known example of this kind of selective disregard.

Selective disregard can be triggered by the location or rough appearance of interface elements. Let's look at an example. The user Cheryl was looking on the U.S. Internal Revenue Service site for information about possible tax deductions for donations made to charities. She had already used global navigation tabs such as *Individuals* and *Businesses* a few times on the site. She selected *Charities & Non-Profits* and then looked at the links in the content area of the page and the topic list on the left. She didn't look at the top, horizontal global navigation—she discounted the menu because she had just used it and didn't need it then. In the first segment of the time Cheryl spent on this page, she fixated on the content area (**Figure 8.21**).

Figure 8.21 Partway into her visit on the IRS site, Cheryl looked at the content area and the topic list on the left side. She did not look at the top horizontal navigation when she did not need it.

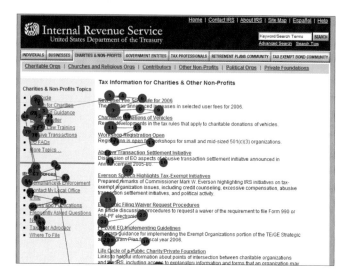

At that point, Cheryl had not even looked at the utility navigation—*Home, Contact IRS, About IRS,* and so on—at the very top of the page. But this is probably because she knew that the type of content that usually appears in utility navigation is administrative. And she knew that it often appears at the very top, based on her experience on other Web sites. Most important, she knew she did not need it and was able to dismiss it.

Once Cheryl felt that she had exhausted the choices in the content and left areas of the page, she turned back to the old standby menu at the top. As a gaze plot of her extended time on this page shows, she fixated on the top, horizontal menu as well as the other areas (**Figure 8.22**).

Figure 8.22 Only after she exhausted the content area and left topic list did Cheryl again turn to the global navigation.

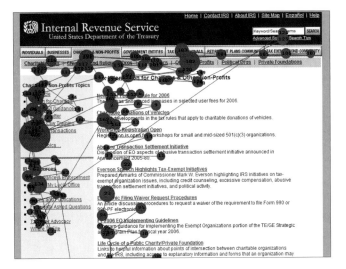

The phenomenon of selective disregard helps illustrate why it's so difficult to interpret eyetracking data without sitting next to users and understanding their thinking as they go about their browsing. Not looking at something might indicate a bad design if it's because users overlooked something they need. But it can also be a result of good design—such as consistent layout—if it's because users are freed from wasting time on something irrelevant.

Post-click Behavior

People typically move forward at lightning speeds on the Web, so why do we sometimes see them fixating on links and buttons after they have already clicked them? Sometimes the looks are a simple confirmation. Other times, they're an indication of doubt or confusion.

Post-click Verification

Users' confidence in a link often dictates their viewing behavior just after they select it. When they select a link that is understandable, they spend the moments until the next page loads looking around at other elements of the page they're on. But when users select a link they are not confident about, they continue to look at it while they wait for the next page. This is called **post–click verification**.

In one example of this, the user Teri was searching for information about dogs. She was on the CNN Web site, which was set as the browser's homepage for this task. (Note that eyetracking technology calls for a start page for all tasks. Often we started with a blank page, but sometimes we selected news sites, just to see whether something would grab people's attention as they started out. This simulates the common scenario of users beginning a new task from the page they ended their last task on.)

Teri looked two times at the site search-scoping radio buttons for the Web and CNN. She confirmed that *The Web* was the selected radio button, as she commented, "I don't think I am going to find this on CNN." She then typed "dogs" in the search field, looked at the *Search* button, and clicked it (**Figure 8.23**). The page remained for just shy of three seconds while the search worked. And Teri's eyes continued to work too, looking at her search query, "dogs," and then at the radio buttons for *CNN.com* and *The Web* (**Figure 8.24**). It was as though she was confirming that she typed a good query and was searching in the right place.

Figure 8.23 The user Teri began her Web search for dogs from the CNN site. She looked at the *Search* button.

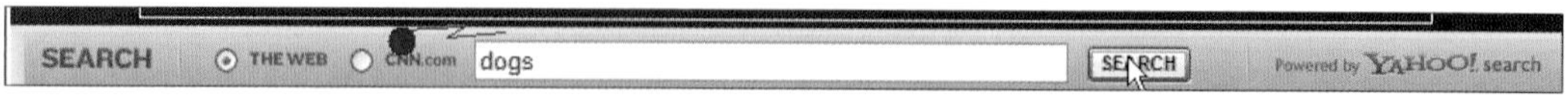

Figure 8.24 Teri then took a moment to confirm that she was, indeed, searching the Web and not just CNN.

Eyetracking Web Usability

Once she confirmed the search selection, she looked further to the left to the first menu choice, *Home Page*. The top position probably attracted her, as did the red background, which was brightly juxtaposed against the dark blue hues nearby. While she continued to wait for the search to process—and remember that this all happened in a matter of a few seconds—Teri confirmed her query yet again, looked at the *Search* button again, and then looked at "dogs" for the last time as the search results loaded (**Figure 8.25**, **Figure 8.26**, and **Figure 8.27**).

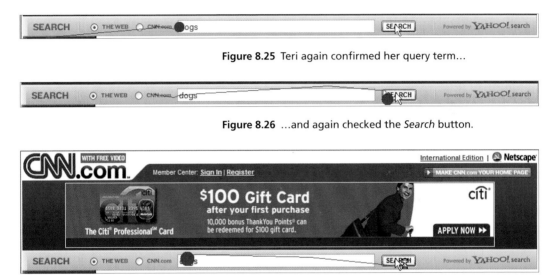

Figure 8.25 Teri again confirmed her query term...

Figure 8.26 ...and again checked the *Search* button.

Figure 8.27 Teri confirmed her search query for a third time just before the search results page loaded.

We know that scoped search often makes users think a bit harder than they need to with a simple search function that has no choices. And we don't usually recommend offering a Web-wide search on most sites because it can confuse people and take up space. It also puts forth a certain arrogance, as if to say, "People spend so much time on our site that they are even going to do their Web-wide searches from it."

That said, the CNNs, Yahoos, and MSNs of the world are possible exceptions to this rule because people often set them as homepages, so they may want to offer Web search as a courtesy. But unless your site is a portal or one of these, usually only very inexperienced users will search the Web from it. Others use search engines and many even have the Google Toolbar downloaded. Teri's example shows a pro and con of doing this even on one of those sites:

- **Pro.** Offering Web search on the site enabled her to move forward from the site without having to go elsewhere.

- **Con.** Having two search choices caused Teri to review them at least three times before she selected one and again even after she constructed and ran her search.

A more problematic example of post-click verification occurred when the user Fred was working with the Web site for Flight 001, which sells retro travel gear. We observed him reexamining menu links he had selected after the pages that appeared did not seem to meet his expectations. In this case, Fred clicked *Entertainment*, looked at the products offered (such as a pocket Scrabble game, a roulette set, and a View-Master), and concluded that they were not all that entertaining. He then backtracked and looked at the *Entertainment* link again. And he did the same thing after he selected the *Carry-on* link. He looked at the bags and then looked back at the link that had brought him to the page like a traveling woman's dream closet.

We consider post-click verifications of menu items like this to be a regression and somewhat negative behavior. We believe this mainly because it means users are second-guessing their selections and their thought processes. They are looking at an item they already selected and wondering whether they made the right choice. Any time a design causes people to believe they may have selected wrong or misunderstood a word, it can damage their experience on a Web site.

> *Looking at a page while waiting for the next page to load comprises post-click looks. This can also involve users looking at parts of a page after making a selection, but not out of hesitation or insecurity about their selections.*

Post-click Looks

Post-click looks are different from post-click verification. They also involve users looking at parts of a page after making a selection, but not out of hesitation or insecurity. Users exhibiting post-click looks are simply looking at the page because they are waiting for another page to load.

An example of post-click looks occurred with the user Sylvia when we asked study participants to go wherever they wanted on the Web. We started Sylvia out on this task on the *International Herald Tribune* Web site. She knew she wanted to go to the site of the television music channel VH1. She didn't even look at the newspaper site but instead typed "www.vh1.com" in the URL field. But after she clicked the *Go* button, she snuck a few peeks at the first headline on the news page (**Figure 8.28**). Why? Because it was there.

Figure 8.28 Sylvia checked out a headline on the *International Herald Tribune* Web site as she waited for the site she had chosen to come up.

Another participant who used the Apple Web site looked at the menu after she had clicked it as she waited for the next page to load (**Figure 8.29** and **Figure 8.30**). It didn't seem that she was confused about her choice but rather that she wanted to keep her train of thought as she waited.

Figure 8.29 A user looked at the menu item as she clicked it on the Apple Web site.

Figure 8.30 She looked at the menu item again after she had clicked it, probably to stay focused on the path she was taking.

Keeping in mind that users will often look at anything on the page they are on as they wait for the page they want to load, designers should consider whether to present a message telling users to wait. For example, on a page where the Apple site sends the message *Loading...Please stand by,* a user read the message *Loading* (**Figure 8.31**). If the wait is

Eyetracking Web Usability

expected to be long, a message like this is likely to be seen and alerts users so that they won't think the site is broken. On the other hand, if there's only a short wait, the message attracts users' attention needlessly and may even overlap some information that they were reading during post-click looks.

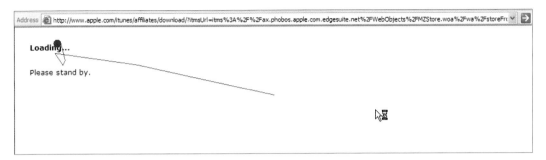

Figure 8.31 A user read the *Loading* message on the Apple site.

Post-click looking sometimes leads users to notice something that they had not paid attention to during their more active use of a page. It is particularly common on e-commerce sites that feature many cross-sales promotions and on news sites with long lists of headlines. If one of these additional items tickles their fancies during post-click looks, users may decide to return to the page after they are finished with the next page. Simply clicking the *Back* button should do the trick, and then they may resume browsing by clicking the new item of interest.

Unfortunately, many of the sites that generate the most user interest during post-click looks also make it the most difficult for users to benefit from these discoveries because they create the featured items dynamically. So, the list will have changed, and the interesting item may be gone when users return to the page. The Amazon site is a prime example of this wasteful design. The site designers probably thought that if they showed something once and users didn't click it, it wasn't of interest to them, so the site is better off showing something else in that space the next time users visit that page. This may work for Amazon, but users who click *Back* often want to return to the exact page they just saw, particularly if they had noticed something of interest during their post-click look.

Perpetual Viewing

When a user constantly looks at something (or nothing) on the screen, we call it **perpetual viewing**. People do this if they are somewhat unsure of the click they just made, or as one page disappears and a blank one draws. They look at the "snowstorm," and some even give it several fixations (**Figure 8.32** and **Figure 8.33**).

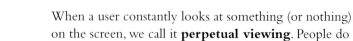

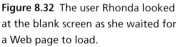
Figure 8.32 The user Rhonda looked at the blank screen as she waited for a Web page to load.

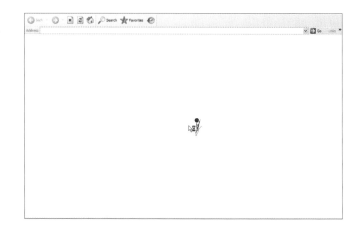

Figure 8.33 She continued to looking at the blank screen, shifting her gaze slightly, as she waited for the page to load.

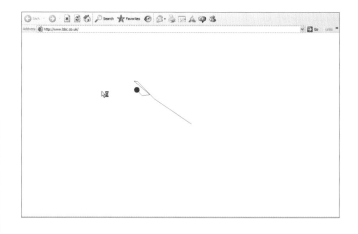

People look at the browser constantly while they are working, exhibiting perpetual viewing. They may look at blank pages, the URL, or the browser buttons. Sometimes they look away from the monitor altogether, but more often they devour what is in front of them.

Impatient Looking

When we observe people looking at useless parts of pages as they appear, we see how impatient users are as they work on the Web. Usually people fixate only once or twice on blank areas before their eyes go to greener pastures such as the browser's progress indicator or the address line. The

Eyetracking Web Usability

address line is especially attractive if users have come to the Web page from a SERP or a link on another site and they are not completely sure where they are about to go.

To the extent that parts of a page render gradually, users will look at the visible bits instead of waiting until the complete page appears. This is particularly true in the case of grandiose designs that take time to load. So, people's first impression of a page may be quite different from that intended by the designer.

In one of many examples, the user Lauren first looked at the blank page as she waited for a site to load and then at the page background after it loaded (**Figure 8.34** and **Figure 8.35**). It was unclear whether she was being impatient or efficient in doing this. Regardless, she looked then at the browser buttons and URL and finally at the page elements as they loaded separately (**Figure 8.36**, **Figure 8.37**, **Figure 8.38**, and **Figure 8.39**).

Figure 8.34 Lauren looked at the blank page as she waited for a site to load.

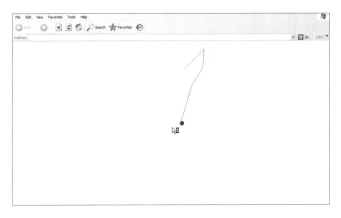

Figure 8.35 She looked at the colored page background once it appeared.

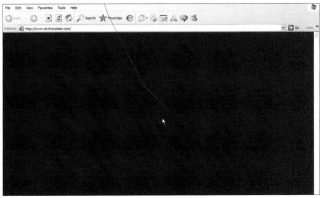

Figure 8.36 She looked at the URL as she waited for the page to fully load.

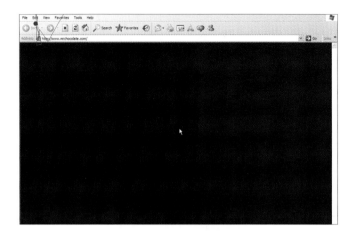

Figure 8.37 She looked at the browser buttons and then again at the page as she continued to wait for it to fully load...

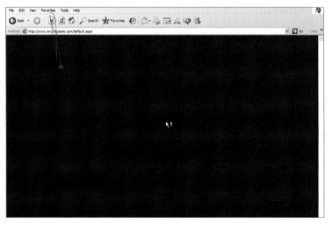

Figure 8.38 ...and again at the page...

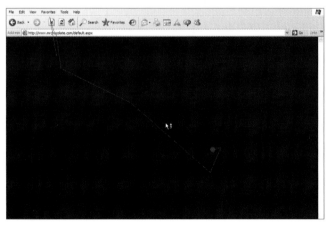

Figure 8.39 ...and finally at the page elements as they become visible on Jacques Torres's Web site, *mrchocolate.com*.

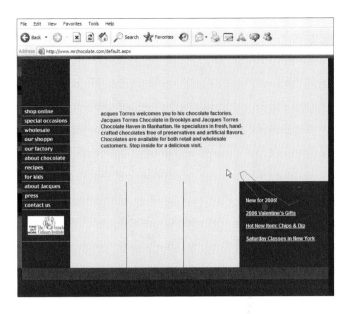

Residual Looks

The first fixation or two on a page as it loads is often just a **residual look** carried over from the spot the user was looking at on the page before. These looks don't necessarily indicate that the person is interested in the content in that area. Designers should be aware of and design for this behavior.

Residual looks that began on a blank page, a SERP, or a different Web site may be relatively less important for designers to consider. For example, the user Rhonda's eye was on the upper-left quadrant of a page before she clicked through to the BBC Web site. She kept her gaze in this position, so when the BBC site loaded, her first look was in the same spot. It happened to land on the second search button on the page. We could conclude that people are attracted to buttons or that she was interested in searching or even preferred the second search over the first one. But actually this was just a residual look—her eye had simply remained in the same position from one site to the next. She instantly looked away once the page loaded.

Considering residual looks can come in quite handy, especially if you are attempting to lead users down a path on your site. If you are highly confident where their eyes were on the previous page, you might show something you think they would want in the same location on the next page they are likely to go to.

Designers have long known that it can be helpful to keep buttons in the same position as users proceed through a linear process. For example, during a checkout process or other linear workflows, users click the *Continue* button on the previous page and usually look in that exact spot on the next page. What if designers could place more items on Web pages so information related to a link on a previous page is in the same spot where that link appeared and where the user may have looked?

Eyetracking Reveals Another Level of User Behaviors

We are quite used to learning by watching what people do as they use the Web. In the interest of making usable designs, we observe, we don't ask. In our studies, we take in everything: where users wave or plant the cursor when they pause to think, what pages they spend time on, where they click, when they click *Back* or scramble for Google, and whether they take a note, sigh, quit, make a comment, lean into or squint at the screen, smile, laugh, snort, or pull a face. We watch exactly what they do and when.

Then the hard part: We analyze the actions to determine why the behavior is happening, whether it is productive and positive, and why or why not. For 16 years now, all of this observation and analysis has helped us design or help others to design better, easier-to-use Web sites.

Now, eyetracking usability research has revealed more mannerisms and activities for us to examine. Eyetracking research provides a much more detailed level of behaviors to watch for and analyze: what users look at, don't look at, fixate on a number of times, look at but do not act upon, look at and act upon later, look at and ignore later, give long fixations to, fixate on many times in a positive or wasteful way, fixate on and have a long saccade before fixating again, fixate on when nothing is there to fixate on, or return to fixating on several times. These behaviors, along with the more traditional noneyetracking behaviors, are subtle but very telling about the usability of Web designs.

Eyetracking is certainly not the end-all usability method, but it is a powerful tool that usability professionals can drop into their bag of tricks and use in their quest to learn about how people act on the Web.

There's certainly no need for eyetracking to observe the most drastic phenomena in Web usability. When visitors to a business-to-business site say that they're leaving because the site doesn't state the price of the services, you know what's wrong and how to fix it without analyzing where people looked (except, of course, if the site does have prices but users didn't spot them). Banner blindness is such a blatant behavior that we documented it back in 1997, purely based on observing how most users ignored anything that looked like an advertisement, even when it was not an ad. Where the newer eyetracking studies offer a value-add is in the kind of detailed information we have presented in this book about what types of ads people do look.

In other words, eyetracking fills in the details. It offers an added level of richness in our analysis of behavioral phenomena. In particular, eyetracking informs our under-standing of how people approach the content on your site and how they react to your words and pictures. The Web is a communications medium, but it differs from all previous media in being interactive. Knowing how to communicate better with interactive content is the ultimate way to enhance the business value of a company's Web presence.

Most companies should not bother conducting their own eyetracking studies. You can double the profitability of your Web site from what you'll learn by sitting down next to a handful of users with no other equipment than a notepad. Almost all sites have such striking usability problems that the simplest of studies will reveal them. But those few companies that have already done large amounts of simple research may find it worth the effort to put their site under the super-enlarging microscope offered by eyetracking.

For most companies, it's fine to stay with cheap and fast user testing and refer to the behaviors we have outlined in this chapter and book to interpret users' reactions to your site. Consider the common behaviors summarized in the glossary to help you imagine how people's eyes will move around your site.

One thing is certain: The way customers look at your site and the way you look at it are totally different. We hope the many examples in this book have opened your eyes to the way users use theirs.

At the risk of sounding altruistic, we hope that, ultimately, eyetracking and the better designs it leads to will make people more productive and happier on your site and on the Web. For sure, you will make more money, given the increased profitability of your site, but we also believe that we can all make the world a little bit better when we design technology for the way human beings actually behave.

Appendix

How Much People Look at Basic Web Interface Elements

This table summarizes how much people look at specific Web interface elements as they use the Web. (Remember that a low number of fixations on navigational elements or other components that are shown to users repeatedly on a site usually indicates that people have already looked at the element and have appropriately chosen to ignore it at that time.)

Web Elements	Average Percent That Were Looked At
Top horizontal navigation	24%
Top horizontal subnavigation	54%
Left-side vertical navigation	49%
Top utility navigation	9%
Bottom utility navigation	4%
Breadcrumbs	31%
Search	16%
Looked for search in upper-right quadrant	56%
Looked for search in upper-left quadrant	44%
Looked for search in lower-right quadrant	3%
Looked for search in lower-left quadrant	2%
Logo	22%
Tag lines and other self-promotions in main site "banner"	7%
Login link or field	26%
Privacy policy link	1%
Contact link	2%
Language selectors	14%
Looked for shopping cart in upper-right quadrant	58%
Looked for shopping cart in upper-left quadrant	42%

Web Elements	Average Percent That Were Looked At
Images	42%
Objects in a simple setting/background	28%
Objects in a crowded setting/background	14%
A single object	26%
Multiple objects	20%
Highly related to page content	29%
Not related or only somewhat related to page content	14%
A person in a simple setting/background	22%
A person in a crowded setting/background	18%
A single person	20%
Multiple people	17%
Attractive people	33%
Less attractive people	9%
Ads (not including SERPs)	36%
Ads when doing a directed task	34%
Ads when freely browsing	39%
Ads that match the style of the site	88%
Text ads	52%
Graphical ads with images separated from text	52%
Graphical ads with text on top of an image	35%
Graphical ads without text: top of pages	27%
Graphical ads without text: right of pages	37%
Animated ads	29%
Sponsored links on SERPs*	51%
SERP sponsored links on top	78%
SERP sponsored links on the right	33%

* SERP = Search Engine Results Page.

Glossary

The following are definitions of the user behaviors and user interface design elements that impact eye movements exhibited in our eyetracking usability research.

Behavior	Description
Ad relativity and competition in UI	All elements on the page, including ads, compete for users' attention. Page elements that are of great interest to users can eclipse advertisements and other UI elements.
Banner blindness	Ignoring elements that peripherally seem to be advertising or banners.
Desired exploration	Multiple fruitful and usually enjoyable fixations, even repeated fixations on the same area.
Exhaustive review[1]	Unconstructive combing of pages and menus. When people repeatedly look at an area, it can indicate that the page is not well organized or is too crowded.
F-pattern of reading	Looking at pages or sections of prose—with few or no bullets, headings, or bolding—in the shape of the letter F. Users look at more words at the beginning of a line than the end, and more words toward to top of the text section than the middle or bottom.
Hot potato	Fixating on an element, finding it is not what it seemed to be about, and instantly looking away—dropping it (and often any others that look like it) like a "hot potato."
Impatient looking	Looking at elements of a page as they appear on the screen. Not waiting for a whole Web page to load but instead looking at even the unfinished parts.
Inferior path	A less direct, sometimes wrong, route that people follow to get their task done.
Logging	Seeing a command or link but not acting on it immediately. Instead, noting it for future reference.

[1] Exhaustive review is related to the long-known eye movements called **regressions**, during which people reread letters and words. In 1989, Keith Rayner and Alexaander Pollatsek found that regressions can represent confusion in higher-level processing of information.

Behavior	Description
Misallocation of screen real estate	Presenting large visual treatments above "the fold" that are of low priority to users and do not get looked at.
Miscues	Elements of design that attract the user's attention at the wrong time.
Mismatched priority	Positioning low-priority elements in a priority spot on a page or putting high-priority elements in what appear to be low-priority locations.
Momentum behavior	Sticking to a chosen approach, even after looking at a better option.
Necessary review	One or a few looks that are necessary to traverse any Web site. These are productive and not frustrating fixations.
Obstacle course	Avoiding large, bright, or low-contrast images that peripherally seem unhelpful but still looking at text and menus that appear around or between those images.
Perpetual viewing	Always looking at something. Sometimes people will look away from the monitor altogether, but more often they devour what is in front of them.
Post-click looks	Looking at a page simply while waiting for the next page to load. (This can also involve users looking at parts of a page after making a selection, but not out of hesitation or insecurity about their selections.)
Post-click verification	Continuing to look at a selected link while waiting for the next page to load because the user is not confident about the selection.
Priority spots	On most pages there is at least one area that has high-visual priority based on: location, size and emphasis, and appearance in relation to the rest of the page. The eye is attracted to priority spots and expects priority information to be in them.
Regression	Rereading letters, parts of words, or words. Regression is a well-known eye behavior, and it often means the word or writing is confusing.
Repeated review	Looking at the same specific element multiple times. This is different from exhaustive review, where the user looks at many different things multiple times. There will be repeated review during an exhaustive review, but there can also be repeated review as a stand-alone behavior.
Residual looks	When the first fixation or two on a page as it loads are looks carried over from the spot the user was looking at on the last page.
Reverse banner blindness	Looking at an ad that appears in an location where the user is expecting to see something else.
Selective disregard	Confidently choosing to ignore things that are available but not needed at the moment.

Index

banner blindness, 75, 92, 96, 116
   ad placement and, 334, 339–341
   early documentation of, 417
   reverse form of, 340, 341
   selective disregard and, 403
Baryshnikov, Mikhail, 252–253
Baseball Almanac Web site, 82–83, 227–228
Baseball Hall of Fame Web site, 77, 250–251, 390–392
Baseball Library Web site, 83–84, 387–390, 392
Baseball Page Web site, 77
Baseball-Reference Web site, 79–81, 383–387, 392
Baskits Web site, 169–171
Batali, Mario, 200
BBC Web site, 415
behavior
   hot potato, 123, 345–347
   impatient viewing, 367
   logging, 402
   momentum, 90, 91, 96, 338, 396–402
   obstacle-course, 200
   post-click, 405–411
   selective disregard, 116, 140, 402–405
   See also user viewing behaviors
Benjamin Moore Web site, 148–149, 298, 307, 308
Berkeley Camera Club Web site, 266
billing forms, 179, 182
black-and-white images, 204
blindness, banner. *See* banner blindness
blood, images of, 260
BNSF Railway Web site, 100–101
BNY Mortgage Web site, 261
bodies
   animal, 255–259
   human, 247–255
   nonsexual parts of, 260–263
   sexual parts of, 247–259
Bourdain, Anthony, 200
branding
   interface elements and, 91
   menu names and, 135–140
breadcrumbs, 156
Brett, George, 76–84, 227, 250–251, 383–391

browsing
   ad views during, 328
   of news pages, 50–53
business goals, xvii, 48–49
buttons, 145–156
   button-looking links, 152
   clickability indicators for, 152
   clickable appearance of, 145–149
   faux buttons, 152–156
   link-looking buttons, 150–152
   status indicators looking like, 152–155

C

cartoon images, 286–287, 288
categories
   consistent naming of, 119
   naming in menus, 119, 136
   navigation images related to, 291–292
   user alienation based on, 131–134
Census Bureau Web site, 88–96, 376–377
Cheap Tickets Web site, 305
Chicago Sun-Times Web site, 366
children
   informational images for, 270–272
   Web studies of, xviii
Circuit City Web site, 49, 374–375
Citi Web site, 351
CityFeet Web site, 206
clickability indicators, 152
CNN Web site, 50–53, 222, 319, 343, 358–359, 363, 406–407
Coast Guard Auxiliary Web site, 277–278
cold zones, 11
color images, 204
Colorado Fishing Network Web site, 209–210
Colorado Ski Country USA Web site, 152
columns on forms, 179, 193
Comedy Central Web site, 147, 265, 321, 365
competition for attention, 335–339, 422
completeness, illusion of, 155
complex backgrounds, 212–213, 230
complicated information, 392–395
Conservation Law Foundation Web site, 273
contact information, 163

content
    ads related to, 335–339
    exciting images related to, 220–222
    people images related to, 242–243
    placement on Web pages, 70–71
    relationship of images to, 218–226, 242–243
contextual ads, 346–347
Continue button, 190
controls, animation, 316–318
corporate research tasks, 27
cost of eyetracking research, 40–43
    eyetracking-related costs, 53
    lost data costs, 42–43
    overall study costs, 41
    recruiting costs, 41–42

D

Danceworks Web site, 252–253
Dansk Web site, 66–67, 146
dark images, 200, 203
data
    collection of, 22–25
    cost of lost, 42–43
Davidson, Scott, 87
defenses against ads, 326–327
delicious-looking food, 266–270
demographics, 23
designing Web pages
    allocation of screen space in, 98–103
    content placement in, 70–71
    discipline required for, 50
    ergonomic considerations in, 398
    example of bad design, 88–96
    featuring important elements in, 103–105
    fundamental elements used in, 158–193
    improving through eyetracking, 108–110
    naming features in, 91–92
    price of miscues in, 105–108
    priority spots in, 72–97
    problem with top-down design in, 65
    sections and headings used in, 69
    standards used for, 64–66
    systematic plan for, 48
    top tasks for, 87

uncluttered approach to, 66–70
usability problems and, 155
visual indicators in, 70–71
See also page layout; Web design elements
desired exploration, 82, 377, 378, 422
dessert photos, 268–269
detailed backgrounds, 230
Details magazine Web site, 13, 247, 281
directional maps, 282
disabled Web users, xviii
display ads, 17
disregard, selective, 116, 140, 402–405
distracting animations, 310–315
Dog Owner's Guide Web site, 288
dog photos, 255–259
drift, 44
drop-down lists, 14, 189–190, 364
Ducks Unlimited Canada Web site, 205
duration of fixations, 12

E

e-commerce, 289–302
    ads viewed while engaged in, 328–331
    navigational images in, 290–294
    post-click looks in, 411
    product images in, 294–302
Edit shopping cart button, 173
eHow Web site, 328–329
elements of Web design. *See* Web design
   elements
e-mail newsletters, xviii
Encyclopedia Britannica Web site, 352–354
Energy Information Administration Web site,
   271
entertainment-oriented Web sites, xvii–xviii
equipment, eyetracking, 3–5, 43–44
ergonomics in Web design, 398
erroneous image ignoring, 283
errors
    cataloguing, 34, 110
    head-motion compensation, 44
    interface, 155
    miscues and, 34–35
    usability, 155

evolutionary responses, 327

exciting, relevant images, 220–222

exhaustive review, 82, 171, 376, 380–392
    baseball Web sites and, 383–392
    complicated information and, 392–395
    definition of, 422
    exhausting nature of, 380–383
    motivators for, 374–376, 378
    regression and, 395
    repeated review and, 393–394

Expedia.com Web site, 72–76, 188–189, 192, 305, 335–336

exposed shopping carts, 172–174

external ads, 356–371
    animation used in, 364–371
    clear, readable text in, 356–359
    magnetic elements in, 359–364
    See also advertisements

Eye Tracking Methodology: Theory and Practice (Duchowski), 5

eyeglasses, 42

eyes
    compared to cameras, 6
    fixations vs. saccades, 6–7
    mind–eye hypothesis, 9
    See also vision

eyetracking
    assistive technology and, 19
    costs of research in, 40–43
    definition of, 3
    early research in, xiv
    gaze plots for, 12–13
    heat maps for, 11–12
    how it works, 4–5
    improving layouts using, 108–110
    input devices based on, 18–19
    recommended books about, 5
    report on research methodology for, xvi, 25
    supplementary reports about, xvi–xvii
    task studies and, 13–16
    technology utilized for, 3–5, 43–44
    usability studies based on, 17–18, 21–44
    user viewing behaviors, 372–418
    visualizing results of, 10–13

Eyetracking the News (Quinn et al.), 5

EzineArticles Web site, 343–344

F

faces
    attractive features of, 230
    smiling, 230, 237, 238, 239, 360–361
    See also people photos

faux buttons, 152–156

faux drop-down lists, 364

Fidelity Web site, 238, 239, 358

fields
    phone number, 188–189
    placing labels for, 178–186
    prompt text in, 191–192
    superfluous, 193
    See also search field

File Forum Web site, 210–211

filler images, 203–204

finding home page elements, 160–162

Fisheries and Oceans of Canada Web site, 286

fixations
    gaze plots of, 12–13
    good vs. bad, 10
    heat maps representing, 11–12
    number vs. duration of, 12
    percentages table indicating, 420–421
    reducing in forms, 192–193
    saccades and, 7
    See also look patterns

Flight 001 Web site, 290, 408

Foley, MaryKate, 87

food photos
    animal bodies in, 261–262
    delicious-looking food in, 266–270

forms, 176–193
    comparing usability of, 178–188
    example of confusing layout for, 176–178, 181
    guidelines for reducing fixations on, 192–193
    phone number fields on, 188–189
    placing field labels on, 178–186
    prompt text in fields on, 191–192
    reviewing user scores for, 187–188
    using short and simple, 189–191

Fortin, Betsy, 87

foveal vision, 6–9

F-pattern of reading, 345, 422
FreshDirect Web site, 68, 116, 174, 215–217, 269, 293–294, 378–379

G

game Web sites, xviii
Gateway Web site, 61–64, 199, 244, 245
gaze patterns, 50–66
  general shopping and, 53–58
  news page browsing and, 50–53
  performing specific tasks, 61–64
  specific item shopping and, 58–60
  Web design standards and, 64–66
gaze plots, 12–13, 183, 319
gaze replay videos, 10
gender differences
  people image looks and, 244–246
  sexual body parts looks and, 247–255
Genentech Web site, 231–233
generic images, 196, 199
genuine-looking people, 230, 241
Gerd Institute Web site, 218–219
Girl Scouts Web site, 143–144
global navigation menus, 58, 114–115
glossary, 422–423
goals
  business vs. user, 48–50
  usability study, 21
Good Dog Foundation Web site, 241–242
Google search engine, 338
Google SERP, 329–330, 331
Google text ads, 343, 344, 346
Google toolbar, 344
GQ magazine Web site, 13, 247, 281
graphical ads, 347–371
  animation of, 364–371
  clear, readable text in, 356–359
  internal promotions as, 348–355
  magnetic elements in, 359–364
  percentage viewed by users, 333, 334
  placement on Web pages, 334
  skin shown in, 362–363
  smiling faces in, 360–361
  text placed over images in, 334
  user interface elements in, 363–364

graphics. *See* images
gray images, 204
Groundhog.org Web site, 85–87

H

Hansen's Natural Web site, 215, 239–240
Harry Potter movie trailer, 308–309, 319–320, 398–401
head position, 4
headings, 69, 142–144
head-motion compensation error, 44
Headset Zone Web site, 70, 154–156, 294, 295
heat maps, 11–12
  number of recordings required for, 25
  video analysis using, 319
high-resolution viewing, 8
Home button, 65
homepage, 160–164
  contact information on, 163
  eyetracking patterns on, 160–161
  finding elements on, 160–162
  language selectors on, 164
  linking to features from, 175
  login features on, 162–163
  obstacle-course behavior on, 200
  privacy policy information on, 163
  shopping cart on, 165
horizontal navigation, 114
hot potato behavior, 123, 345–347, 422
hot zones, 11
hotels.com Web site, 176–178
How2 Web site, 312–314
human body images, 247–255

I

iconic images, 209–212
  definition of, 209
  using multiple, 212
ignored images, 196, 197, 283
illusion of completeness, 155
illustrations, 285–289
  cartoon-like, 286–287
  instructional, 289
  photos vs., 285–286

images, 194–322
album cover, 299
animals in, 255–259, 261–263
animated, 302–318, 364–371
attractive people in, 237–243
backgrounds of, 212–213, 230
black-and-white, 204
bodies viewed in, 247–255
cartoons used as, 286–287, 288
color vs. shades of gray in, 204
contrast and detail in, 204–206
dark or low-contrast, 200–203
deciphering detail in, 204–206
drawing attention to, 196–197, 204
e-commerce, 289–302
exciting and relevant, 220–222
expectations related to, 206–209
faces used in, 230
filler, 203–204
food in, 261–262, 266–270
gender differences in viewing, 244–246
human bodies in, 247–255
iconic, 209–212
ignored by users, 196, 197, 283
illustrations as, 285–289
informational, 270–280
magnetic, 197, 226–270
maps used as, 280–282
motivation for viewing, 206–209
moving, 302–322
nonsexual body parts in, 260–263
objects of attention in, 264–266
as obstacles, 197–204
originality of, 213–218
people in, 231–255, 260–261
pornographic, 254
product, 294–302
quality of, 204–206
real-looking people in, 230, 241
related to content, 218–226
resembling advertisements, 283–285
screen resolution and, 244
sexual body parts in, 247–255
sexually explicit, 255
simple vs. complex, 212–213

stock-art, 213–214
text placed over, 334, 356
thumbnail-size, 296
TV and movie, 319–321
unexciting but relevant, 222–226
user responses to, 196, 200
Web video, 319–321
impatient viewing, 367, 412–415, 422
inferior path, 396, 422
information
complicated, 392–395
problems prioritizing, 155
information architecture (IA), 114–142
branding and, 135–140
category names and, 119
global navigation, 114–115
marketing and, 135–140
persistent and simple, 116–118
subnavigation, 118–121
user alienation and, 131–134
utility navigation, 140–142
vanishing, 121–131
Web search vs., 115
informational images, 270–280
animations as, 312–315
examples of good and bad, 277–280
illustrations as, 286, 289
kids' Web pages and, 270–272
screenshots as, 275
information-bearing words, 144
input devices
assistive technology and, 19
eyetrackers as, 18–19
instructional images. See informational images
interactive ads, 17
interfaces. See user interfaces
internal promotions, 348–355, 370
Internal Revenue Service (IRS) Web site,
403–405
International Herald Tribune Web site, 409
Internet pornography, 254
intranets, xix

J

Jacob, Robert J. K., 18
Jacques Torres Web site, 268–269, 415
JCPenny Web site, 102–103, 150–151, 181–183, 187–188, 277
JetBlue Airways Web site, 69
John F. Kennedy Presidential Library & Museum Web site, 225, 317–318

K

Kiehl's Web site, 121–129, 151, 179–181, 187–188, 235–237, 304
knot-tying instructions, 277–280

L

La Guardia, Fiorello, 226, 345–346
labels
    field, 178–186
    left-aligned, 185–186
language selectors, 148, 164
layout. *See* page layout
Learnthings Web site, 340, 341
left-aligned labels, 185–186
Liberty Travel Web site, 305
light pages, 66–70
Likert scale, 32
links, 142–144
    buttons looking like, 150–152
    information-bearing words for, 144
    looking like buttons, 152
    presenting features vs., 175
    sponsored, 328–331
LiveScience Web site, 340, 341
Living Cities Web site, 224
Loading... message, 410–411
logging process, 402, 422
login/out features, 65, 162–163, 175
logos, 65, 164
Lohan, Lindsay, 247, 248
Lonely Planet Web site, 208–209
look patterns, 50–66
    general shopping and, 53–58
    news page browsing and, 50–53

performing specific tasks, 61–64
perpetual viewing and, 412–416
post-click looks and, 409–411
residual looks and, 415–416
specific item shopping and, 58–60
table of percentages for, 420–421
Web design standards and, 64–66
    See also fixations; user viewing behaviors
low vision, 401
low-contrast images, 201, 202, 203
low-resolution viewing, 8

M

magnetic elements, 226–270
    animals as, 255–259
    drawing users to, 104, 105
    faces as, 230, 237, 238, 239, 360–361
    graphical ads using, 359–364
    human bodies as, 247–255
    images as, 197, 226–270
    nonsexual body parts as, 260–263
    objects of attention as, 264–266
    people used as, 231–246
    sexual body parts as, 247–255
    skin as, 260–261, 362–363
    smiling faces as, 230, 237, 238, 239, 360–361
    user interfaces as, 363–364
magnifying the screen, 401
MapQuest Web site, 337
maps, 280–282
marketing
    menu names and, 135–140
    See also advertisements; promotions
measures, 30–35
    of errors, 34, 110
    of miscues, 34–35, 109–110
    of subjective satisfaction, 30–33, 110
    of success, 34, 110
    of time, 33, 110
men
    fixations on images of, 246
    people image looks by, 244–246
    sexual body part looks by, 247–255
Men.style.com Web site, 247, 248

O

obstacle courses, 98, 197, 200, 201, 423
obstacles, images as, 197–204
online advertisements, 17–18
organization of Web pages, 66–110
   allocating screen space, 98–103
   content placement and, 70–71
   example of bad design, 88–96
   important elements and, 103–105
   improving through eyetracking, 108–110
   miscues and, 105–108
   priority spots and, 72–97
   sections/headings and, 69
   top tasks for, 87
   uncluttered approach to, 66–70
   visual indicators and, 70–71
originality of images, 213–218

P

page layout, 46–110
   allocating screen space in, 98–103
   content placement in, 70–71
   discipline in designing, 50
   example of badly designed, 88–96
   featuring important elements in, 103–105
   gaze patterns and, 50–66
   improving through eyetracking, 108–110
   naming features in, 91–92
   page organization and, 66–110
   price of miscues in, 105–108
   priority spots in, 72–97
   problem with top-down design of, 65
   sections and headings in, 69
   site goals and, 48–50
   systematic planning of, 48
   top tasks for, 87
   uncluttered approach to, 66–70
   visual indicators in, 70–71
   Web design standards and, 64–66
Panasonic Web site, 130–131, 291–292, 297–298, 309–310, 311
Panic Goods Web site, 296–297
past experience of users, 96

people photos, 231–246
   attractive people in, 237–240
   bodies looked at in, 247–255
   gender differences in viewing, 244–246
   nonsexual body parts in, 260–261
   objects of attention in, 264–265
   real-looking people in, 241
   relevance to content, 242–243
   sexual body parts in, 247–255
   user look patterns and, 231–237
percentages table, 420–421
perceptible menus, 64
perceptual psychology, xiv
peripheral vision, 6–9, 283
perpetual viewing, 412–416
   definition of, 423
   impatient looks and, 412–415
   residual looks and, 415–416
personal weblog sites, xvii
photos
   illustrations vs., 285–286
   See also images
Pioneer Electronics Web site, 101, 283–284
placement of ads, 334–341
poor affordance, 155
pornography Web sites, 254
portal pages, 358, 407
post-click behavior, 405–411
   post-click looks, 409–411, 423
   post-click verification, 405–408, 423
Postmodern Web site, 263
Priceline Web site, 306–307
Prioritizing Web Usability (Nielsen and Loranger), xvi
priority spots, 72–97
   definition of, 423
   design elements indicating, 72
   example of poorly designed, 88–96
   mismatched priority and, 79, 84, 96
   plotting on a page, 97
   unclear, 76–84
   user tasks and, 85–87
privacy policy information, 163
Proceed to Checkout button, 173

product images, 294–302
    album cover art, 299
    names of items in, 298
    thumbnail-size, 296
progress indicators
    animated, 303–310
    whimsical, 307–310
progressive disclosure, 187
promotions
    animated, 370
    assessing, 354–355
    internal, 348–355
    tag lines and, 164
    See also advertisements
prompt text in fields, 191–192
pull media, 322
Pupil Center Corneal Reflection (PCCR)
    technique, 44
push media, 322

Q

qualitative methods, 24–25
    measures utilizing, 30
    test tasks and, 28–29
quantitative methods, 24–25
    measures utilizing, 30–35
    test tasks and, 26–27

R

Ramirez, Manny, 252
rapid evolutionary response, 327
rapid-fire tasks, 332
rating scales, 32
reading
    F-pattern of, 345, 422
    test tasks in, 27
realistic task performance, 36–38
Realknots.com Web site, 279
real-looking people, 230, 241
recruiting costs, 41–42
red-colored features, 93
regression, 395, 408, 423

relativity of ads, 335–339, 422
relevance of images, 218–226
repeated review, 393–394, 423
representative users, 35
research
    cost of conducting, 40–43
    criteria for valid, 35–40
    data collection in, 22–25
    equipment used in, 43–44
    measures used in, 30–35
    qualitative vs. quantitative, 24–25
    session logistics in, 26
    tasks utilized in, 26–29
    test sessions in, 25–35
    See also usability studies
residual looks, 415–416, 423
resolution, screen, 43, 244
retail product presentations, 379
reverse banner blindness, 340, 341, 423
review of Web pages, 374–396
    complicated information and, 392–395
    desired exploration, 377, 378
    exhaustive review, 374–376, 378, 380–392
    motivators for, 374
    necessary review, 377, 378
    regression, 395
    repeated review, 393–394
Rupp, Heather A., 255

S

saccades, 7, 12, 176
Schade, Amy, xviii, 33
scoped search, 406–407
screen magnification, 401
screen real estate, 98–103
screen resolution
    eyetracking research and, 43
    images and, 244
screenshots, 275
search engine results pages (SERP), 50
    percentage of ad views on, 333
    position of ads on, 335
    report about user behavior on, 335
    sponsored links on, 342–343

text
    ads consisting of, 328–331, 332, 333,
       342–347
    animation using, 315
    graphical ads with, 334, 356–359, 363
    placed over images, 334, 356
    prompt, 191–192
text ads, 342–347
    e-commerce tasks and, 328–331
    hot potato behavior and, 345–347
    non-SERP pages and, 343–345
    percentage viewed by users, 332, 333
    position on Web pages, 335
    SERPs and, 342–343
    See also sponsored links
thumbnail-size images, 296
time measures
    ad fixations, 326
    task completion, 33, 110
T-Mobile Web site, 104–105, 117, 145–146,
    184–186, 187–188
Tobii 1750 Eyetracker, 43
Tobii Technology Web site, 44
Tollesbury Sailing Club Web site, 315
top banner blindness, 334
top tasks, 87
top-down design, 65
travel Web sites
    progress indicators on, 305–307
    promotions on, 336–337
Travelocity Web site, 206–207
TV content, 319–321, 322

U

unclear priority spots, 76–84
unclear terminology, 96
UnderwaterTimes Web site, 362
unexciting, relevant images, 222–226
United Airlines Web site, 307, 308
U.S. Census Bureau Web site, 88–96, 376–377
U.S. Coast Guard Auxiliary Web site, 277–278
U.S. Internal Revenue Service (IRS) Web site,
    403–405
USA Today Web site, 357

usability
    interface errors and, 155
    questions related to, 14
    Web vs. application, 17–18
usability studies, 17–18, 21–44
    cost of conducting, 40–43
    criteria for valid, 35–40
    data collection in, 22–25
    demographics of, 23
    equipment used in, 43–44
    goals of, 21
    measures used in, 30–35
    qualitative methods in, 24–25, 28–29, 30
    quantitative methods in, 24–25, 26–27, 30
    report on methodology used in, xvi, 25
    representative users for, 35
    session logistics in, 26
    simple approach to, 418
    tasks used in, 26–29, 36–38
    test sessions in, 25–35
    variety of Web sites for, 38
    weighing the evidence of, 38–40
Usability Week conference, 14, 15, 16
useit.com Web site, xvi, 10
user interfaces (UIs)
    ads using elements of, 363–364
    errors related to, 155
    eyetrackers as part of, 18–19
    faux elements of, 364
    look patterns for elements of, 162
    usability studies of, 14
user viewing behaviors, 372–418
    complicated information and, 392–395
    desired exploration, 377, 378
    exhaustive review, 374–376, 378, 380–392
    impatient viewing, 412–415
    logging process, 402
    momentum behavior, 396–402
    necessary review, 377, 378
    perpetual viewing, 412–416
    post-click behavior, 405–411
    reasons for staying on sites, 374
    regression, 395
    repeated review, 393–394
    residual looks, 415–416
    retail product presentations and, 379

user viewing behaviors *(continued)*
   revealing through eyetracking, 416–418
   selective disregard, 402–405
   See also look patterns
users
   alienation of, 131–134
   goals of businesses vs., 48–49
   past experience of, 96
   representative, 35
   satisfaction of, 30–33, 110
   viewing behaviors of, 372–418
utility navigation, 65, 140–142

V

vanishing navigation, 121–131
verification, post-click, 405–408
vertical navigation, 114
VH1 Web site, 367, 409
videos, 319–322
   eyetracking of, 319
   issues about using, 303
   sound added to, 310
   Web evolution and, 322
   See also animated images
viewing
   high-resolution, 8
   impatient, 367, 412–415
   low-resolution, 8
   perpetual, 412–416
   See also user viewing behaviors
virtual tours, 317–318
Visa card verification image, 277
vision
   foveal vs. peripheral, 6–9
   low, and momentum behavior, 401
   See also eyes
visual indicators, 70–71

W

Wallen, Kim, 255
Warner Bros. Web site, 308–309, 319–320, 398–401

Web browsing
   ad views during, 328
   of news pages, 50–53
Web design elements, 158–193
   contact information, 163
   forms or applications, 176–193
   homepage, 160–164
   language selectors, 164
   login features, 162–163
   logos, 164
   presenting vs. linking, 175
   privacy policy information, 163
   shopping carts, 165–174
   tag lines, 164
   viewing percentages for, 162
   See also designing Web pages
Web sites
   advertisements on, 324–371
   allocating space on, 98–103
   animations on, 302–322, 364–371
   breadcrumbs on, 156
   buttons on, 145–156
   design standards for, 64–66
   ergonomics of designing, 398
   fundamental elements on, 158–193
   images used on, 194–322
   links and headings on, 142–144
   look patterns on, 50–66, 420–421
   media types used on, 196
   menus designed for, 114–142
   naming features on, 91–92
   navigation elements on, 142–157
   organization of, 66–110
   percentages table for views on, 420–421
   position of ads on, 334–341
   priority spots on, 72–97
   promotions matching style of, 332, 348–355
   retail product presentations on, 379
   searching/researching, 26–27
   systematic planning of, 48
   usability studies of, 17–18, 108–110
   user viewing behaviors on, 373–418
   variety in testing, 38
   video on, 319–322
   See also specific sites by name

Web videos, 319–322
    evolution of, 322
    eyetracking of, 319
    issues about using, 303
    sound added to, 310
    See also animated images
whimsical animations
    distracting, 312–313
    progress indicators as, 307–310
white space
    field labels and use of, 193
    preferred over poor images, 102, 204
Wikipedia Web site, 220, 274–275
women
    fixations on images of, 246
    people image looks by, 244–246
    sexual body part looks by, 247–255
words, information-bearing, 144

Y

Yahoo search box, 338, 339
Yahoo SERP, 331
Yahoo Travel Web site, 305
YouTube Web site, 322

Z

Zales Web site, 165–168
zigzag layouts, 193